The Globalisation of Real Estate

T0330838

Individual foreign investment in residential real estate by new middle-class and super-rich investors is re-emerging as a key issue in academic, policy and public debates around the world. At its most abstract, global real estate is increasingly thought of as a liquid asset class that is targeted by foreign individual investors who are seeking to diversify their investment portfolios. But foreign investors are also motivated by intergenerational familial security, transnational migration strategies and short-term educational plans, which are all closely entwined with global real estate investment. Government and local public responses to the latest manifestation of global real estate investment have taken different forms. These range from pro-foreign investment, primarily justified on geopolitical and macro-economic grounds, to anti-foreign investment for reasons such as mitigating public dissent and protecting the local housing market. Within this changing geopolitical context, this book offers a diverse range of case studies from Canada, Hong Kong, Singapore, Russia, Australia and Korea. It will be of interest to academics, policymakers and university students who are interested in the globalisation of local real estate.

The chapters in this book were originally published in the *International Journal of Housing Policy*.

Dallas Rogers is Senior Lecturer at the Sydney School of Architecture, the University of Sydney, Australia.

Sin Yee Koh is Assistant Professor of Geography in the Institute of Asian Studies at Universiti Brunei Darussalam, Brunei.

The Globalisation of Real Estate

The Politics and Practice of Foreign
Real Estate Investment

Edited by
Dallas Rogers and Sin Yee Koh

LONDON AND NEW YORK

First published 2018
by Routledge
2 Park Square, Milton Park, Abingdon, Oxon, OX14 4RN, UK

and by Routledge
52 Vanderbilt Avenue, New York, NY 10017

First issued in paperback 2020

Routledge is an imprint of the Taylor & Francis Group, an informa business

British Library Cataloguing in Publication Data
A catalogue record for this book is available from the British Library

Typeset in Times New Roman
by RefineCatch Limited, Bungay, Suffolk

Publisher's Note
The publisher accepts responsibility for any inconsistencies that may have
arisen during the conversion of this book from journal articles to book chapters,
namely the possible inclusion of journal terminology.

Disclaimer
Every effort has been made to contact copyright holders for their permission to
reprint material in this book. The publishers would be grateful to hear from any
copyright holder who is not here acknowledged and will undertake to rectify
any errors or omissions in future editions of this book.

ISBN 13: 978-0-367-57229-7 (pbk)
ISBN 13: 978-1-138-57785-5 (hbk)

Contents

CONTENTS

Citation Information

The chapters in this book were originally published in the *International Journal of Housing Policy*. When citing this material, please use the original page numbering for each article, as follows:

Chapter 1
Introduction: The globalisation of real estate: the politics and practice of foreign real estate investment
Dallas Rogers and Sin Yee Koh
International Journal of Housing Policy, volume 17, issue 1 (March 2017), pp. 1–14

Chapter 2
Global China and the making of Vancouver's residential property market
David Ley
International Journal of Housing Policy, volume 17, issue 1 (March 2017), pp. 15–34

Chapter 3
The (geo)politics of land and foreign real estate investment in China: the case of Hong Kong FDI
Karita Kan
International Journal of Housing Policy, volume 17, issue 1 (March 2017), pp. 35–55

Chapter 4
Courting the 'rich and restless': globalisation of real estate and the new spatial fixities of the super-rich in Singapore
C.P. Pow
International Journal of Housing Policy, volume 17, issue 1 (March 2017), pp. 56–74

Chapter 5

The geopolitics of real estate: assembling soft power via property markets
Mirjam Büdenbender and Oleg Golubchikov
International Journal of Housing Policy, volume 17, issue 1 (March 2017),
pp. 75–96

Chapter 6

*Transnational real estate in Australia: new Chinese diaspora, media
representation and urban transformation in Sydney's Chinatown*
Alexandra Wong
International Journal of Housing Policy, volume 17, issue 1 (March 2017),
pp. 97–119

Chapter 7

*Chinese investment in Australian housing: push and pull factors and
implications for understanding international housing demand*
Sha Liu and Nicole Gurran
International Journal of Housing Policy, volume 17, issue 4 (December 2017),
pp. 1–23

Chapter 8

*Ethnic connections, foreign housing investment and locality: a case study
of Seoul*
Hyung Min Kim
International Journal of Housing Policy, volume 17, issue 1 (March 2017),
pp. 120–144

For any permission-related enquiries please visit:
http://www.tandfonline.com/page/help/permissions

Notes on Contributors

Mirjam Büdenbender is a Doctoral Researcher at KU Leuven, Belgium. Her research interests include urban political geography, critical and post-socialist studies, energy geography and sustainable cities.

Oleg Golubchikov is Senior Lecturer in Human Geography at Cardiff University, UK.

Nicole Gurran is Professor at the Sydney School of Architecture, Design and Planning, University of Sydney, Australia. Her research focuses on comparative land use planning systems and approaches to housing and ecological sustainability.

Karita Kan is Assistant Professor in the Department of Applied Social Sciences, The Hong Kong Polytechnic University. Her research interests include the political economy of rural transformation in China, Chinese land and property rights reform, contentious politics related to land disputes, as well as state building and social governance at the rural-urban grassroots.

Hyung Min Kim is Lecturer in Urban Planning at the University of Melbourne, Australia. His teaching and research activities focus on economic and spatial dynamics of cities including globalisation and global cities, urban and environmental economics, liveability, healthy cities and the Asia-Pacific region.

Sin Yee Koh is Assistant Professor of Geography in the Institute of Asian Studies at Universiti Brunei Darussalam, Brunei. Her research covers migration and mobilities, citizenship, colonial legacies and urbanisation.

David Ley is Professor in the Department of Geography, the University of British Columbia, Canada. He is currently studying housing bubbles in several Pacific Rim cities, the causes, social consequences and policy responses to high-priced and volatile housing markets in cities open to global flows of capital and labour.

NOTES ON CONTRIBUTORS

Sha Liu is a PhD candidate at the University of Sydney, Australia. Her research focuses on analysing the growing interactions between domestic housing policies and international housing markets.

C.P. Pow is Associate Professor in the Department of Geography, National University of Singapore. His research interests include critical geographies of the urban built environment and urban landscape, urban environmentalism and nexus between urban culture, nature and power, and globalisation and urban cultural politics in Asia.

Dallas Rogers is Senior Lecturer at the Sydney School of Architecture, Design and Planning, the University of Sydney, Australia. His research and teaching focuses on the relationships between poverty, wealth, urban planning and governance in global cities.

Alexandra Wong is an Engaged Research Fellow at the Institute for Culture and Society, Western Sydney University, Australia. Her research explores the interplay of innovation/creativity, culture and urban theories which covers a wide range of topics such as cultural economy, knowledge cities, migration, housing, multiculturalism, innovation and entrepreneurship.

INTRODUCTION

The globalisation of real estate: the politics and practice of foreign real estate investment

Dallas Rogers ⓘ and Sin Yee Koh ⓘ [1]

Foreign investment in residential real estate – especially by new middle-class and super-rich investors – is re-emerging as a key political issue in academic, policy and public debates. On the one hand, global real estate has become an asset class for foreign individual and institutional investors seeking to diversify their investment portfolios. On the other, a suite of intergenerational migration and education plans may also be motivating foreign investors. Government and public responses to the latest manifestation of global real estate investment have taken different forms. These range from pro-foreign investment, primarily justified on geopolitical economic grounds, to anti-foreign investment for reasons such as mitigating public dissent and protecting the local housing market. Within this changing global context, the six articles in this special issue on the globalisation of real estate present a diverse range of empirical case studies from Canada, Hong Kong, Singapore, Russia, Australia and Korea. This editorial highlights four methodological challenges that the articles collectively highlight; they are (1) investor cohorts and property types, (2) regulatory settings, (3) geopolitics and (4) spatial differences and temporal trajectories.

Introduction

Foreign investment in residential real estate is re-emerging as a key political issue in several Anglo-sphere and Asian countries. The global real estate activities of the Four Asian Tiger countries (i.e., Hong Kong, Singapore, South Korea and Taiwan) in Anglo-sphere markets in the 1980s are well documented. The increasing foreign investor activity of new middle-class and super-rich investors from Brazil, Russia, India, China and South Africa (known collectively as the BRICS) in global real

---

[1]Sin Yee Koh started work on this special issue while she was Postdoctoral Fellow at the Department of Public Policy at City University of Hong Kong.

estate markets has introduced or revived some deep-seated cultural and political sensitivities (Rogers, Lee, & Yan, 2015).

Government and public responses to the latest manifestation of global real estate investment has taken different forms. On the back of the well-reported rise in Chinese investment in local real estate in Australia, for example, in 2014, the federal government conducted a parliamentary inquiry into individual foreign investment in residential real estate. In Canada, under mounting pressure to take action on housing affordability, the government reviewed their investment visa programme. In London, a 300-strong group of protestors picketed against foreign real estate investment outside The World Property Market international real estate event. Meanwhile, European Union countries such as Spain, Greece, Cyprus and Turkey have introduced visa schemes targeting investors from Asia, Russia and North America in an attempt to attract global capital to their local real estate markets. In Asia, the Chinese government tightened up foreign investment rules for real estate in 2010, and the Singaporean and Hong Kong governments introduced staged 'cooling measures' with implications for foreign investment in real estate beginning in 2009 and 2010, respectively. In the fluid regulatory environment in Hong Kong, the government suspended their Capital Investment Entrant Scheme in January 2015.

Within this changing global context, the six articles in this special issue on the globalisation of real estate present a diverse range of empirical case studies from Canada, Hong Kong, Singapore, Russia, Australia and Korea. David Ley (2015) examines the impact of international real estate investment on the local housing market in Vancouver, Canada. Choon-Piew Pow (2016) exposes the strategies that are used by investors and the government in Singapore to create and seek out new safe havens within which to 'park' and 'grow' super-rich wealth. Karita Kan (2016) moves beyond culturally essentialist analyses of global real estate transactions to show how Hong Kong investors have made inroads into the Mainland Chinese market. This analysis draws attention to geopolitical questions at the abstract level of the nation-state as well as the more embodied level *on the ground*. Mirjam Büdenbender and Oleg Golubchikov's (2016) article also considers geopolitical questions. It demonstrates that global real estate and property markets play an increasingly important role in international relations, and in this Russian case study, foreign investment has emerged as a form of soft geopolitical power. Hyung Min Kim's (2016) article shows how foreign investment is organised socio-spatially in Seoul, Korea. In this case, a knowledge of local conditions, which is often built through previous residency or a shared ethnicity, is important in shaping the spatial distribution of foreign investment in the city. Finally, Alexandra Wong focuses on Mainland Chinese foreign real estate investments into Sydney's Chinatown district, with Chinatown being an important global-urban node within the emerging Chinese foreign real estate market in Sydney.

This editorial contextualises these articles with recent scholarship on the globalisation of real estate to speculate on the methodological challenges this special issue might expose. We are not suggesting that this is a definitive list of the methodological challenges that will confront further empirical and theoretical scholarship in this area. Certainly, there are many more methodological challenges that we have not covered, such as the financialisation of real estate (Fields, 2015), reports of black and grey financial channels, lucre and suspect money sources, and corruption (Rogers & Dufty-Jones, 2015), or the financial, digital and global commodification of real estate (Madden & Marcuse, 2016; Rogers, 2016b). Nonetheless, reading across the articles we find four methodological challenges that deserve a short exposé in this editorial; they are (1) investor cohorts and property types, (2) regulatory settings, (3) geopolitics, and (4) spatial differences and temporal trajectories.

Investor cohorts and property types

There are important differences between the various foreign investor and property categories within the global real estate sector. Individual foreign investors are different from institutional investors. A new residential apartment in a middle-class suburb in Sydney is different from an 'ultra-expensive condominium' in New York's recently rebranded 'Billionaire's Row' (Madden & Marcuse, 2016, p. 39). These properties are different again from a large cattle station or other large agricultural properties that are purchased by foreign commercial entities. The different investor groups and property types are not always fully teased out in the academic scholarship and they are regularly conflated in the public debate.

Although contested, there are broadly four meta-individual foreign investor cohorts that are beginning to frame the renewed focus on foreign real estate investment (Koh, Wissink, & Forrest, 2016). These are largely conceptualised as a set of financial 'disposable asset' categories – to the exclusion of the first cohort listed below, which is class-based. The investor cohorts are: (1) the new middle-class (NMC); (2) high-net-worth individuals (HNWI); ultra-high-net-worth individuals (UHNWI); and ultra-ultra-high-net-worth individuals (UUHNWI). The NMC is a term that increasingly refers to the expanding middle-class in the BRICS countries. HNWI are often defined as people who hold disposable assets that exceed US$1 million (Hay, 2013, p. 4). UHNWI are defined as individuals with asset holdings in excess of US$30 million (Hay, 2013, p. 4). According to one professional super-rich wealth manager, UUHNWI are defined as people who hold an 'absolute bare minimum' of US$50 million in disposable assets that can be solely contributed to a wealth management fund (Harrington, 2016, p. 71 citing an interview with a global wealth manager). These three 'disposable asset' categories (HNWI, UHNWI and UUHNWI) exclude primary residences, collectables and other consumables (Atkinson, 2016, p. 1307; Harrington, 2016; Hay, 2013; Rogers, 2016a, p. 8). Wealth management funds might include a portfolio of ultra-expensive residential or commercial real estate properties in cities such as London or New York (Atkinson, 2016; Fields, 2015; Harrington, 2016; Madden & Marcuse, 2016; Rogers, 2016a).

Within this context, the articles by Kim (2016), Wong (2016) and Kan (2016) call into question the utility of rigid financial 'disposable asset' investor categories for global real estate analyses. These articles show that there are additional ways to further augment these financially defined investors cohorts, including by class (Koh et al., 2016), mobility (Atkinson, 2016), familial relationships (Robertson & Rogers, in press), and age and gender (Knowles, 2016), to name a few. Contemporary global real estate practices unhinge any class, capital or culturally essentialist assumptions we might use to frame these categories, because the global real estate industries, which are central to moving human and financial capital around the world, are increasingly blurring the cultural boundary between the 'West' and the 'East' (Rogers, 2016a, p. 134). Thus, we get both the separating out and the bringing together of different class, cultural and wealth groups within the literature and public debate about foreign real estate investment (also see: Forrest, Koh, & Wissink, in press-a).

For example, the rise of Chinese foreign real estate investment has made the cultural demarcations of this particular investor cohort more prevalent. These types of culturally mediated analyses show that individuals from the Asia-Pacific region have become the greatest contributors to the HNWI and UHNWI cohorts (Hay, 2013, p. 5). This follows on from mid-1980s scholarship by Goldberg (1985) and others which argued that Asian investments into Pacific Rim countries favoured real estate as an investment strategy. In 2012, Wealth-X (2012) estimated that there were 11,730 UHNWI real estate investors in Asia with at least 13% of their net worth held in real estate. Brooke Harrington (2016, p. 11) argues, 'as world wealth has grown to record levels ... to an estimated US$241 trillion – inequality has also grown, with 0.7 percent of the global population owning 41 percent of the assets'. Remarkably, UHNWI real investors from the six markets of China, Hong Kong, India, Indonesia, Malaysia and Singapore constitute 87% of the population of UHNWI real estate investors in Asia, and hold 91% of the net worth that is held in real estate in Asia (calculated from Wealth-X, 2012, p. 7). More recently, a survey of UHNWI investments in 2015 (Knight Frank, 2015) shows that the global average in property investments in the overall investment portfolio is 32%, with higher allocations in Australasia (42%), the Middle East (40%), Asia (38%) and Europe (33%).

The personal motivations of international investors are important too, and they can extend far beyond any financial considerations to include, for example, the intersection of familial, migratory and education considerations (Robertson & Ho, 2016; Robertson & Rogers, in press). Wong (2016) and Kim's (2016) articles explore the ethno-cultural dimensions of foreign real estate investment. They draw attention to the roles that migrant- and diaspora-led real estate intermediaries play in mediating the global connections between different investors and across nation-state borders. They expose a range of culturally responsive services that facilitate foreign real estate investment via a suite of new multi-cultural investor-buyer networks (also see: Ley, 2015; Rogers et al., 2015).

Wong (2016) shows how foreign investors are motivated by the opportunities that exist in Australia, particular as they relate to their own migration plans, their children's education and the financial security that Australian real estate supposedly guarantees. Equally, China's state-led housing cooling measures that apply to local real estate markets in Chinese cities are suggested to be motivating Mainland Chinese investors and developers to seek out foreign investment opportunities for their surplus capital. Within this broader shift in the global landscape of property investments, Wong argues that the knowledge-based economy of Sydney has attracted large numbers of Mainland Chinese skilled migrants, who prefer to live in the central business district where Chinatown is located.

Kim (2016) finds an explicit spatial pattern to foreign real estate investments in different neighbourhoods in Seoul, Korea. Kim's geospatial analysis of three neighbourhoods covers: (1) Yeonhee dong, (2) Yongsan and (3) Gangnam. Yeonhee dong attracts the *Hwagyo* (non-Korean Asians), who include the Taiwanese and Mainland Chinese diaspora who have been living in Korea for more than a century. Yongsan, north of the Han River, attracts a more diverse composition of foreign investor-buyers and residents. The famous Gangnam district, south of the Han River, attracts Korean emigrants and the returning diaspora community. Kim argues that a working knowledge of the local social, cultural, economic and political landscape of each neighbourhood – either acquired through previous residency or accessible through shared ethnicity – shapes foreign real estate investments in these specific localities. Therefore, the practices of the foreign real estate investors are shaped by more than financial motives. In this case, there are complex ethno-cultural dimensions that shape foreign real estate investment and the way various diaspora communities and investments impact the urban landscape (also see: Bose, 2014; McGregor, 2014).

Focusing on investments from Hong Kong into Mainland China's real estate markets, Kan's (2016) article further complicates the notion of 'foreign' and 'local' within global of real estate analyses. Her analysis shows how the constructed 'foreignness' of Hong Kong developers in Mainland China worked for, and subsequently against, the developers at different times and places. In the first two decades of the reform period in Mainland China, Hong Kong developers were seen as cultural compatriots contributing to China's modernisation. These developers enjoyed privileged access to the local real estate market, which was unavailable to other foreign developers and investors. In recent years, however, the 'foreignness' of Hong Kong developers was developed as a political strategy to mobilise public discontent around issues of housing affordability, the local politics of land rent extraction and the loss of cultural built heritage in Chinese cities. Kan's (2016) article traces the ebbs and flows of a 'glocal' economy of foreign real estate investment in a 'zone of exception' that has been created as a result of the intertwining of the social, economic and political histories of Hong Kong and Mainland China (also see: Shen, 2003). Notwithstanding the particularities of the Hong Kong–Mainland China case, Kan's work highlights more broadly how 'foreignness' is a contested term within the globalisation of real estate practices.

Beyond this special issue, Atkinson (2016, p. 1309–1310) identifies an additional three types of HNWI and UHNWI investors in terms of their global mobility, which are also useful concepts. The first are the globally mobile 'free-floating' investors who travel around the world, stopping off in various global cities. This group is suggested to have little allegiance to place. The second are those that move between multiple residences, and have place attachments to the cities or neighbourhood that their properties are located in. The third group live in, or send their spouse and/or children to live in the house they have purchased, and, therefore, have an allegiance to place. These groups have very different socio-spatial experiences in the city, they will interact with local infrastructure in different ways (if at all), and will, thus, impact and engage with the city in different ways (see also: Forrest, Koh, & Wissink, in press-b). In London, for example, neighbourhoods with high concentrations of HNWI and UHNWI investors may appear to be (or may be) devoid of people, and local businesses can become unviable in these neighbourhoods (Webber & Burrows, 2016), to say nothing about the broader questions relating to neighbourhood life.

Therefore, the arrival of foreign capital is not always accompanied with the arrival of new permanent inhabitants for the city. Indeed, the way capital hits the ground and intersects with the local real estate market is dependent on who is investing capital, into what properties capital is being placed, and through which investment vehicles capital is being invested and stored. Therefore, it is a conceptual trap to assume that NMC, HNWI, UHNWI and UUHNWI will have the same effects on the housing landscapes of different cities around the world. This lack of conceptual clarity is amplified by a further methodological challenge. Absentee foreign real estate investors might be reportedly common in cities such as London, New York, Vancouver and Sydney. However, capturing the different manifestations and effects of absentee investors, including accurately locating their properties, has proved difficult to achieve with analytical rigour at the level of the city, let alone conducting comparative analysis across different cities (see Andy Yan's scholarship covering Vancouver for some innovative methodologies).

There is also the question of access to the different investor cohorts by researchers. Looking at the wealth management profession, Harrington (2016, p. 20) provides an insight on how wealth managers assess their UHNWI clients' needs, which goes far beyond wealth management and tax avoidance. The way they diversify their client's wealth globally 'depends on the client's country of origin, he or she may also need help protecting the family fortune from corrupt government officials, kidnappers, or frivolous lawsuits. Other clients may wish simply to avoid paying their debts', writes Harrington (2016, p. 20). Many HNWI, UHNWI and

UUHNWI go to great lengths to protect their privacy and to isolate themselves from public scrutiny. Recent studies have shown that gaining access to the economic, social and political spaces of the HNWI, UHNWI and UUHNWI can be a difficult task, with each group presenting different challenges (see the following authors for methodologies suited to HNWI, UHNWI and UUHNWI studies: Atkinson, 2016, p. 1309; Harrington, 2016, p. 22; Webber & Burrows, 2016).

Regulatory settings

The relationship between the global real estate industry and the nation-state is a strange one (Rogers, 2016a, 2016b). Much like the wealth management industry, it 'is a state-building force in some respects and a state-destroying force in others' (Harrington, 2016, p. 21–22). In one sense, many of the professions and professionals that are working within the global real estate industries – such as real estate sales agents, migration professionals, real estate lawyers and wealth managers – repeatedly undermine the nation-states' regulatory settings (Harrington, 2016; Rogers, 2016a). In another sense, these very actors, and the international sale of property across nation-state borders more broadly, are only possible because of the regulatory rules and laws that are enabled by nation-state sovereignty. Without the nation-states there would be no foreign investment laws and immigration policies, and therefore, no loopholes for the global wealth and real estate industries to seek out and manipulate (Harrington, 2016, p. 21).

At the national level, pro-foreign investment and business immigration policy is often justified and defended via one of two related arguments (Rogers & Dufty-Jones, 2015). At times of prosperity, the first narrative is one of 'financial benefits', which suggests that foreign real estate investment will be good for the local economy and could have secondary benefits, such as jobs growth through targeted skill migration and business development. At times of hardship, the second narrative is one of 'economic necessity', which suggests that the country will be at an economic disadvantage if they refuse the global capital.

In this special issue, Ley's (2015) analysis of Canada's Business Immigration Programme (BIP), and its role in the globalisation of Vancouver's local housing market, shows that the Canadian government attempted to 'reboot a troubled regional economy' (p. 1) by inviting Asian capitalists to transfer their entrepreneurial skills to Canada. This study is located within an emerging suite of work that focuses on the way HNWI and UHNWI foreigners acquire citizenship-like status through a real estate purchase or transnational business strategy (Sumption & Hooper, 2014).

As is the case in many global cites, Ley (2015, p. 1) argues that in Vancouver, '[h]ouse prices have risen rapidly and the detached housing market is now unaffordable to most Vancouver residents'. There are increasing calls from a range of actors for government intervention in the area of housing affordability, and this makes the politics of these regulatory systems an important site for further research. Ley's (2015) analyses also contribute to recent work on the global real estate industry, which appears in this special issue (Wong, 2016) and other places (Rogers, in press). He shows that a sophisticated trans-Pacific real estate industry developed to facilitate the flow of capital from Asia to Canada. In this industry, off-the-plan property sales and the offshore marketing of Vancouver property in the Asia Pacific were used to close sales with 'wealthy BIP migrants at or before their arrival in Canada' (Ley, 2015, p. 1).

The effects of the regulatory settings in the home countries of the foreign investors are important too. More than a decade ago, Smart and Lee (2003, p. 161) argued that Hong Kong was moving toward a financialised regime of accumulation where 'the government, the business sector, and individual households have ... treat[ed] buying and selling real estate as a central part of their investment activities ... and in which real estate has become a key driving force in the economy'. Indeed, the embodied practise of investing in real estate and capitalising on the returns has contributed to the development of local and foreign real estate investment mentalities (Rogers, 2016a), which are increasingly essential to the regulatory settings that underwrite the 'global economies' of cities such as London, New York, Vancouver and Sydney.

Thus, how the home is conceptualised is important for analyses of global real estate. Exploring the home as a repository for capital in relation to the differences between the investor cohorts is an important empirical task moving forward. David Madden and Peter Marcuse (2016, p. 4) put it this way, 'there is a conflict between housing as lived, social space, and housing as an instrument for profitmaking – a conflict between housing as *home* and as *real estate.*' Increasingly, the home is viewed as repository for placing, storing and building capital (Rogers, 2016b), and this view of the *home as real estate* stands in stark contrast to other notions of home as a lived space (Rogers, 2013; Smith, 2008). The motivations of the NMC from Asia to invest in countries like Canada and Australia are being shaped by a suite of intergenerational migration and education plans that involve the whole family (Robertson, 2013; Robertson & Ho, 2016; Robertson & Rogers, in press). These could prove to be very different to the actions of UHNWI and UUHNWI investors (Harrington, 2016; Knowles, 2016; Webber & Burrows, 2016), and ultimately, they may require different regulatory responses.

Fernandez, Hofman, and Aalbers (in press) recently analysed the global real estate activity of UHNWI and UUHNWI investors in London and New York. They developed the idea of a 'safety deposit box' as a way of talking about how UHNWI and UUHNWI investors are seeking ultra-expensive global city real estate assets within which to store their wealth. It might no longer be appropriate to understand ultra-expensive global city real estate in locations such as New York as a repository for capital that investors may or may not live in or rent out while they are chasing a capital gain. Ultra-expensive global city real estate, at least in the case of UHNWI and UUHNWI investors, might increasingly be used as a part of a wealth management and diversification strategy. In other words, ultra-expensive global city real estate is becoming an asset class that can be brought together with other asset classes to build a diversified investment portfolio, which, in this form, completely alienates the dwelling from its other 'use value' uses (Madden & Marcuse, 2016, p. 53–83). This type of asset class is far removed from the concept of the home as a lived space that is inhabited (Darcy & Rogers, 2014; Rogers & Darcy, 2014); a place that is alive with living memories of the past and plans for the future (Madden & Marcuse, 2016; Rogers, 2013).

Geopolitics

Geopolitical scholarship is working its way into analysis of foreign real estate investment (Rogers, 2016a; Rogers & Dufty-Jones, 2015, p. 223), and this special issue adds two contributions to this field. Büdenbender and Golubchikov (2016) show how Russian foreign investment has emerged as a soft geopolitical strategy within European international relations. They show how the Russian state uses foreign investment as an explicit strategy of state power *in-* and *ex-territory*. In other words, local real estate becomes a technology through which the nation-state performs a modern form of statecraft in both the national and global arenas. Foreign real estate investment becomes a technology of the state in the Russian case in three ways. First, the export of an institutionalised housing finance system enhances state influence over foreign territories through their respective real estate markets. Second, foreign real estate investments, by the state and private actors, act as a conduit to the foreign outposts, which is used to exercise a form of extraterritorial power. Third, major real estate projects – especially mega projects – project an image of the state beyond its own territory. Pushing beyond common understandings of residential real estate as a repository for *financial capital*, this article highlights how property and real estate construction and consumption can be converted into *political capital* by the nation-state.

Kan (2016) also mobilises an analysis that moves from nation-state concerns down to the everyday lived experiences of people who are operating within the geopolitical structures that frame foreign real estate investment. The shifting geopolitical and cultural dynamics that exist between Hong Kong and Mainland China – as we outlined earlier – call into question the very notion of 'foreign' within foreign real estate investment debates. Rather than foreign people and foreign capital being static terms, in this case, these terms are always in a state of geopolitical contention.

Spatial differences and temporal trajectories

The articles in this special issue show that various cultural, social, political and historical real estate processes and practices develop their own spatial and temporal genealogies in different cities and countries around the world. Indeed, the analysis of the globalisation of real estate is replete with fabulous spatial metaphors and conceptual tools that are place-specific, such as the *alpha territories of the super-rich* in London (Atkinson, 2016; Webber & Burrows, 2016), the *safety deposit box* metaphor in New York (Fernandez et al., in press), the *tycoon city* metaphor in Hong Kong (Wissink, Koh, & Forrest, in press) or the globally focused *real estate/financial complex* (see work by Manuel Aalbers et al.). Looking across the articles in this special issue reminds us that it is a mistake to assume that foreign investment in Sydney or Hong Kong might manifest along similar cultural, social, material and political lines as foreign investment in London or Seoul.

The importance of considering the conceptual tools in relation to the specific context that is under investigation is clear from this collection of articles. In other words, when we borrow various conceptual tools that are developed for one context, it is important to critically reassess the epistemological and/or methodological utility before they are applied to another context.

One article from this special issue highlights this point well. Pow (2016) deploys the term 'spatial fix' to analyse the local super-rich housing market in Singapore at two scales of analysis. Pow (2016, p. 2) writes, it 'is worth noting that the term 'spatial fix' is often associated with the Marxist geographer David Harvey'; but in his article, Pow 'extends the notion of spatial fix by examining the dialectical tensions and contradictions associated with the spatial fixities of the super-rich and the Singapore state through investments in the secondary circuit of capital via prime real estate properties' (p. 3). At the local/national scale, Pow shows how the Singaporean state's spatial fix is made manifest in its deliberate attempt to attract HNWI and UHNWI to live and invest in the city-state. At the national/global scale, the spatial fix of HNWI and UHNWI investors is visible in their willingness to park their capital in the 'safe haven' of Singapore. In Pow's analysis, Singapore is an exemplar of Haila's (2015) 'property state', which is demonstrated by the active mobilisation of *land as a strategy* to capture and (re)produce HNWI and UHNWI capital in the city-state. While other nation-states and local governments may marvel at the relative success and ability of the city-state to attract foreign capital, Pow points to the 'contested housing landscapes' (p. 15) and rising 'social-spatial polarisation' (p. 11) to demonstrate that the pockets of luxury and private housing are created as foreign investor enclaves, rather than as homes for local Singaporeans. Pow's careful application of Marxist theory to the Singaporean case is instructive, and there are many additional spatial and temporal questions in the global real estate space that warrant more detailed conceptual retooling like this.

The articles in this special issue provided insight into the usefulness of looking beyond the so-called first tier global cities like New York and London to understand the changing dynamics of global real estate investment more generally. More comparative work, which investigates the similarities and differences between the commonly reported cities of London, New York, Vancouver and Sydney, is needed.

The experience of second and third tier cities, like Melbourne or Manchester, or the many cities is the global South and Asia, has been little explored and may prove to have very different cultural, social, material and political dynamics than the first tier global cities. Whatever analytical tools and categories are deployed within these studies, it might be useful for comparative analyses to draw on scalar notions of space to frame the analysis. This could include country-to-country, city-to-city, neighbourhood-to-neighbourhood or street-to-street comparisons.

It might also be useful to move beyond these rigid notions of scale, to explore the emerging global sphere or assemblage of real estate practices and activity. Recent work has used assemblage theories to explore the ways in which global real estate and other professionals are acting beyond the governance structures of nation-states, by networking complex real estate, financial, education and immigration information together in ways that might be used to circumvent the rules of different nation-states (Robertson & Rogers, in press; Rogers, 2016a).

Furthermore, Atkinson's (2016) work in London is interested in the way HNWI and UHNWI investors engage with the material spaces of the city. He shows how these investors create spaces of isolation, anonymity, exclusion and retreat, through which the super-rich develop and maintain elaborate strategies to circumvent their entanglement with other social groups (p. 1303). There is perhaps, therefore, some methodological utility in framing questions about the super-rich and cities using concepts such as gentrification, or indeed, planetary gentrification (Lees, Bang Shin, & López-Morales, 2016).

Finally, there is also an emerging body of temporally directed scholarship that is focusing on the historical underpinnings of various real estate and wealth management industries and practices that currently underwrite the globalisation of real estate (Harrington, 2016; Rogers, 2016a; Short, 2013). Indeed, Brooke Harrington (2016, p. 4) provides a fitting concluding remark for this editorial; she writes, '[h]istorically, land ownership has been the primary source of great fortunes globally' (p. 4), and the 'original purpose of wealth management was to ensure the smooth transfer of landed estates – free of taxation and legal encumbrances – from one generation to another' (p. 15). At this historical moment it could be important to return to the relationship between global wealth accumulation, global land claiming and global real estate practices (Rogers, 2016a). We hope this special issue prompts new spatial and temporal conceptual interventions within the scholarship of global real estate.

Acknowledgments

We would like to thank the contributors to this special issue for their excellent articles. Dallas Rogers received funding from Western Sydney University [grant number IG] to complete this special issue. Sin Yee Koh's postdoctoral fellowship (Feb 2014–May 2015) was supported by a grant from the ESRC/RGC Joint Research Scheme sponsored by the Research Grants Council of Hong Kong and the Economic and Social Research Council [grant number ES/K010263/1].

Disclosure statement

No potential conflict of interest was reported by the authors.

ORCID

Dallas Rogers ⓘ http://orcid.org/0000-0002-9359-8958
Sin Yee Koh ⓘ http://orcid.org/0000-0001-9350-1119

References

Atkinson, R. (2016). Limited exposure: Social concealment, mobility and engagement with public space by the super-rich in London. *Environment and Planning A, 48*(7), 1302–1317. doi:10.1177/0308518x15598323

Bose, P.S. (2014). Living the way the world does: Global Indians in the remaking of Kolkata. *Annals of the Association of American Geographers, 104*(2), 391–400. doi:10.1080/00045608.2013.858571

Büdenbender, M., & Golubchikov, O. (2016). The geopolitics of real estate: assembling soft power via property markets. *International Journal of Housing Policy, 17*(1), 75–96. doi:10.1080/14616718.2016.1248646

Darcy, M., & Rogers, D. (2014). Inhabitance, place-making and the right to the city: Public housing redevelopment in Sydney. *International Journal of Housing Policy, 14*(3), 236–256. doi:10.1080/14616718.2014.934157

Fernandez, R., Hofman, A., & Aalbers, M.B. (in press). London and New York as a safe deposit box for the transnational wealth elite. *Environment and Planning A, 48*(12), 2443–2461.

Fields, D. (2015). Contesting the financialisation of urban space: Community orgainsations and the struggle to preserve affordable rental housing in New York City. *Journal of Urban Affairs, 37*(2), 144–165. doi:10.1111/juaf.12098

Forrest, R., Koh, S.Y., & Wissink, B. (in press-a). In search of the super-rich: Who are they? Where are they? In R. Forrest, S.Y. Koh, & B. Wissink (Eds.), *Cities and the super-rich: Real estate, elite practices, and urban political economy* (pp. 1–18). London: Palgrave Macmillan.

Forrest, R., Koh, S.Y., & Wissink, B. (Eds.). (in press-b). *Cities and the super-rich: Real estate, elite practices, and urban political economy*. London: Palgrave Macmillan.

Goldberg, M.A. (1985). *The Chinese connection: Getting plugged in to Pacific Rim real estate, trade, and capital markets*. Vancouver: University of British Columbia Press.

Haila, A. (2015). *Urban land rent: Singapore as a property state*. London: Wiley-Blackwell.

Harrington, B. (2016). *Capital without borders: Wealth managers and the one percent*. London: Harvard University Press.

Hay, I. (2013). Establishing geographies of the super-rich: Axes for analysis of abundance. In I. Hay (Ed.), *Geographies of the super-rich* (pp. 1–25). Cheltenham: Edward Elgar Publishing.

Kan, K. (2016). The (geo)politics of land and foreign real estate investment in China: the case of Hong Kong FDI. *International Journal of Housing Policy, 17*(1), 35–55. doi:10.1080/14616718.2016.1248607

Kim, H.M. (2016). Ethnic connections, foreign housing investment and locality: A case study of Seoul. *International Journal of Housing Policy, 17*(1), 120–144. doi:10.1080/14616718.2016.1189683

Knight Frank. (2015). *The wealth report 2015: The global perspective on prime property and wealth*. London: Knight Frank Research.

Knowles, C. (2016). *Young Chinese migrants in London*. Retrieved from http://www.gold.ac.uk/media/documents-by-section/departments/sociology/Young_Chinese_Migrants_in_London.compressed.pdf

Koh, S.Y., Wissink, B., & Forrest, R. (2016). Reconsidering the super-rich: Variations, structural conditions and urban consequences. In I. Hay & J. Beaverstock (Eds.), *Handbook on wealth and the super-rich* (pp. 18–40). Cheltenham: Edward Elgar Publishing.

Lees, L., Shin, H.B., & López-Morales, E. (2016). *Planetary gentrification*. Cambridge, MA: Polity Press.

Ley, D. (2015). Global China and the making of Vancouver's residential property market. *International Journal of Housing Policy, 17*(1), 15–34. doi:10.1080/14616718.2015.1119776

Madden, D., & Marcuse, P. (2016). *In defense of housing*. New York, NY: Verso.

McGregor, J. (2014). Sentimentality or speculation? Diaspora investment, crisis economies and urban transformation. *Geoforum, 56*, 172–181. doi:10.1016/j.geoforum.2014.07.008

Pow, C.P. (2016). Courting the 'rich and restless': Globalisation of real estate and the new spatial fixities of the super-rich in Singapore. *International Journal of Housing Policy, 17*(1), 56–74. doi:10.1080/14616718.2016.1215964

Robertson, S. (2013). *Transnational student-migrants and the state: The education-migration nexus*. Basingstoke: Palgrave Macmillian.

Robertson, S., & Ho, E.L.-E. (2016). Temporalities, materialities and connecting locales: Migration and mobility in Asia-Pacific cities. *Journal of Ethnic and Migration Studies, 42*(14), 2263–2271. doi:10.1080/1369183X.2016.1205804

Robertson, S., & Rogers, D. (in press). Education, real estate, immigration: Brokerage assemblages and Asian mobilities. *Journal of Ethnic and Migration Studies*.

Rogers, D. (2013). The poetics of cartography and habitation: Home as a repository of memories. *Housing, Theory and Society, 30*(3), 262–280. doi:10.1080/14036096.2013.797019

Rogers, D. (2016a). *The geopolitics of real estate: Reconfiguring property, capital and rights*. London: Rowman & Littlefield International.

Rogers, D. (2016b). Uploading real estate: Home as a digital, global commodity. In N.T. Cook, A. Davison, & L. Crabtree (Eds.), *Housing and home unbound: Intersections in economics, environment and politics in Australia* (pp. 23–28). Abingdon: Routledge.

Rogers, D. (in press). Becoming a super-rich foreign real estate investor: Globalising real estate data, publications and events. In R. Forrest, S.Y. Koh, & B. Wissink (Eds.), *Cities and the super-rich: Real estate, elite practices, and urban political economy* (pp. 85–104). London: Palgrave Macmillan.

Rogers, D., & Darcy, M. (2014). Global city aspirations, graduated citizenship and public housing: Analysing the consumer citizenships of neoliberalism. *Urban, Planning and Transport Research, 2*(1), 72–88. doi:10.1080/21650020.2014.906906

Rogers, D., & Dufty-Jones, R. (2015). 21st Century Australian housing: New frontiers in the Asia-Pacific. In R. Dufty-Jones & D. Rogers (Eds.), *Housing in twenty-first century Australia: People, practices and policies* (pp. 221–236). Aldershot: Ashgate.

Rogers, D., Lee, C.L., & Yan, D. (2015). The politics of foreign investment in Australian housing: Chinese investors, translocal sales agents and local resistance. *Housing Studies, 30*(5), 730–748. doi:10.1080/02673037.2015.1006185

Shen, J. (2003). Cross-border connection between Hong Kong and Mainland China under 'Two Systems' before and beyond 1997. *Geografiska Annaler. Series B, Human Geography, 85*(1), 1–17. doi:10.2307/3554377

Short, J.R. (2013). Economic wealth and political power in the second Gilded Age. In I. Hay (Ed.), *Geographies of the super-rich* (pp. 26–42). Cheltenham: Edward Elgar Publishing.

Smart, A., & Lee, J. (2003). Financialization and the role of real estate in Hong Kong's regime of accumulation. *Economic Geography, 79*(2), 153–171. doi:10.1111/j.1944-8287.2003.tb00206.x

Smith, S.J. (2008). Owner-occupation: At home with a hybrid of money and materials. *Environment and Planning A, 40*(3), 520–535.

Sumption, M., & Hooper, K. (2014). *Selling visas and citizenship: Policy questions from the global boom in investor immigration.* Washington, DC: Migration Policy Institute.

Wealth-X. (2012). *Real estate and the Asian UHNW investor.* Retrieved from http://www.wealthx.com/wp-content/uploads/2013/01/Real-Estate-And-The-Asian-UHNW-Investor.pdf

Webber, R., & Burrows, R. (2016). Life in an alpha territory: Discontinuity and conflict in an elite London 'village'. *Urban Studies, 53*(15), 3139–3154. doi:10.1177/0042098015612983

Wissink, B., Koh, S.Y., & Forrest, R. (in press). Tycoon city: Political economy, real estate and the super-rich in Hong Kong. In R. Forrest, S.Y. Koh, & B. Wissink (Eds.), *Cities and the super-rich: Real estate, elite practices, and urban political economy* (pp. 229–252). London: Palgrave Macmillan.

Wong, A. (2016). Transnational real estate in Australia: New Chinese diaspora, media representation and urban transformation in Sydney's Chinatown. *International Journal of Housing Policy, 17*(1), 97–119. doi:10.1080/14616718.2016.1210938

Global China and the making of Vancouver's residential property market

David Ley

This paper examines the role of international investment in the construction of a local housing market in Vancouver, Canada. The background political economy included the attempt by Canadian governments to reboot a troubled regional economy through an infusion of activity from the growth region of Asia Pacific. An important investment tool was a Business Immigration Programme (BIP), which welcomed capital and invited capitalists to transfer their entrepreneurial skills to Canada. The BIP was very popular in Greater China, attracting wealth migration to Vancouver from Hong Kong and Taiwan in the 1980s and 1990s, and from Mainland China since 2000. An intricate trans-Pacific real estate market developed, with off-plan sales and offshore marketing of Vancouver property in Asia Pacific, and sales to wealthy BIP migrants at or before their arrival in Canada. House prices have risen rapidly and the detached housing market is now unaffordable to most Vancouver residents. Despite public discontent about the likely role of investors in boosting prices, provincial and local governments, who value the revenues of high property prices and BIP fees, have shown little desire to intervene.

Introduction

While conventional analyses have regarded residential property prices to be largely a product of local conditions, there is clear evidence of the internationalisation of real estate markets in gateway cities. Vancouver (Canada) is a prominent example, and has been regarded in the global media for the past 25 years as a prototype of real estate investment from East Asia (Claiborne, 1991; Dorfmann, 2015; Economist, 2014; Kolet & Quinn, 2013; Le Corre, 1994; Yu & Donville, 2011). This paper places such capital (and related migration) flows within a broader histor-ical context, highlighting the active role of Canadian governments in soliciting trade, investment, and migration from Asia Pacific since the early 1980s. Household and corporate capital from Greater China (Hong Kong, Taiwan, and the People's

15

Republic of China Mainland) did not arrive unannounced, nor indeed uninvited. For the Canadian state, in search of financial and human capital to rejuvenate a stagnant economy, especially in the Pacific Coast province of British Columbia (BC), established a number of policies and instruments to facilitate trans-Pacific economic flows.

British settler societies, including Canada, Australia, and New Zealand, have always been territories where capital and labour have been imported with sometimes volatile results for local housing markets (Daly, 1982; Wynn, 1992). Britain, and then the United States, dominated investment in these states up to the 1970s. Thereafter, the rise of Japan and the Asian Tigers led to significant foreign direct investment in real estate, the resource sector, and manufacturing. Edgington (1996) examined the distinct sectoral and geographical patterning of Japanese real estate investment in Canada, notably in Vancouver and BC, before the bursting of its property bubble in the early 1990s. In a valuable longitudinal study, Hajdu (1994) identified the transition in central Sydney and Melbourne in commercial property investment, as UK and US property owners gave way to East Asian investment from Japan and the Tiger economies. But in the past decade another player has emerged. With growing liberalisation of its national economy, Chinese global investments have risen from less than US$1 trillion in 2004 to $6.4 trillion in 2015, and a projected $18 trillion in 2020 (Hanemann & Huotari, 2015). 'Today', they write: 'We are on the verge of a massive growth in China's cross-border capital flows, which will result in major shifts in the global financial landscape'(Hanemann & Huotari, 2015, p. 9). These investments have been directed at a number of sectors, including real estate. The downturn in the Mainland real estate market in 2013–2015 encouraged development and insurance companies to diversify their property holdings in gateway cities like London, New York, Los Angeles, and Sydney; overseas purchases of commercial real estate exceeded $10 billion for the first time in 2014 (CBRE, 2015). These recent corporate forays are accompanied by, and in some cities have followed, the overseas housing market investments of individual households, many of them immigrants, in selected cities. Their activity will be the focus of this discussion.

The paper will first establish the broader political economy accompanying the development of Canada's Asia Pacific outreach. It will then highlight tools employed by the state to benefit from the vibrant economic development of Asia Pacific, notably the Business Immigration Programme (BIP), entry streams intended to transplant Asian economic vitality to Canada through the recruitment of successful entrepreneurs and investors. Permanent residence and later citizenship would be the reward for the geographical relocation of their human and financial capital across the Pacific. Third, the paper analyses the placement of Vancouver in a trans-Pacific residential property market, which accompanied existing networks of information, migration, and capital. Fourth, we examine the concomitant inflation of residential property prices in Vancouver, the most popular destination of business migrants to Canada, particularly the wealthiest, with accompanying stresses including local unaffordability and serious mortgage debt. Finally, we observe the impasse that has occurred in public policy with governments and their allies in the property sector in denial that the deregulated space of flows accompanying the globalisation they have so actively promoted could be a primary cause in the creation of a property asset bubble.

Vancouver plays an anomalous role in Canadian housing markets. While national analyses stress either post-2008 stability (Carter, 2012) or instability (Walks, 2014) in the Canadian market, Vancouver supports both arguments. Despite by far the highest house prices and acute unaffordability that recently led the UBS Global Real Estate Bubble Index to classify Vancouver as 'significantly over-valued' (UBS, 2015), the same week a report from the Canada Mortgage and Housing Corporation regarded the Vancouver market as stable with 'weak evidence of problematic conditions' (CMHC, 2015, p. 3). CMHC's assessment derives from the long-standing and seemingly predictable role of global capital in shaping a high-priced market. A quantitative start has been made to analysing these effects of globalisation on Vancouver's residential market (Ley & Tutchener, 2001; Moos & Skaburskis, 2010). This paper offers a more intensive interpretation of the creation of a global housing market over the past 30 years, highlighting the specific roles of policy-led wealth migration and the trans-Pacific real estate networks that developed with it. The paper also emphasises the state's agency in facilitating globalisation, and thus its responsibility in the ensuing impacts.

The research is based on extended observation that has included database analysis, and interviews and conversations with representatives of the real estate sector, government, the media, and civil society, including immigrant households. The paper covers the period from 1986 to 2015, covering two waves of business immigrants and capital, principally from Hong Kong and Taiwan from 1986 to 1997, and from Mainland China after 2000. Sources will also include the grey literature of newsletters, media sources, and private and public sector reports.

Canada and a Pacific Rim political economy

While the 1970s in Canada represented the fullest expression of a Keynesian society with a well-developed welfare state (Lemon, 1993), the decade also prefigured the significant challenges that would lie ahead. Punishing recessions accompanying the OPEC oil shocks contributed to a deepening national debt, a steadily deteriorating unemployment rate, to exceed an average of 9% through the 1980s, and alarming declines in productivity and per capita GDP growth. The recession of the early 1980s was particularly savage, with the economy shrinking 3% in 1982. Cutbacks followed, including the abandonment of Canada's social housing programme by senior government, never to be revived. Stagnation behind national borders made deregulation and the establishment of larger trading zones attractive, and led, albeit with significant disagreement, to the Free Trade Agreement with the USA in 1989 extended to include Mexico in 1994.

Economic conditions during the 1980s were even more severe in Canada's Pacific Coast province of British Columbia. A housing bubble in Vancouver burst in 1980 with a devastating 40% deflation in home prices (Skaburskis, 1988). The resources-led provincial economy contracted 8% in 1982, while unemployment raced ahead into double digits for much of the decade (Barnes, Edgington, Denike, & McGee, 1992). Under these conditions, the right-wing provincial government inaugurated a dramatic series of market-oriented reforms; its neo-liberal menu included privatisation, deregulation, welfare state rollbacks, and anti-union measures. So precipitous were these policies that the Solidarity Coalition, a strong oppositional movement, emerged and British Columbia barely escaped a general strike (Resnick, 1987). An important part of the entrepreneurial agenda of BC government policies was the planning of a world's fair, Expo 86, a familiar piece of place marketing to 'bring the world' to Vancouver in 1986.

In these critical economic circumstances, the extraordinary growth of the Asia Pacific region could not be overlooked. All three levels of Canadian government – municipal, provincial, and federal – undertook repeated trade missions to Japan, the four Asian Tiger nations, and, later China, through the 1980s and 1990s. The enhancement of trade, capital flows, and immigration shaped their agenda. In 1985, for example, after securing sister city status with Guangzhou in South China, the Mayor of Vancouver conducted a mission to Hong Kong, Singapore, and Kuala Lumpur with the primary place marketing objective, 'To establish Vancouver's commitment to fostering two-way trade and investment, as well as a full range of linkages and relationships with the Asian Pacific Rim' (City of Vancouver, 1985, p. 2).

Part of the trip's mandate was to publicise Expo 86, the six-month world's fair in Vancouver. Following the fair, the Provincial Government sold off the 82-hectare site on the edge of downtown Vancouver as a single land holding, guaranteeing that only the largest global developers could enter the bidding competition. Trumping an offer from local entrepreneurs, the winning joint submission came from three of Hong Kong's largest development companies, led by Li Ka-shing's Cheung Kong Holdings (Olds, 2001). Li, nicknamed 'Superman' for his business achievements, held celebrity status as the richest man in Hong Kong. Powerful trans-Pacific property capital had made its landfall by invitation. Sometime later a Chinese-Canadian real estate insider explained to me how Li's deal had brought smaller Hong Kong investors to Vancouver, for 'where the big fish swim, the smaller fish follow' (Ley 2010, p. 55).

The initial 1989 gathering of APEC, the Asia Pacific Economic Co-operation network, provided a loose institutional network for Canada's Pacific Rim manoeuvres, while the urgent search for bilateral economic relations to rejuvenate the national economy was elevated to a new level by the five 'Team Canada' trade missions to Asia undertaken by the Chrétien government between 1994 and 2002. An important policy tool in the bilateral discussions was a liberalised immigration regime. In the late 1960s, Canada had decisively moved away from the historic privilege granted to immigrants from Europe, and within a decade, a major re-configuration of source regions towards Asia occurred. A sign of things to come was a spike in arrivals from Hong Kong through the new skilled worker stream fol-lowing the serious pro-Mainland (and anti-British) riots and bombings in 1967. A middle-class exodus to Canada brought newcomers who would be well positioned as middlemen to welcome the much larger migration that would follow the confir-mation of the Sino-British Joint Declaration on the future of Hong Kong in 1985. Hong Kong was then a small territory of 5.4 million, yet for a decade after Expo 86 it became the leading source of immigration to Canada. For this later and more sub-stantial population movement, new means of immigrant entry were in place, provid-ing a convenient exit strategy for the wealthiest members of the colony.

Wealth migration: the business immigration programme

Provision for business immigration to Canada existed as early as 1978, when a sub-category of the skilled worker stream allowed for applicants holding significant financial capital and possessing entrepreneurial experience. This *entrepreneurial stream* was finessed many times in the following years, but basically required estab-lishing a business in Canada and employing at least one Canadian. More novel was the *investor stream* established in 1986 with an eye, according to sources at Citizenship and Immigration Canada (CIC), to recruiting wealthy residents of Hong Kong who were apprehensive about their assets with the colony's return to Main-land China in 1997. Investors had to commit greater resources than entrepreneurs, initially in unpredictable venture capital projects, but later in guaranteed provincial funds, returnable but without interest after five years. The BIP was to be a primary vehicle for bringing High Net Worth Individuals (HNWIs) from Greater China to the Vancouver housing market.

Business immigration was in principle a masterstroke, transferring embodied capital to the receiving country, conveying not just financial capital but also its enterprising creator. Not surprisingly, the innovation diffused quickly and Tseng (2000) enumerated some 30 nations who had adopted business immigration policies by *fin de siècle*. That figure has grown substantially, notably since the Global Finan-cial Crisis, as countries facing serious economic challenges, for example, in South-ern Europe and the Baltic States, have sought to offer permanent residence to international entrepreneurs and investors in return for cash or investments, and often property (Sumption, 2012; Sumption & Hooper, 2014). Residential property is a major investment interest to HNWIs, and thus to the global property and wealth management companies that serve them. Knight Frank's *Wealth Report* includes detailed profiles of the characteristics and investment preferences of the 190,000 global HNWIs with net assets of over $30 million (Knight Frank, 2013; Paris, 2013). In recent years, property has become the leading item in their investment portfolio. Savills real estate consultancy has tracked the property spending of global HNWIs, and has estimated that they hold over $5 trillion in residential real estate investment globally (Savills, 2013). Their analysis noted both the disproportionate recent growth of this cohort in Asia, and also the Asian HNWI preference for property investment.

Canada has proven very successful in recruitment in the international marketplace for HNWIs and other business immigrants (Ley, 2010; Wong, 2003). From 1980 to 2001, almost 330,000 people landed in Canada through the various streams of the business programme, the largest response for any nation. Up to 2001, the entrepreneur stream was the more popular, but since then the programme has been dominated by wealthier investor arrivals who make a larger financial contribution, $400,000 per household from 1999, rising to $800,000 later. While entrepreneurs had more challenging hands-on requirements to start a business whose progress was monitored by immigration officials, investors in contrast played a much more passive role, required only to contribute funds to the government for a five-year loan period.

The profile of BIP arrivals in Canada has been consistently dominated by Greater China, especially for the investor stream, comprising 74% of all investor enlistees between 1986 and 2008 (Ware, Fortin, & Paradis, 2010). Hong Kong prevailed up to the late 1990s, while Mainland China has dominated the inflow since. Relevant to housing market impacts are the destinations selected by these wealthy arrivals, restricted largely to Toronto, Montreal, and Vancouver, the smallest of the cities but the most popular destination. Among the richer investor class, provincial data showed that BC (essentially Vancouver) led with 49% of all landings from 1986 to 2008 (Ware et al., 2010). But this data overlooks secondary migration, the relocation of BIP migrants from their stated provincial destination − where they will make their required financial investment − to a subsequent province where they will live. An early analysis suggested net gains for Toronto and Vancouver, and net losses elsewhere, with Vancouver's share of business immigrants rising substantially (CIC, 2000). More recently, inter-metropolitan relocation after landing in Canada has risen further, contributing to a grand total of over 60,000 new arrivals in BC through the investor programme from 2002 to 2014 (Young, 2015a). To these arrivals a smaller group of lesser wealth who have landed through the entrepreneur stream of the BIP must be added.

Out of China: capital and capitalists

In the 1980s and 1990s, affluent Hong Kong and Taiwanese families in the geopolitical shadow of the Mainland looked to overseas business immigration programmes where they might attain 'passport insurance' should political directions in China become ominous (Salaff, Wong, & Greve, 2010). In addition, quality of life and educational opportunities for children in English-speaking countries provide weighty attractions to emigrate (Waters, 2008). More recently, in the more liberalised migration regime of twenty-first-century China, wealthy Mainland families cite similar reasons for departure (Hurun Report, 2011, 2014). There is also an additional unmentioned anxiety, coinciding with the PRC government's anti-corruption drive, as the state's arm reaches even beyond national borders through its Fugitive Repatriation and Asset Recovery Office. In 2015, the Office published a top 100 most wanted list among its diaspora, asserting charges that included corruption and money laundering. Among this list, 26 individuals were believed to have taken refuge in Canada, including a successful property developer living in Vancouver under an assumed name. The PRC has petitioned Canada for his extradition.

Wealth management firms have identified the migration propensities of affluent Mainland families. The Hurun Report is a well-established source on Chinese HNWIs, defined as those with liquid assets of over 10 million RMB (US$1.6 million); by 2014, there were estimated to be over a million Mainland HNW households. A striking finding from a survey of 980 HNWIs was that 60% were considering emigration, or in the process of emigrating, with both the USA and Canada preferred by two of every five potential leavers (Hurun Report, 2011). Two subsequent surveys of HNWIs found 46% and 56% who responded positively to similar questions on emigration (Wang, 2013). A follow-up Hurun study examined migration preferences of 141 HNWIs emigrating or considering doing so (Hurun Report, 2014). Amongst a global range of options, the West Coast cities of Los Angeles, San Francisco, and Vancouver were each selected as first choice by 13%−14% of respondents, followed by New York and Toronto; Vancouver was more popular as a destination than New York and Sydney combined. Significantly, real estate was by far the most favoured form of overseas investment, with Vancouver ranked third globally as an investment location behind the much larger cities of Los Angeles and San Francisco. For a metropolitan area of 2.5 million, there are major implications for Vancouver from a continuing stream of millionaire migrants intent on residential property investment.

These emigration proclivities have been realised as increasing numbers of Chinese HNWIs have moved to the USA and Canada. The number of formerly undersubscribed EB-5 investor visas released by the USA rose from 1443 in 2008 to 10,692 in 2014, while the proportion allocated to Mainland Chinese citizens inflated from 25% in 2008 to 85% of the 2014 releases (IIUSA, 2014). Consistent with the trends identified by the Hurun Report, the rise of EB-5 investor immigration has been associated with the rapid escalation of residential purchases. Chinese households surpassed Canadians to become by far the leading foreign purchasers of US residential property both by value and by the number of transactions in 2014−2015, with Californian cities being the most popular locations (National Association of Realtors, 2015). Chinese homebuyers also paid the highest prices among national groups, US$831,800 per transaction, more than three times the average price of $255,600 paid by Americans. Despite these expensive outlays,

70% of transactions were cash-based, in contrast to 25% for domestic buyers, revealing significant wealth reserves (National Association of Realtors, 2015). The role of cash purchases of this magnitude is notable because the existing capital controls in China limit personal transfers overseas to US$50,000 a year. The depressed Mainland real estate market in 2013–2015 encouraged portfolio diversification overseas, and the US economic recovery provided an incentive; for some, the anti-corruption drive by the Beijing government begun in 2013 has added palpable urgency.

This movement to selected US cities is not unique. Anderlini's (2015) sources indicate that Chinese purchasers 'have become the biggest [foreign] buyers of housing in many major western cities, including New York, London, Sydney, Vancouver, Toronto and Auckland'. A recent Credit Suisse analysis in Australia revealed that residential real estate purchases from China rose from AU$2.5 billion in 2008–2009 to AU$8.7 billion in 2013–2014 (McMartin, 2015). While Chinese settlers to Australia spent the majority of residential property funds in 2008–2009, by 2013–2014 they were displaced by investors, defined as 'temporary residents, foreign investors and developers'. In the most recent year, both groups together were purchasing 20% of the new-build market in Melbourne and 23% in Sydney.

Measured by the volume of business immigration, connections with Greater China have been stronger in Vancouver than in Sydney. Between 2005 and 2012, 81% of immigrants who landed directly in BC through the investor category were from Greater China, four-fifths from the Mainland. Many others relocated to BC after first landing in Quebec, taking the total from business investors alone to 60,000 between 2002 and 2014 (Young, 2015a). Interest seems unabated. When the Canadian government unexpectedly aborted the BIP in 2014, there was a backlog of 50,000 Chinese investor applications headed for Vancouver whose submissions were terminated (Marlow, 2014).

East Asian capital and the Vancouver housing market

We have only glimpses of the scale of capital that has accompanied this wealth migration to Canada over the past 30 years. Reviewing a number of studies, Mitchell (2004) estimated that several billion dollars a year were reaching Canada from Hong Kong in the busiest years from the late 1980s to the mid-1990s. Major flows were also arriving from Taiwan after the liberalisation of foreign exchange controls in 1987. A senior Vancouver banker confided to me that his bank received $100 million in just one month from a branch in Taiwan, coinciding with threatening offshore exercises by the Chinese navy in 1995. During the 1990s, the BC government published occasional annual data that included the size of verified liquid assets among business immigrants, 70% of them originating in Hong Kong or Taiwan (Ley, 2010). For the entrepreneur class, the average available funds for a household ranged in different years from $1.2 to $1.6 million; for the investor class, the range was \$2–2.5 million. Extrapolating this information to the 1988–1997 period, the decade of the Hong Kong exodus, would lead to a conservative total of \$35–\$40 billion in personal liquid funds available for all business immigrants to use after their arrival in Vancouver.

Comparable data are no longer published to permit a similar assessment of the post-2000 period, when the entrepreneur stream of the BIP shrank, and the investor stream became dominated by richer arrivals from Mainland China. However, government data of the addresses of business class landings in Vancouver between 2006 and 2011 showed a highly concentrated distribution in two dozen census tracts in the region's wealthiest districts: the Westside neighbourhoods in the City of Vancouver, West Vancouver municipality, locations of the top state and independent schools, and a group of tracts in Richmond, a suburb adjacent to the City and the international airport. In contrast, the spatial pattern is more dispersed for business immigrants who landed earlier, in the 1980s and 1990s, supporting the view that Mainland arrivals through the BIP since 2000 have access to considerably greater capital.

The Hurun Report (2014) repeats a long-established fundamental for business immigrants from Greater China – their ingrained commitment to property ownership as the primary building block of both family life and an investment portfolio. Property was the most favoured overseas investment by 43% of HNWI respondents. Upon settlement in Canada, therefore, it was not surprising that business immigrants from Greater China showed a keen interest in property purchase. In the early days of BIP arrivals, a special tabulation of the 1996 Census showed that among ethnic Chinese immigrants landing in Vancouver in the previous decade, 85%–90% were already homeowners in 1996, a remarkable figure in Canada's most expensive city, and far above the figure of 59% for the whole population (Ley, 2010; also Hiebert 2009a). Aside from their own experience with ownership and wealth acquisition in East Asia, they observed the example of earlier compatriots who had left Hong Kong after the 1960s riots and had made money in Vancouver property. Particularly notable was David Lam, a banker who landed in Vancouver in 1967, and quickly made a large fortune in real estate. He was a well-respected public figure, a Christian philanthropist, and sponsor of harmonious intergroup relations. In an act of immense symbolic significance, he was appointed as Lieutenant Governor of BC in 1988. Other early immigrants established real estate fortunes, and served as models to the large groups of post-1986 arrivals.

Chinese-Canadian real estate companies introduced two important innovations to the Vancouver industry, off-plan (pre-build) selling and offshore marketing. A significant property-selling network was established between Vancouver and principal cities in Asia Pacific, especially Hong Kong, Seoul, Singapore, and Taipei, and later Shanghai and Beijing. Early in the development of the offshore business it was estimated that 30 Vancouver condominium buildings had already sold out in East Asia without any marketing at all in Canada (Hamilton, 1988). Substantial sales to investors, some of whom might later be immigrants, were achieved at weekend property fairs. One agent described her work in Hong Kong for a large Vancouver-based company (Ley, 2010, p. 133):

> I sold a lot of property through exhibitions. We would hold exhibitions in five-star hotels with a large room costing $20,000 for a weekend. We would be selling condos, single-family lots. I would sell half a dozen properties myself an average weekend. They would be lining up. The exhibition area would take 200, and the hotel security would have to turn people away. I also sold in Taiwan but did not do as well there.

Offshore sales launches remain a very important market model in Vancouver, like other gateway cities including London, where in 2013, over 1800 new-build dwellings were sold in Hong Kong and Singapore, 10% of all London residential completions that year (CBRE, 2014). Now, however, online marketing and virtual tours of available properties have expanded the flexibility of trans-Pacific networks between buyers and sellers (cf. National Association of Realtors, 2015; Rogers, Lee, & Yan 2015).

Transnational sales are orchestrated by companies either within Vancouver's ethnic enclave economy or by older companies that have shown some nimbleness in adding Cantonese- and Mandarin-speaking agents. The ethnic specificity of some companies was almost complete, as an interview made clear with an agent at Keystone Realty, established in 1987 to reach the post-1986 Greater China migration: 'At its peak, Keystone had 125 agents. We always had 5−6 Caucasian agents' (Ley, 2010, p. 140). The largest immigrant-serving agency is Royal Pacific Realty, a successful company most active in Vancouver's high-end Westside neighbourhoods, while Macdonald Realty is an older company that has expanded its reach, operating in the same elite districts, the most expensive in Greater Vancouver.

Royal Pacific Realty was founded in 1995 with 30 real estate agents, and by 2015 employed 1200 staff in four Vancouver offices. Its President and co-founder, David Choi, began his business life selling Vancouver property in East Asia, marketing 'entire subdivisions of multi-million dollar single-family homes in Hong Kong and Taiwan' (Jordan, n.d.). The company sold almost $10 billion worth of residential property in 2014, a remarkable 18% of all sales by value in the Real Estate Board of Greater Vancouver (REBGV) region (Royal Pacific Realty, 2015). Confirming their emphasis at the top end of the market, the average sales price was $1.15 million, 40% above the REBGV average. Twenty-three of the firm's top 25 selling agents in 2014 were Chinese-Canadians, led by Winnie Chung, who has sold more than 100 properties each year since 1990. Between 2009 and 2014, her sales total amounted to $660 million in Vancouver's blue-chip neighbourhoods. As of June 2015, her website listed 60 available properties in these neighbourhoods with a total price tag of some $240 million (Chung, 2015). Her sales have been primarily within the ethnic Chinese market, including immigrants, residents, and investors. Her properties have been advertised in Vancouver's *Sing Tao*, *Ming Pao*,

World Journal (Taiwan), and the *China Journal*, providing seamless coverage to buyers from Hong Kong, Taiwan, and the PRC.

In contrast, Macdonald Realty is long-established and has grown in the past 25 years from its Westside Vancouver origins to a large entity with almost 1000 agents in 19 BC offices and residential sales of over $6 billion in 2014 (Macdonald Realty, 2015). Its current President was born in Taiwan, and has spearheaded the expansion of the company; in its Westside Vancouver office, a third of the 190 staff is Chinese-Canadians. The firm has disclosed that 70% of all its 2014 sales above $3 million (detached, townhouse, and condominium) in the City of Vancouver were to buyers originating in Mainland China. The figure fell to 21% for prices from $1 to $3 million, and 11% for lower prices (Lee-Young, 2015). Macdonald Realty has opened a sales office in Shanghai and launched a Chinese website to reach its Mainland market. Its habitual top-selling realtor is Manyee Lui, in the top 1% of REBGV selling agents for 16 years. Her listings appear in *Ming Pao* and *Sing Tao*, the English-language *Real Estate Weekly*, and also *Luxury Portfolio International*, as befits the leader of the Westside carriage trade. Her website currently shows 228 listings, with 14 of them priced above $10 million; each of her three women sales associates is fluent in English, Cantonese, and Mandarin (Lui, 2015). In 2014, she sold dwellings with list prices amounting to almost $150 million.

These agents are among the most prominent of a large, successful industry selling primarily to the wealthy ethnic Chinese buyer. Others include Victor Kwan of RE/MAX who sold 60 Westside properties in 2014 for over $220 million; his advertising brochure announces, 'We have buyers and investors who are looking for and ready to buy properties in your neighbourhood'. Meanwhile, another RE/MAX agent, Danny Deng, whose team also speak English, Mandarin, and Cantonese, claims to be the top RE/MAX seller in Westside neighbourhoods. Deng states that he has 'lots of cash buyers waiting to purchase your property... strong international connections with wealthy buyers' (*Westside and Downtown edition*, 2015).

Such advertising highlights the continuing role of East Asian investors in Vancouver's most expensive districts. In 1971, there were only 30,000 ethnic Chinese living in Greater Vancouver. But now with a total of 400,000, including tens of thousands of business immigrants, there is also a good deal of upgrading from buyers already in residence. However, their source of funds frequently remains offshore, for business immigrants have achieved minimal economic success in Canada. Despite their high levels of human capital at landing, tax filer data show that their declared incomes have been lower than any other visa category, *including refugees* who commonly arrive in Canada traumatised and with broken families (Hiebert 2009b; Ley, 2003; 2010). Home purchases by BIP households as well as foreign investors derive from wealth secured elsewhere.

Any calibration of the extent of foreign capital in the Vancouver housing market – a perennially disputed issue– is muddied by the variable locations of capital and buyers. It is offshore capital that continues to drive the top end of Vancouver's market even though buyers may be temporary or permanent residents of Canada (Young 2015b). Business immigrants are simply not generating enough local revenue to permit purchase. Even detecting the existence of foreign buyers is complex because of transnational social networks stretched across the Pacific, allowing local residents or property professionals to stand in as proxy buyers for distant investors. There have been many cases in Vancouver's high-priced neighbourhoods of home purchases by students at a local university. These may be the children of later migrant households or, if migration is not planned, the property becomes a short-term investment that will be sold (or rented) once the child's education is completed. In a transnational network spanning national borders, foreign capital, one way or another, is usually routed through local buyers (Ley, 2010; Young, 2015b).

House prices and local demand

In January 2013, Bloomberg's 'Chart of the Day' graphed Vancouver's house price inflation since 1991 against the growth of China's GDP (Kolet & Quinn, 2013). The synchronicity of the two trend lines was evident, and was even closer after 2002, as Mainland migration networks replaced Hong Kong in trans-Pacific flows of information, capital, and people. A coincidence of trend lines, of course, does not require causality without a corresponding contextual argument. The earlier sections of this paper have presented such an argument based largely upon wealth migration facilitated by Canada's welcoming policies on immigration and international investment, and activated by real estate intermediaries with a trans-Pacific orientation, especially at the top end of the housing market.

Unexplored so far, however, have been potential drivers in the local economy, more conventional factors in house price analysis. Local incomes evidently do not have the capacity to drive such a high-priced market. Over the period from 1977 to 2006, real median family incomes in the Vancouver metropolitan area reached a peak of $61,800 in 1980 and had fallen to $54,900 by 2006; during this same period average real house prices almost doubled. More recent data from the 2011 Household Survey support the same conclusion. Despite enduring the highest house prices in Canada, Vancouver residents, even those with post-secondary education, have modest incomes. In a ranking of individual incomes in the 10 largest Canadian cities, Vancouver residents aged 25–55 with a bachelor's degree scored 10th and last, with incomes only 65% of those in top-ranked Toronto (Yan, 2015). Wage growth has remained slow; between 2001 and 2014, average wages increased 36%, while average home values rose 63% in the metropolitan area, and 211% in the City of Vancouver (Vancity, 2015).

Another regional factor that might be related to house prices is domestic in-migration from the rest of Canada. Figure 1 compares the relative importance of net international and net domestic migration against a standardised measure of

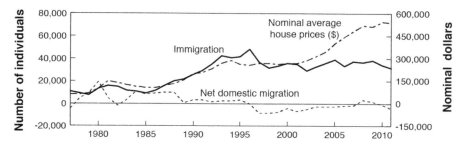

Figure 1.   House prices, net immigration, and net domestic migration, Greater Vancouver, 1977−2011.

Vancouver dwelling prices from 1977 to 2011. Net population in-migration from the rest of Canada peaked in 1980 and has fallen steadily since, with a net loss in some years. Overall, there is a negative correlation ($r = -0.56$), with prices rising even as net domestic migration declined. In contrast, prices have risen consistently with net immigration ($r = 0.76$), and until 2002 immigration closely paralleled the inflating house price line. In recent years, prices have outpaced immigration, coinciding with the convergence of cheap mortgage money and HNWI investment.

Certainly, the Vancouver market has proven a rewarding investment. The REBGV benchmark price for a typical detached property, which excludes the distortions of high values, had reached $1.2 million in Greater Vancouver by October 2015, a 10-year increment of 103%. For the City's Westside neighbourhoods, the equivalent price was $2.8 million with a 10-year growth of 162%. But the more disturbing consequence of these statistics is the extreme unaffordability for local entrants to the market. The RBC Housing Affordability index computes the share of a typical household's pre-tax income that would be consumed by servicing the costs of buying a typical family home. In the first quarter of 2015, the index continued its irrepressible upward march reaching the unlikely level of 86% of gross household income required for servicing an average Greater Vancouver bungalow (*Housing trends and affordability*, 2015). A second metric is provided by the annual affordability assessment of metropolitan markets by the Demographia consultancy, which compares median house prices with median household incomes. A score equal to or less than 3.0 defines an affordable market, while a score above 5.1 defines the worst category, severe unaffordability. As usual, in 2014, Vancouver was second only to Hong Kong in unaffordability, and its excessively high score of 10.6 was the most extreme since the survey had begun (Demographia, 2015).

There is no space here to detail the social and economic consequences of the acute lack of affordability in Vancouver housing. They include difficulty in retaining key employees, out-migration of young workers (Vancity, 2015), crowding and the downsizing of condominium units to microsuites, heavy debt loads (Walks,

2013), long commutes (Angus Reid, 2015), the (necessary) rise of illegal suites in detached homes, and young adults remaining in the family home well into their 20s. Family reproduction is affected as the necessity of two wage earners in a family delays (or prohibits) child-raising. While parents may be involved in financing purchases for some adult children, especially for first-time condominium buyers, significant penalties endured by the young are self-evident (Moos, 2014).

As the issue of affordability was becoming finally politicised in the spring of 2015, a survey of over 800 residents in Greater Vancouver showed the extent of inter-generational inequality (Angus Reid, 2015). A large majority of respondents aged over 55 could be described as happy or comfortable with their housing conditions, while a large majority of those aged 18–34 were uncomfortable or miserable: most of these two unhappy groups agreed with the statement, 'I'm seriously thinking of leaving Metro Vancouver because of the cost of owning a home here.' Long-term homeowners in small households with a paid-off mortgage and no commute were the happiest. Those describing themselves as miserable included renters and mortgage-holding owners; most had at least one child and a sizable commute, yet were also the most educated. Their profile fits the new suburbs, and Walks (2013) has drawn attention to the high incidence of mortgage and overall household debt in these municipalities. Almost every neighbourhood in Greater Vancouver has an average household debt to disposable income level that is above the national average; in many parts of the new suburbs, debt loads are more than twice the national average, identifying a precarious status vulnerable to any economic ill wind.

Another credible report further aggravated emerging public concerns. The largest regional credit union published an alarming forecast on labour market–housing market relations. The report anticipated significant out-migration by qualified workers driven from Vancouver by their desire for affordable homeownership of a single-family home (Vancity, 2015). With current trends, in only five years and even assuming dual-income households, the median incomes of 82 of 88 in-demand positions, including police officers and general practitioners, would fall below the necessary house price threshold. The housing crisis would precipitate a labour crisis. This extraordinary mismatch between wage returns and unaffordable housing costs overturns any conventional model of a symbiotic relation between local incomes and local house prices.

Spring 2015: no data, no policy, no worries

At a Singapore conference in April 2015, Laurence Fink, Chairman and CEO of BlackRock, the world's biggest asset manager, offered his advice on successful investment: 'The two greatest stores of wealth internationally today is [sic] contemporary art… and two, the other store of wealth today is apartments in Manhattan, apartments in Vancouver, in London' (Burgos & Ismail, 2015). This forthright investment recommendation placed Vancouver residential property at the forefront of global asset classes. Fink's judgement was cited by David Eby, an opposition Member in the BC Legislature, the following month in a question he posed to Rich Coleman, Deputy Premier and Minister Responsible for Housing. As Vancouver housing affordability had tumbled to its lowest level ever, and with its housing market serving as a global investor's honey pot, Eby asked whether the minister would collect data measuring the relative extent of international (relative to domestic) speculative investment in Vancouver's market.

Minister Coleman responded:

> I will tell the member that it has virtually nothing to do with the ministry for housing at all... Government doesn't have any policy around this... we do not discriminate against foreign ownership... the reason it [housing] is attractive internationally is because it's pretty reasonable compared to other cities like London, Singapore, Tokyo... There's no initiative at this time in government to go and interfere in the marketplace with regards to housing. (Hansard, 2015)

Three features in this meandering promise of non-response draw attention. First was the unsustainable claim that Vancouver house prices were 'pretty reasonable' compared to others – though the RBC, Demographia, Vancity, and Angus Reid reports all showed Vancouver's affordability to be dire. Second was the Minister's reticence to gather ownership data to identify the extent of foreign investment in the housing market (standard data elsewhere), an action requested by rising public pressure, but rejected as interference in the marketplace. In an earlier television interview, he had made a similar reply to a question on foreign ownership: 'It's not come up as an issue for us' (CTV, 2015). Third and most important is the claim that the question of foreign ownership had nothing to do with government. Yet it most certainly did, for governments had for 30 years led trade and investment missions to Asia, and had used the tool of business immigration to draw in entrepreneurs and their capital.

Though the Minister Responsible for Housing had told the Legislative Assembly that no studies and no data were available on foreign residential investment, a few weeks later, Premier Clark, under fire from growing public dissent (Young, 2015b), drew upon a short report by the Ministry of Finance, using data and interpretation from the BC Real Estate Association. The flimsy analysis – quickly debunked by local critics – denied that foreign investment was a significant factor in the housing market, a process of denial dating back to the first round of sharp house price increases after 1988 (Gold, 2015; Mitchell, 2004). The Premier's source of authoritative data, the vested interest of the BCREA, revealed a convergence of institutional objectives. For the province's coffers, as well as property industry bottom lines, have both benefitted greatly from East Asian capital flows. Each investor household in the BIP selecting BC as a destination brings the province a share of their interest-free $800,000 loan. No wonder that CIC managers in Ottawa had informed me that the provincial governments were the principal lobbyists for the

BIP. Indeed, when the federal government had turned the screws on the BIP in the late 1990s over tax avoidance, the then social democratic government of BC had been one of its strongest advocates (Ley, 2013). In addition to the bounty from the BIP, property tax plus the property transfer tax (a residential sales tax) from spiralling housing prices contributed $3 billion (6.8%) to provincial revenues in 2013–2014 (Government of BC, 2014). Every $1 million residential sale is worth $18,000 in transfer tax to the provincial government. While acknowledging criticisms of the transfer tax, Premier Clark admitted her government's dependence on it: 'this year we brought in $928 million in revenue' (CBC, 2015).

Conclusion

Structural defects in the BC economy exposed by a severe recession led three levels of government to develop networks with the growth region of Asia Pacific from the early 1980s. The objectives, to augment trade and investment, were aided by neoliberal tools that included open borders, deregulation, a place-boosting world's fair, liberalised immigration policies, and a development-ready province pushing back the gains of labour and the welfare state. An innovation that gained significant take-up was the Business Immigration Programme, with Vancouver, the closest major city to East Asia and with a high quality of life, the most popular destination especially for the wealthiest investor newcomers. Although the BIP was open to affluent residents of all nations, in the past 35 years, 80%–85% of investor class immigrants originated in Greater China.

The state's Asia Pacific outreach has proven successful in reaching its economic goals. In 2014, 37% of BC's exports were Asia-bound. Piecing together various sources, and including secondary migration, I estimate wealth migration of 200,000 immigrants to Vancouver through the three streams of the BIP between 1980 and 2012, the equivalent of 8%–9% of the metropolitan population in 2011. Massive amounts of capital moved across the Pacific; the estimated liquid capital available to business immigrants arriving in Greater Vancouver between 1988 and 1997 alone was $35–$40 billion. Some of this was surrendered to the provincial government as a requisite interest-free loan. Newcomers moved quickly into homeownership in Canada's most expensive city and their housing impact was elevated by their preference for property as an early site for further investment and rental income.

While real incomes have atrophied for several decades, the Greater Vancouver benchmark price for detached properties is now $1.2 million, and is once again on a tear, having risen by 20% in the past 12 months. Both provincial and municipal government revenues have benefitted from property-based taxation, and are reluctant to harm the goose that lays the golden egg. Wealth generated in asset hotspots in a deregulated globalised economy can generate huge public revenues as well as private returns. The convergence, even without collusion, of private and public sector property interests in BC creates immense momentum that precludes meaningful policy responses to inequities that include excessive housing unaffordability, precarious mortgage indebtedness, and disillusioned out-migration. The default housing policy position has become minimal response and the cultivation of ignorance concerning actual trends. In this neo-liberal policy environment, community costs assume the status of acceptable collateral damage.

Acknowledgements

The author is grateful to Dan Hiebert and to audiences at Harvard and Goldsmiths Universities for comments on an earlier draft of this paper.

Disclosure statement

No potential conflict of interest was reported by the author.

Funding

This work was supported by the Social Sciences and Humanities Research Council under their Canada Research Chairs programme.

References

Anderlini, J. (2015). Chinese take lead among foreign buyers of US homes. *Financial Times*. Retrieved from http://www.ft.com/intl/cms/s/0/351606a8-159b-11e5-be54-00144feabdc0.html

Angus Reid. (2015). *Lotusland blues*. Vancouver: Angus Reid Institute. Retrieved from http://angusreid.org/vancouver-real-estate/

Barnes, T., Edgington, D., Denike, K., & McGee, T. (1992). Vancouver, the province and the Pacific Rim. In G. Wynn, & T. Oke (Eds.), *Vancouver and its region* (pp. 171–199). Vancouver: UBC Press.

Burgos, J., & Ismail, N.I. (2015). New York apartments, art top gold as stores of wealth, says Fink. *Bloomberg Business*. Retrieved from http://www.bloomberg.com/news/articles/2015-04-21/new-york-apartments-art-top-gold-as-stores-of-wealth-says-fink

Carter, T. (2012). The Canadian housing market: No bubble? No meltdown? In A. Bardhan, R. Edelstein, & C. Kroll (Eds.), *Global housing markets* (pp. 511–534). Hoboken, NJ: John Wiley.

CBC. (2015). BC property transfer tax could be cut, Premier Christy Clark hints. *CBC News British Columbia*. Retrieved from http://www.cbc.ca/news/canada/british-columbia/b-c-property-transfer-tax-could-be-cut-premier-christy-clark-hints-1.2963133

CBRE. (2014). *Supplying London's housing needs; building to match demand*. London: Author.

CBRE. (2015). *The expanding role of Chinese capital in global real estate markets*. London: Author.

Chung, W. (2015). Retrieved from http://www.winniechung.com/

CIC. (2000). *Recent immigrants in the Vancouver metropolitan area*. Ottawa: CIC Strategic Research and Review.

City of Vancouver. (1985). *Vancouver economic mission to Hong Kong, Singapore and Kuala Lumpur, 2 July-14 July, 1985*. Vancouver: Economic Development Office.

Claiborne, W. (1991). The new 'hongs ' of Vancouver: Canadian city becomes a haven for Hong Kong's wealthiest families. *Washington Post*, p. H1.

CMHC. (2015). *Housing market assessment: Canada*. Ottawa: Author. Retrieved from http://www.cmhc-schl.gc.ca/odpub/esub/68456/68456_2015_Q04.pdf?fr = 1446749233245

CTV. (2015). One-third of Vancouver house units scooped up by foreign buyers. *CTV News Vancouver*. Retrieved from http://bc.ctvnews.ca/one-third-of-vancouver-house-units-scooped-up-by-foreign-buyers-1.2364478

Daly, M. (1982). *Sydney boom, Sydney bust*. Sydney: George Allen & Unwin.

Demographia. (2015). *Eleventh annual Demographia international housing affordability survey: 2015*. Belleville, IL: Demographia. Retrieved from http://www.demographia.com/dhi.pdf

Dorfmann, J. (2015). New wealth seeks a 'home': The rise of the hedge city. *Harvard International Review, 36*(3). Retrieved from http://hir.harvard.edu/new-wealth-seeks-a-home-the-rise-of-the-hedge-city/

Economist. (2014). Housing in Vancouver: The B.C. bolthole. Retrieved from http://www.economist.com/blogs/americasview/2014/06/housing-vancouver

Edgington, D. (1996). Japanese real estate involvement in Canadian cities and regions, 1985−1993. *Canadian Geographer, 40*, 292−305.

Gold, K. (2015). First step: Accept there's a problem. *Globe & Mail,* p. S6.

Government of BC. (2014). *Budget and fiscal plan 2014/15-2016/17*. Victoria: Ministry of Finance. Retrieved from http://bcbudget.gov.bc.ca/2014/bfp/2014_budget_and_fiscal_plan.pdf

Hajdu, J. (1994). Recent cycles of foreign property investment in central Sydney and central Melbourne. *Urban Geography, 15*, 246−257.

Hamilton, G. (1988, December 16). Li promises local sale for Expo project, Taylor says. *Vancouver Sun,* p. A14.

Hanemann, T., & Huotari, M. (2015). *Chinese FDI in Europe and Germany: Preparing for a new era of Chinese capital*. Berlin: Mercator Institute for Chinese Studies and Rhodium Group. Retrieved from http://www.merics.org/fileadmin/templates/art/aktuelles/COFDI/Download/PDF/COFDI-EN-WEB.pdf

Hansard. (2015). Coleman to Eby, House in Committee, Legislature of British Columbia. Vol. 26, No. 6, pp. 8541−2. Retrieved from http://www.leg.bc.ca/hansard/40th4th/20150514am-Hansard-v26n6.htm#

Hiebert, D. (2009a). Newcomers in the Canadian housing market: a longitudinal study, 2001−2005. *Canadian Geographer, 53*, 268−287.

Hiebert, D. (2009b). The economic integration of immigrants in Greater Vancouver. *Choices, 15*, 2−42.

Housing trends and affordability. (2015). *RBC Economics*. Retrieved from http://www.rbc.com/newsroom/_assets-custom/pdf/20150622-HA.pdf

Hurun Report. (2011). *White paper on Chinese people's private wealth management*. Shanghai: Hurun Research Institute.

Hurun Report. (2014). *Immigration and the Chinese HNWI 2014*. Hurun Report and Visas Consulting Group. Retrieved from http://up.hurun.net/Humaz/201406/20140606132402353.pdf

IIUSA. (2014). FY2014 statistics reveals important trends in EB-5 visa usage, market diversification. Retrieved from https://iiusa.org/blog/research-analysis/economic-impact-research-analysis/department-state-dos-fy2014-statistics-reveals-important-trends-eb5-visa-usage-market-diversification/

Jordan, D. (n.d.). David Choi — bucking the trend. *Business in Vancouver*. Retrieved from http://royalpacific.com/about/profile.asp

Knight Frank. (2013). *The wealth report 2013: the global perspective on prime property and wealth*. London: Knight Frank.

Kolet, I., & Quinn, G. (2013). China growth sets Vancouver home prices: Chart of the day. *Bloomberg Business*. Retrieved from http://www.bloomberg.com/news/articles/2013-01-20/china-growth-sets-vancouver-home-prices-chart-of-the-day

Le Corre, P. (1994). Canada's Hong Kong. *Far Eastern Economic Review, 157*(6), 36–37.

Lee-Young, J. (2015). Mainland Chinese 'dominating' high-end Vancouver real estate market. *Vancouver Sun*, p. A2.

Lemon, J. (1993). Social planning and the welfare state. In L. Bourne & D. Ley (Eds.). *The changing social geography of Canadian cities* (pp. 267–280). Montreal: McGill-Queen's University Press.

Ley, D. (2003). Seeking *homo economicus*: The strange story of Canada's Business Immigration Program. *Annals, Association of American Geographers, 93*, 426–441.

Ley, D. (2010). *Millionaire migrants: Trans-Pacific life lines*. Oxford: Wiley-Blackwell.

Ley, D. (2013). Does transnationalism trump immigrant integration? Evidence from Canada's links with East Asia. *Journal of Ethnic and Migration Studies, 39*, 921–938.

Ley, D., & Tutchener, J. (2001). Immigration, globalization and house prices in Canada's gateway cities. *Housing Studies, 16*, 199–223.

Lui, M. (2015). Retrieved from http://www.manyeelui.com/.

Macdonald Realty. (2015). Retrieved from http://www.macrealty.com/.

Marlow, I. (2014). Chinese investors' immigration cases fail. *Globe & Mail*, p. S2.

McMartin, P. (2015). Why don't we have real estate data? *Vancouver Sun*, p. A4.

Mitchell, K. (2004). *Crossing the neoliberal line: Pacific Rim migration and the metropolis*. Philadelphia, PA: Temple University Press.

Moos, M. (2014). Generational dimensions of neoliberal and post-Fordist restructuring: The Changing characteristics of young adults and growing income inequality in Montreal and Vancouver. *International Journal of Urban and Regional Research, 38*, 2078–2102.

Moos, M., & Skaburskis, A. (2010). The globalization of urban housing markets: Immigration and changing housing demand in Vancouver. *Urban Geography, 31*, 724–749.

National Association of Realtors. (2015). *2015 profile of home buying activity of international clients for the twelve month period ending March 2015*. Washington, DC: National Association of Realtors.

Olds, K. (2001). *Globalization and urban change: Capital, culture and Pacific Rim megaprojects*. Oxford: Oxford University Press.

Paris, C. (2013). The homes of the super-rich: multiple residences, hyper-mobility and decoupling of prime residential housing in global cities. In I. Hay (Ed.), *Geographies of the super-rich* (pp. 94–109). Cheltenham: Edward Elgar.

Resnick, P. (1987). Neoconservatism on the periphery: the lessons for BC. *BC Studies, 75*, 3–23.

Rogers, D., Lee, C.L., & Yan, D. (2015). The politics of foreign investment in Australian housing: Chinese investors, translocal sales agents and local resistance. *Housing Studies*. Advance online publication. doi:10.1080/02673037.2015.1006185

Royal Pacific Realty. (2015). Record breaking year for Royal Pacific Realty Group. Retrieved from http://www.royalpacific.ca/record-breaking-year-for-royal-pacific-realty-group/

Salaff, J., Wong, S.L., & Greve, A. (2010). *Hong Kong movers and stayers: Narratives of family migration*. Urbana: University of Illinois Press.

Savills. (2013). *Around the world in dollars and cents: How private money moves around the real estate world*. London: Savills and Wealth-X.

Skaburskis, A. (1988). Speculation and housing prices: A study of Vancouver's boom-bust cycle. *Urban Affairs Quarterly, 23*, 556–580.

Sumption, M. (2012). *Visa for entrepreneurs: How countries are seeking out immigrant job creators*. Washington, DC: Migration Policy Institute.

Sumption, M., & Hooper, K. (2014). *Selling visas and citizenship: Policy questions from the global boom in investor immigration*. Washington, DC: Migration Policy Institute.

Tseng, Y.-F. (2000) The mobility of entrepreneurs and capital: Taiwanese capital-linked migration. *International Migration, 38*, 143–168.

UBS. (2015). *UBS global real estate bubble index 2015*. Zurich: Author. Retrieved from https://www.ubs.com/global/en/wealth_management/wealth_management_research/global-bubble-index.html

Vancity. (2015). *Help wanted: Salaries, affordability and the exodus of labour from Metro Vancouver*. Vancouver: Vancouver City Savings Credit Union. Retrieved from https://www.vancity.com/SharedContent/documents/News/Help_Wanted_May_2015.pdf

Walks, A. (2013). Mapping the urban debtscape. *Urban Geography, 34*, 153–187.

Walks, A. (2014). Canada's housing bubble story: Mortgage securitization, the state, and the global financial crisis. *International Journal of Urban and Regional Research, 38*, 256–284.

Wang, Z. (2013). Why China's new rich want to emigrate. *The Diplomat*. Retrieved from http://thediplomat.com/china-power/why-chinas-new-rich-want-to-emigrate/

Ware, R., Fortin, P., & Paradis, P.E. (2010). *The economic impact of the immigrant investor program in Canada*. Montreal: Analysis Group. Retrieved from http://sciencessociales.uottawa.ca/grei-rgei/fra/documents/Ware_Fortin_Paradis_Canada_IIP_Report_English.pdf

Waters, J.L. (2008). *Education, migration and cultural capital in the Chinese diaspora*. Amherst, NY: Cambria Press.

Westside and Downtown edition. (2015). *Real Estate Weekly*.

Wong, L. (2003). Chinese business migration to Australia, Canada and the United States: State policy and the global immigration marketplace. *Asian and Pacific Migration Journal, 12*, 301–336.

Wynn, G. (1992). The rise of Vancouver. In G. Wynn, & T. Oke (Eds.), *Vancouver and its region* (pp. 69–145). Vancouver: UBC Press.

Yan, A. (2015, April 2). *Rethinking the housing affordability crisis*. Paper presented at the 3rd Annual Symposium of the Rethinking the Region Series, Urban Studies Program, Vancouver.

Young, I. (2015a). Millionaire migration to Canada didn't fall after investor scheme's axing – it rose, new data reveals. *South China Morning Post*. Retrieved from http://www.scmp.com/comment/blogs/article/1843069/millionaire-migration-canada-didnt-fall-after-investor-schemes-axing

Young, I. (2015b). Something is grotesquely wrong with Vancouver's housing market, and the time for denialism is over. *South China Morning Post*. Retrieved from http://www.scmp.com/comment/blogs/article/1804916/something-grotesquely-wrong-vancouvers-housing-market-and-time

Yu, H.-Y., & Donville, C. (2011). Chinese spreading wealth make Vancouver homes pricier than NYC. *Bloomberg*. Retrieved from http://www.bloomberg.com/news/print/2011-05-16/chinese-spreading-wealth-make-vancouver-homes-pricier-than-nyc.html

The (geo)politics of land and foreign real estate investment in China: the case of Hong Kong FDI

Karita Kan

Market reforms and the relaxation of rules governing inbound investment have contributed to the growth of foreign investment in Chinese real estate. Although the property sector remains one of the most tightly regulated, property developers from Greater China have enjoyed relative success in the mainland market. Conventional explanations of such investment outcomes have often drawn attention to economic complementaries and cultural proximities. By tracing the development of Hong Kong investment in China's real estate from the late 1970s to the present, this paper demonstrates the importance of considering (geo)politics at both the national and ground levels in analysing bilateral economic relations. The geopolitical prerogatives of national sovereignty structure economic interactions between the Chinese state and the Special Administrative Region, while popular politics from the ground level up interacts with state-level geopolitics to affect and change policy outcomes. The shifting dynamics demonstrate that the cultural meaning and value of foreign capital are not static or fixed but rather open to continuous re-negotiation and contestation.

Introduction

The landscape of urban China has undergone tremendous changes in the past three and a half decades. An agent behind the on-going territorial transformation is foreign real estate capital, which has become increasingly active in the mainland market since China opened its door to foreign direct investment (FDI) in the late 1970s. A significant proportion of the real estate FDI China receives originates from Asian property developers based in Hong Kong, Taiwan, Japan, South Korea and Southeast Asian countries such as Singapore and Malaysia. Specifically, capital from Hong Kong, Taiwan, and Macau accounted for approximately 60% of foreign real estate investment in the People's Republic as of 2010 (Hui & Chan, 2014). That such a large proportion of China-bound property capital comes from constituents of Greater China puts into perspective the ascribed foreignness of the real estate investment China receives, but also sheds important light on the robustness of trans-boundary linkages within the regional economy and the geopolitics that structure and underpin such capital flows.

Existing studies of foreign real estate investment in China have often focused attention on the mutually beneficial relationship between domestic economic development and inbound FDI. Liberalisation policies pursued by the Chinese government and rapid growth rates have contributed to increased foreign investments in real estate (Hui & Chan, 2014). Overseas investors have focused on large cities in coastal areas where market institutions are most developed and where perceived returns on capital are highest (He, Wang, & Cheng, 2011; He & Zhu, 2010). The growth in FDI has in turn bolstered economic performance at home as real estate remains one of the largest sectors to attract foreign capital in China (Broadman & Sun, 1997; Jiang, Chen & Isaac, 1998). A strong real estate sector creates employment opportunities in related industries from raw materials and construction to property management and home decoration (Fung, Huang, Liu, & Shen, 2006). The inter-city competition to attract foreign investment also spurs state investments in infrastructure and invigorates place promotion activities by local governments (Wu, 2002). On the ground, foreign capital has participated in the production of new urban spaces in Chinese cities. Studies have noted how, through introducing foreign planning ideals, designs and practices, overseas property investment has contributed to the modernisation and internationalisation of Chinese urban landscapes (Cartier, 2005; Gaubatz, 2005; He & Wu, 2005; Zhu, Sim, & Zhang, 2006).

The bolstering effect of foreign real estate investment in recipient countries, however, has not been uncontested. While they are generally seen as being conducive to economic growth, inward investment flows have also been viewed as intrusive and harmful to local interests. The housing studies literature has highlighted the cultural politics that often underlies foreign investment in residential real estate. In recent years, the increased global activity of Asian investors in Western housing markets has enlivened sociocultural anxieties and contributed to the growth of protectionist and xenophobic discourses surrounding issues of housing affordability and insider/outsider relations (Ley, 2010; Rogers, Lee & Yan, 2015). Manifestations of local parochialism are not limited to residential and housing concerns, but have also found expressions in broader claims-making about citizenship, territoriality and sovereignty (Rogers & Dufty-Jones, 2015). There is thus an important geopolitical dimension pertaining to foreign real estate investment, both in the traditional sense of inter-state relations, national interests and foreign policy, and in the critical sense that gives emphasis to geopolitical discourses of the everyday and the lived experiences of actors on the ground (Dittmer & Sharp, 2014; Ó Tuathail & Dalby, 1998; Rogers, 2016).

While existing studies of foreign real estate investment in China have primarily focused on its contribution to China's economic growth and urbanisation, this paper seeks to develop a more nuanced understanding of the geopolitical and cultural dynamics that both facilitate and constrain capital flows. The study of Hong Kong real estate FDI provides a uniquely interesting case for the examination of such dynamics in the Chinese context given the particular geopolitical status of the territory as a Special Administrative Region (SAR) of the People's Republic. A British colony from the mid-nineteenth century until the handover in 1997, Hong Kong investment in China has been classified as 'foreign' and remains so following the resumption of Chinese rule as the territory is now governed under a 'one country, two systems' framework and given autonomous decision-making power.

By examining Hong Kong investment in Chinese real estate from the 1980s to the present, this paper aims to unpack and scrutinise the shifting geopolitics at both the national and ground levels that has conditioned and structured cross-border flows in a changing context. It argues that the cultural meaning and (economic) value of 'foreign' capital are not static or fixed but rather open to continuous re-negotiation and contestation. While in the early reform years the geopolitical projects of national re-unification and global economic rise had contributed to the privileged status and success of Hong Kong investors, in recent years popular politics from the ground level up with its socioeconomic concern for housing affordability and critique of the dominant pro-growth agenda has complicated, even undermined, the territory's investment in the mainland. These shifting dynamics highlight the fluid meaning of foreign capital in post-socialist China and lend insight into the country's changing landscape of investment and urbanisation.

Identity, geopolitics and capital flows between Hong Kong and China

The role of Hong Kong capital in China's market reform is well documented. Since the late 1970s pioneer capital from the city has played an agential part in spurring rural industrialisation and urbanisation particularly in southern China (Smart & Smart, 1991; Sit & Yang, 1997). Research on Hong Kong-mainland economic relations in the early reform years has focused on economic complementarities and comparative advantage in explaining the formation of a cross-border regional production system (Shen, 2003). A spatial division of labour was established where industrial investment transferred out from Hong Kong's restructuring economy was directed northwards to invigorate manufacturing in the mainland (Sit, 1998).

In comparing the geographical origins of China-bound FDI, existing studies have drawn attention to ethno-cultural proximity as an important explanatory or intervening variable in accounting for the prominence of investments from Hong Kong. The territory's business community consists of many first- and second-generation immigrants whose native places lie in cities, towns and villages in southern China. Their investments in their respective hometowns have been seen as constitutive of distinct economic orders characterised by social ties, relational networks and cultural affinity (Crawford, 2000). In this respect, Hong Kong investment shares similarities with foreign investments made by other overseas Chinese where ethnic social capital and cultural networks play key roles in facilitating economic exchanges (Hsing, 1996; Jean, Tan, & Sinkovics 2011; Smart & Hsu, 2004; Tseng, 2002; Wong, 1998; Wong, 1999; Zhang, 2005). Building on trust, reciprocity and obligatory norms, these informal connections are found to enhance information sharing and prevent defection (Rauch & Trindade, 2002), with the effect of improving responsiveness in policy-making (Chen, 2000) and mitigating risks in business transactions (Chen & Chen, 1998; Wang, 2000). The multivocality of Hong Kong investors' identity as both Chinese and foreign has given them distinct advantages: The cultural proximity of Chineseness has granted them privileged access to the mainland market and competitive edge over non-Chinese investors, while their outsider status has enabled them to capture economic benefits exclusive to foreign investment and to conduct business without the constraints that govern domestic enterprises (Smart & Smart, 1998).

Cultural identity, however, is not an inherent essence or static property to be possessed and owned (Siu, 1993; Nonni & Ong, 1997; Tseng, 2002). Its meaning and value are rather fluid and in-the-making, open to re-presentation and re-interpretation by social groups and powerful actors as it is differentially activated and mobilised in accordance with changing agendas and objectives. In highlighting ethno-cultural proximity in explanations of economic and investment relations, therefore, attention should also be directed to the forces that participate in the on-going construction of the meanings and functions of identity. In the extant case, a consideration of geopolitics is crucial in contextualising the articulation of identity and economic interactions in Hong Kong-China relations. Informed by critical geopolitical scholarship, geopolitics is taken here to refer not only to the strategic statecraft that guides nation-states' policy making, but also to the production and consumption of geopolitical discourses and representations by academics, officials, and popular media and people's everyday practices and lived experiences (Dittmer & Dodds, 2008; Dittmer & Gray, 2010). Geopolitics both structures formal decision-making at the high level and 'saturates' the everyday at the ground level in people's daily encounters and media consumption (Ó Tuathail & Dalby, 1998).

In the Hong Kong-China context, the geopolitics of sovereignty and unification forms the important background in conceptualising bilateral relations and identity construction. In the Chinese national imaginary, Hong Kong represents a formerly colonised territory to be fully re-integrated and re-unified with its motherland. The SAR constitutes a 'zone of exception' to normalised Chinese rule, created to generate conditions for its re-absorption into the Chinese sovereign landscape (Ong, 2004). As Ong (2004) argues, the geopolitical construct of 'Greater China' is part and parcel of the Chinese national project of using zoning technologies to economically integrate disarticulated political entities, with the aim of achieving eventual political integration. Such prerogatives have found manifestation in a variety of mainland Chinese policies towards Hong Kong both before and after the handover, from the central leadership's cooptation of the city's political and financial elites (Goodstadt, 2009) and the signing of a free trade agreement, to the relaxation of tourism restrictions across the Hong Kong-mainland border (Rowen, 2016).

According politics a central role in explaining foreign investment also requires taking into account the disaggregated, non-unitary nature of the Chinese state. Indeed, the market-oriented reforms that have contributed to China's ascendance in global economic and geopolitical prominence have been characterised by active agency on the part of subnational actors. The devolution of administrative and fiscal authority has led to a rescaling of politics in China's political economy, with the outcome of empowering local governments (Chung, 2001; Yeung, 2000). The reform era has seen the rise of pro-growth, entrepreneurial local states that politically prioritise the creation of good business climates for furthering capital accumulation (Zhu, 1999; Zhang, 2002; Wu, 2003). These local state actors have been active in soliciting investments and forging growth coalitions with both domestic and foreign capital, and have played a key role in the internationalisation of China's real estate.

Statist projects and prerogatives, however, are by no means constant and unchanging but may shift as a result of changes in policy agendas and societal demands. Foreign investment in Chinese real estate has not always been seen in a positive light; rather, the influx of foreign money particularly since the mid-2000s has been represented by official and media discourses as unfavourable and harmful, with the undesirable consequences of driving up domestic home prices and contributing to structural imbalances in housing development (Cao, 2015). Such practical and popular geopolitics interacts with policy-making at the state level. Recent scholarship has for instance observed the move towards a more socially conscious brand of entrepreneurialism in Chinese local governance that gives greater emphasis to social redistribution and housing concerns in response to societal sentiments (Wang, 2011b). This paper thus pays attention to how both state and social forces participate in the attribution of meaning and value to foreign capital and as such influence policy outcomes.

To examine the above, this paper both analyses primary documentary sources and draws on empirical observations. National-level policy documents concerning foreign investment, the real estate industry and land management from the late 1970s to the present are surveyed. The examination of media sources is commonly used in popular geopolitical analysis (Dittmer & Sharp, 2014). Chinese-language news sources related to Hong Kong or foreign real estate investment in China are collated, with a particular focus on leading Hong Kong developers' mainland investments. In addition to documentary sources, this paper also draws on empirical observations made during fieldwork in mainland China, which has focused on investigating rural and urban neighbourhood redevelopment projects involving local and foreign real estate capital. Site visits and fieldwork involving interviews and participant observation were carried out in the Pearl River Delta cities of Shenzhen and Guangzhou between 2011 and 2015.

Contextualising Hong Kong real estate investment in China

Foreign real estate investment is often considered risky and costly due to the highly localised nature of the industry. In reform-era China, whose transition from a socialist economic system has created additional institutional constraints including uncertain property rights and weak legal procedures, the land and real estate market presents significant entry barriers to foreign investors. Western companies are often restricted to making indirect investment through establishing and selling real estate investment trusts or purchasing and operating built property (Hsing, 2006). By comparison, Hong Kong property capital has been much more extensively involved in the mainland market. Investments made by the territory's developers have reached both first- and second-tier Chinese cities along the coast and further inland. They have also diversified from commercial real estate and hotel development to residential projects and neighbourhood redevelopment.

Real estate has long played a key role in Hong Kong's economy where land rent constitutes an important source of government revenue (Haila, 2000; Jessop & Sum, 2000). The property developers of Hong Kong are transnational business conglomerates with subsidiaries operating in a wide range of sectors from infrastructure and retail to utilities and telecommunication. The largest dozen of these rank amongst the 2015 Forbes list of the world's biggest two thousand public companies; some of their owners also top the list of the richest twenty real estate billionaires worldwide. The most established of these companies, including the Cheung Kong-Hutchison group, Sun Hung Kai Properties, Henderson Land Development, New World Development and the Wharf-Wheelock conglomerate, are controlled by their respective founding families, whose members own between 40% and 80% of the firm's shares.[1]

The ascendance of the property elite in colonial Hong Kong dates back to the late 1940s, when the end of the Second World War and Communist victory in China brought huge waves of immigration into the British-ruled colony and invigorated industrial activities, creating a spike in demand for factories and housing. Investing the revenues accumulated through industrial activities in land acquisition and property development, the company founders built up significant land reserves by purchasing land in the rural hinterlands of Hong Kong (Poon, 2010). They also expanded their companies by taking over land and property assets from retreating British firms in the late 1960s when the Chinese Cultural Revolution heightened fears of political instability, and in the early 1980s when uncertain prospects raised by negotiations over Hong Kong's return to Chinese rule led to the further departure of foreign capital (Goodstadt, 2009; Wong, 2015). By the 1980s, the developers have established themselves as powerful players as they further expanded their corporate profiles through extensive acquisition of public utilities and transportation companies. Their financial strength and the influence they possessed both with the British colonial leadership and within Hong Kong society made them ideal partners for the Chinese state at the national and local levels.

The national politics of cooptation and economic integration

The city's property elites were targets of political cooptation by the central leader-ship, an objective that became closely intertwined with broader processes of eco-nomic integration. Hong Kong's property elites were sought by the Chinese government as mediators in the years leading up to the signing of the Sino-British Joint Declaration of 1984, the document that confirmed the British colony's immi-nent return to Chinese sovereignty (Goodstadt, 2009). Following the 1989 Tiananmen tragedy, which exacerbated anxieties in Hong Kong over reversion to Chinese rule and triggered a wave of emigration, the need for supporters with high standing in local society further compelled Beijing to reinforce its commitment in enlisting the property elites as its local partners (Baum, 1999; Wong, 2015).

Economically, the late 1970s and 1980s saw the gradual opening up of China's real estate market to Hong Kong investors. In 1978, Chinese officials negotiated an agreement with six Hong Kong developers to build China Hotel, the country's first joint-venture luxury hotel located in Guangzhou (Chen, 2015). The Guangzhou Garden Hotel, which also opened in the mid-1980s, was likewise developed with property investment from Hong Kong. In these early reform years, Hong Kong developers' 'foreign but Chinese' identity provided an important ground for busi-ness interactions at a time when the dust was far from settled concerning the debate between the socialist and capitalist paths. The labelling of overseas Chinese invest-ors as 'compatriots' helped reform-minded factions in Beijing navigate the apparent conflict between economic pragmatism and ideological symbolism (Smart & Hsu, 2004). As the 'foreignness' of capitalist investment was mediated by the geopoliti-cal and ethnocultural proximities of Hong Kong, Chinese leaders with pro-business inclinations could open up to 'patriotic' foreign capital while still proclaiming ideo-logical adherence to socialism. By producing landmark outcomes such as the China Hotel, Hong Kong capital helped buttress pro-reform forces and played a part in precipitating and deepening the liberalisation of foreign investment in China.

The subsequent ascendance of reform leaders in Chinese politics meant that the developers were granted further connections and market access. Hong Kong's prop-erty elites were appointed policy advisors to the State Council and given seats on the influential Chinese People's Political Consultative Conference (Ye, 2014). The loosening of foreign real estate investment restrictions in the early 1990s further provided opportunities for the developers to expand their investments. Hopewell Holdings, the company responsible for overseeing the construction of China Hotel, branched out to power plant and superhighway construction and earned lucrative rights to develop residential apartments and shopping centres along major transpor-tation thoroughfares. By 1992, the mainland had already eclipsed Hong Kong as Hopewell's primary investment, accounting for 60-70% of the company's portfolio (China Business Review, 1993). Lee Ka-shing's Hutchison Whampoa similarly engaged in infrastructure development and expanded the company's presence by building container ports for coastal cities. The extension of market privileges in turn strengthened the political partnership between the two sides as networks of power and accumulation became increasingly intertwined.

The local politics of land finance and territorial development

While geopolitical and economic considerations at the national level shaped and structured the broader currents of capital flows, it is local governments on the ground to which such investments have accrued and with whom foreign developers have actively cooperated. The activism of local governments in attracting external investment is a direct product of the decentralisation of administrative and fiscal authority in the reform era, which has enhanced the agential role of local governments in urban development and created local economies dependent on land-derived revenues.

To begin with, the downward transfer of power has given local governments greater autonomy in overseeing infrastructural construction and planning territorial development (Yeh & Wu, 1999). Financially, local governments were empowered by the opening up of the economy to FDI and Beijing's decision to allow local authorities to set up financing platforms for fund raising. Reform of the land management system further opened up an entirely new stream of revenue for municipal coffers. The introduction of a market track in the urban land system created a nascent leasehold market where commercial users could now purchase the use rights of urban land from the state by paying conveyance fees (Lin & Ho, 2005). Because local governments are the designated representatives of state ownership for the land under their jurisdiction, they have been the largest beneficiaries of the commodification of urban land (Hsing, 2010).

The activism of municipal leaders in auctioning off premium land in cities helped engineer the real estate boom of the early 1990s (Huang & Yang, 1996). The interest rate cuts in 1990 and 1991 and the availability of loans spurred an influx of investment in Chinese real estate (Jiang, Chen, & Isaac, 1998). The amount of realised real estate FDI rose from US$0.5 billion in 1991 to US$3.4 billion in 1992, of which an approximate US$1.5-2.5 billion originated from Hong Kong (China Business Review, 1992b). Media reports of the time noted how Hong Kong developers had signed up for Chinese projects 'at a frantic pace', issuing special shares to raise funds and transferring money out of European and American projects to capitalise on a 'window of opportunity that may disappear within a few years' (China Business Review, 1992b). Sun Hung Kai, New World Development and Kerry Properties signed contracts worth a total of US$645 million with Beijing in 1992, while Shanghai and Guangdong province each secured no less than eight agreements with Hong Kong developers. Deals were also successfully concluded, as joint ventures with Chinese companies, with the local governments of Tianjin, Zhejiang, Fujian, Hainan, Shandong and Sichuan. By the end of the year, Hong

Kong developers had gained rights to develop an estimated 200 million square feet of land in China (China Business Review, 1992a). Most of these projects were retail, residential, and commercial developments, with several involving the redevelopment of entire districts into mixed-use neighbourhoods.

The land-centred mechanism of bolstering municipal finances became imperative for many local governments after the 1994 tax reform, which significantly reduced municipal budgetary revenues and forced local governments to turn to off-budget sources including land conveyance fees (Chung, 2001; Yang, 2006).[2] The reliance on land rents intensified competition between cities as the ability to attract investment became crucial to economic success. As a result, a distinct turn towards urban entrepreneurialism could be observed in China's first- and second-tier cities. The rise of pro-growth economic considerations in political thinking, as characteristic of the entrepreneurial city, has brought about closer cooperative relations between local bureaucracies and enterprises and foreign capital, who shared similar interests in the maximisation of land rents (Hubbard & Hall, 1998; Zhu, 1999; Zhang, 2002; Wu, 2003).

For local governments, cooperation with foreign developers offered financial resources, technical expertise, and reputational prestige. Compared with their mainland counterparts Hong Kong developers were able to raise a large amount of capital within a short period of time, an advantage that cash-strapped local governments might find attractive (Wu, 2000). The ability to secure contracts with Hong Kong developers also improved other foreign investors' confidence in the city and helped accumulate further investment. In terms of expertise and prestige, property capital from Hong Kong was seen as a vehicle of modernisation and internationalisation that matched with the territorial ambitions of local officials in constructing world-class urban landscapes. In the reform era, the production of international spaces such as central business districts, convention halls and skyscrapers has become the most visible form of political achievement municipal leaders could hope to demonstrate.

Signing of free trade agreement

From the mid-1990s to the early 2000s, foreign real estate investment in China remained at a relatively constant level. Following Hong Kong's return to Chinese sovereignty in 1997, economic exchanges between the two sides had further deepened. The geopolitical project of re-absorption through economic integration and the cultivation of vestedness found clearest expression in the signing of the Closer Economic Partnership Arrangement (CEPA), the first free trade agreement between China and Hong Kong, in 2003. Designed to attract the financial elite, CEPA granted Hong Kong's service industries effective market access to China's service sector by lowering entry thresholds. Specifically, it extended privileged treatment to the real estate sector in two important ways (Hong Kong Trade and Development

Council [HKTDC], 2003a, 2003b). First, Hong Kong developers could now set up wholly-owned holding companies to manage their assets in China, without being required to set up a joint venture for each mainland project. This freedom to choose between sole ownership and equity joint venture and the eased restrictions on direct capital flow significantly lowered development costs. Second, CEPA allowed property-related service providers to enter the mainland market. This facilitated Hong Kong developers' operation as complete industry chains, as architecture and design firms that developers have a working relationship with could now enter the mainland.

The extension of preferential treatment through CEPA further enhanced the competitiveness of Hong Kong real estate capital amongst foreign investors. A week after the signing of CEPA, over ten major developers were invited for a group visit to Shanghai where they met with local leaders and negotiated a combined investment of 25 billion yuan in the municipality (HKTDC, 2003b). Unfavourable market conditions at home due to the outbreak of the Severe Acute Respiratory Syndrome further motivated Hong Kong's property elites to revise their corporate strategy and shift investments northwards. The Wharf, for example, made high-profile acquisitions of twelve land sites in Chengdu, Hangzhou, Suzhou, Chongqing, Nanjing, Changzhou and Wuxi in 2007 and 2008, and invested a further 30 billion yuan from 2009 to 2012 to secure another 34 plots of land for residential and commercial development. By the 2010s, many of the developers have built up significant reserves of developed and developable land in China through successful acquisitions in both investment properties and development properties (Table 1). Cheung Kong, Henderson, Wharf and Shui On each possesses 10 to 20 million square metres of land bank in gross floor area, while New World tops the list with a land bank of 27.5 million square metres.

The account of Hong Kong real estate investment in China presented in this section aptly demonstrates the centrality of geopolitical and economic considerations in explaining the apparent success of property capital from the former British colony in comparison to investment from other regions. It highlights the importance of considering the transborder capital flows in question within broader geopolitical and economic frameworks, which in the extant case are structured by the Chinese project of national sovereignty at the central level, and the land-centred model of development at the local level. At both scales, the mediated foreignness of Hong Kong capital allowed them privileged access to the mainland market and facilitated capital accumulation for both state actors and foreign investors.

Contested developments: Popular politics and changing responses to foreign investment

Throughout the 1990s and 2000s Hong Kong developers had steadily expanded their investment in mainland China, making extensive acquisitions of land parcels

Table 1. List of select Hong Kong developers and their land banks in mainland China. Source: Compilation from company reports and newspaper articles.

Hong-Kong-based Company	Market capitalisation (HK$)	Land bank in gross floor area (sq. m.)
Sun Hung Kai Properties	363,657,282,313	7.4 million
Cheung Kong Property Holdings	246,440,472,225	19.7 million
Henderson Land Development	176,074,905,952	10.8 million
The Wharf (Holdings)	157,916,523,737	10.2 million
Hang Lung Properties	104,511,583,111	2.3 million
New World Development	91,210,574,557	27.5 million
Sino Land	78,990,950,347	2.0 million
Kerry Properties	43,807,474,208	3.4 million
Shui On	18,059,917,925	11.8 million

in both coastal and inland cities. Their relative success was conditional upon favourable policy and governance frameworks. Into the recent decade, however, shifts in public sentiments and state concerns have led to changing priorities in policy making. Two issues stood out in particular, namely growing public dissatisfaction over the decline in housing affordability and increasing concern, articulated by affected residents and civil society groups in particular, over the negative consequences of demolition and eviction in urban redevelopment projects. The emergence of the two issues in policy agendas have led to changing attitudes towards real estate investment. While Hong Kong capital is certainly not alone in precipitating such developments, given its limited role in Chinese urban real estate in comparison to domestic developers, its very foreignness engenders a distinct geopolitical dimension. The literature has discussed how protectionist cultural politics may lead to characterisations of foreign investment as invasive (Rogers & Dufty-Jones, 2015). Such geopolitical discourses, in contrast to the cultural politics of ethnic identity which appears to mediate difference, have rather drawn attention to the undesirable aspects of foreign real estate investment.

Housing affordability and land banking

Housing affordability has emerged as a public issue since the financialisation of the Chinese housing sector in 1998 (Wu, 2015), and the influx of foreign money in domestic real estate since the mid-2000s has brought this to the foreground of local politics. Foreign money has been seen as a chief cause of housing price inflation and has been associated with the skewed development of the housing market given foreign investors' focus on high-end luxury housing (Cao, 2015). The home price increases have raised social discontent and exacerbated perceived inequality as low-income groups have borne the brunt of the deterioration in housing affordability (Ye, Song & Tian, 2010).

The concern over housing affordability has directed public attention to the phenomenon of land banking by property developers. The corporate practice involves a so-called 'buy low, sell high' approach to land acquisition: developers purchase land parcels while prices are low, then leave sites idle or develop them at a slow pace as they wait for land prices to go up. Accumulated land stocks can be used as collateral to obtain bank loans or as valuable assets to boost share prices of listed companies, which in turn generate additional capital for further investment (Wang, 2011a). Although there are national regulations disciplining the practice,[3] local governments have low incentives in enforcing them as this might jeopardise investors' relations and reduce investment inflows. Indeed local governments may themselves benefit from land scarcity and rising urban property prices as this translates into higher land-granting premiums of which they are direct beneficiaries.

Land banking is widely seen as contributing to home price increases as it reduces the supply of land for development. A study conducted by the financial research centre of Beijing Normal University estimates that a 70-percent increase in housing prices could be attributed to the phenomenon of land stockpiling (China.org.cn, 2007). It is estimated that over 70 percent of China's idle land has been designated for residential use. The increase in housing costs further feeds into the perverse incentives of local governments in maintaining a measure of scarcity in order to generate high land premiums. The lucrative income local governments receive from leasing land also reduces their willingness to assign land for welfare housing, which is to be allocated free of charge (Wang, 2011a).

As public discontent over rising home prices grows, property developers have been subject to tighter scrutiny over their corporate behaviour. While the practice of land banking is not unique to Hong Kong developers, their status as foreign investors has heightened sensitivity towards cases of their alleged malpractice. Speculating on land and property price increase, Hong Kong developers have acquired the use rights to many land sites in mainland China throughout the 1990s and 2000s and kept them in reserve. New World China Land has for example built up a land bank of 27.5 million square metres in gross floor area, of which completed properties accounted for only 2.5 million square metres while the rest was reportedly under development or held for future development.[4]

Hong Kong developers have featured in media campaigns against land banking. The mainland press has made ironic references to the 'Hong Kong model of stockpiling land to plant gold' (Zhongguo Jingying Bao, 2012). China Central Television, the country's national broadcaster, has openly criticised a Hong Kong developer for 'blatant land hoarding' (Ming Pao, 2009). Popular news provider Netease even created an interactive web feature tracking the stockpiling practices of four prominent Hong Kong developers, with maps indicating projects suspected

of land banking by Cheung Kong, Sun Hung Kai, New World and Henderson.[5]
Developers have been criticised for their practice of leaving land sites idle for
extended periods and the tactic of breaking down a single project into multiple
phases that each took years to complete. Local newspapers reported that governments had been wary of challenging such behaviour given its potentially adverse
impact on municipal revenues, especially with established developers like Cheung
Kong that invested not only in real estate but also in infrastructure and logistics
(Time Weekly, 2014). A Sun Hung Kai project in Shanghai has been dubbed a
'marathon construction project', with a development cycle spanning seven years
that reportedly earned the company a profit margin of almost 100% (HKTDC,
2012).

In 2010, the Ministry of Land and Resources launched a nationwide campaign
to rein in land banking behaviour. Notably, the campaign turned on a Hong Kong
developer for violating rules on the disposal of idle land. In March 2010, the Beijing
Bureau of Land and Resources made an example of Pacific Century Premium
Developments for leaving an acquired site idle, a company then chaired by Richard
Li, the son of property tycoon Li Ka-shing. According to reports, Richard Li's company obtained the use rights of a land parcel in the Chaoyang district of Beijing in
2005 by paying 510 million yuan in premium. Instead of proceeding with development, the land was reportedly kept in reserve and subsequently sold to another
Hong Kong developer for 806 million yuan in 2009, generating some 230 million
yuan in pre-tax profits for the company (China Daily, 2010). The developer was
fined and prohibited from making new land purchases in the capital city (Wall
Street Journal, 2010).

This high-profile move targeting a foreign developer was widely circulated
within the mainland press and interpreted as a sign of Beijing's resolve to curb
increases in housing costs.[6] Given the prevalence of the corporate practice, it was
notable that Beijing has chosen a Hong Kong developer to showcase its commitment to the social goal of housing affordability. Following the incident local news
remarked on 'the demise of the Hong Kong model' of land banking which relies on
land stockpiling, slow development, and speculation on future price increase
(Netease, 2015). The Chinese government's determination in tackling the practice
may present future challenges to Hong Kong developers' operation in the mainland.

Property rights, historic preservation and redevelopment

Real estate investment from Hong Kong has also become embroiled in contentious
dynamics surrounding property rights and heritage preservation. These often
involved redevelopment projects whose visible impact on local livelihoods has
made them increasingly controversial, from the displacement of residents to the
destruction of rural and cultural landscapes. In reform-era China, redevelopment
has evolved from a welfare-oriented policy of reconstructing old and dilapidated

houses for low-income households to a profit-oriented enterprise that involves entrepreneurial leaders and enthusiastic investors (He & Wu, 2005). It is a lucrative undertaking as the demolition of old neighbourhoods and the creation of high-value, high-density spaces on their site allows officials and developers to capitalise the enhanced ground rent (Smith, 1996).

Hong Kong developers have been extensively engaged in mainland property-led redevelopment projects. Shui On, for example, is well-known for pioneering the property-led redevelopment model with its Xintiandi project in Shanghai, a commercial and recreational development based on the revitalisation of historic architecture (He & Wu, 2005). In the 1990s, the company made headlines for undertaking 'the most efficient' large-scale eviction in its relocation of 3,800 households within 43 days (Nanfang Dushibao, 2013). The developer has subsequently replicated the same model of public–private partnership in Chongqing, Wuhan, Dalian, and Foshan, completing four megaprojects under its successful Tiandi brand.

Redevelopment has also involved the remaking of rural landscapes and the urbanisation of rural communities (Kan, 2016). Hong Kong developers have been active in rural redevelopment projects in the Pearl River Delta cities such as Guangzhou, where they enjoy relatively established presence. For example, Sun Hung Kai is involved in the redevelopment of Liede, a formerly rural community situated in Guangzhou's new financial district. The company also reached a deal with the rural cadres of Linhe to redevelop the urban village, which occupied 65,000 square metres of prime land near the Guangzhou East railway station, into a commercial-residential neighbourhood. Given the considerable rent gap, the redevelopment of villages often yields rich financial rewards that are shared primarily between rural cadres, local governments, and property developers.

The disruptive impact redevelopment effects upon resident communities and the often unequal distributive outcomes engendered have made it an increasingly contentious undertaking. Public opinion and societal forces are playing a more significant role in shaping popular discourses about development and urbanisation in China, as they begin to vocally question the singular focus on growth and challenge the legitimacy of undertaking large-scale demolition and forced eviction in the name of development. The kind of property-led redevelopment that Hong Kong developers champion has thus come under increased scrutiny. As Shui On expanded its real estate ventures, for example, *Nanfang Metropolis Daily*, a liberal-leaning newspaper, has criticised its 'outdated' model of profit-driven redevelopment that 'leaves no room for the representation of indigenous residents' rights' (Nanfang Dushibao, 2013). The paper further challenged local governments' active complicity as 'champions of real estate interests' in their desire to create political achievements for themselves (Nanfang Dushibao, 2013).

The growth in public concern over the loss of cultural heritage has also animated resistance to development. A Hong Kong developer was pulled into a controversy in 2013 when its mainland subsidiary was charged with the unauthor-ised demolition of two historic buildings in Guangzhou (South China Morning Post, 2013). The destruction led to an angry outpour in the mainland media, with local public opinion leaders including university professors and members of the local people's congress joining the censure (Nanfang Ribao, 2013). The news was quick to point out that the company was then chaired by the chief of the Hong Kong Tourism Board. A local newspaper printed an editorial criticising the demoli-tion as representative of the 'extraordinary expansion of real estate power' and the hijacking of public policy making by private property interests (Yangcheng Wan-bao, 2013). The Guangzhou government was prompted to react strongly by dealing out punitive measures and the company issued a public apology. As in the case of land banking, these incidents are by no means exclusive to developers from Hong Kong. Nonetheless, the nationalistic trope of the expansion of foreign capital inter-ests at the expense of local welfare may have particular resonance amongst the local population in these cases of perceived misbehaviour, one that mainland civil society and the commercial press will find efficacious to employ in their reaction toward what is seen as collusion and the erosion of rights.

Conclusion

If the particular brand of foreignness that Hong Kong property capital embodies, exported under the trope of compatriotism in the early reform years, has facilitated its entry into Chinese real estate and given it distinct advantages over other foreign investors, recent developments presented in the previous section serve as a poignant reminder that the meaning of foreignness is socially constructed and, therefore, fluid and open to re-interpretation. In the first two decades of reform, when China was navigating its path toward the development of a market economy, developers from Hong Kong were welcomed by reform leaders as compatriots contributing to China's modernisation. Their mediated foreignness, as a result of ethnic and cultural ties, gave them privileged access to the Chinese real estate market that was not readily available to other foreign investors. The growing entrenchment of their economic interests in China was also seen as desirable by the Chinese government, whose geo-political project of national re-unification has sought to combine elite cooptation with economic integration. At the subnational level, the foreignness of Hong Kong invest-ment was desired by local governments for its economic and reputational value. Its symbolism of modernity and internationalism generated both political and financial returns in the creation of valorised urban landscapes that attracted further property investment, with lucrative outcomes for both state and capital.

But if Hong Kong capital has been seen as an agent of modernisation and of the mediation of Chinese cities' transition to transnational metropolises, it has also engendered geographies of displacement as it participates in the remaking of local landscapes. As socioeconomic goals such as housing affordability and alternative ideals such as historic preservation come to the foreground of local politics, the profitable arrangements between local governments and foreign developers that are based on land rents extraction have come under increasing scrutiny. In recent years we find instances where foreignness becomes a focal point for the organisation and mobilisation of public discontent.

All in all, the analysis presented in this paper highlights the importance of combining geopolitical, economic, and cultural perspectives in the study of foreign real estate investment and housing studies. Looking ahead, the state of Hong Kong real estate investment in China will continue to be shaped by the confluence of factors identified. Continuing state concerns over profiteering and speculative activities, and the need for the Chinese leadership to shore up legitimacy through the implementation of welfare-oriented policies such as the provision of affordable housing, mean that real estate will remain one of the most tightly regulated sectors. Foreign developers have also been faced with intensifying competition from China's own developers as the mainland real estate industry matures (Cao, 2015). Studies have already shown how local governments may accord partial treatment to domestic developers, which are backed by powerful ministries and bureaucracies within the Chinese state (Hsing, 2006). Finally, local governments and both domestic and foreign developers alike can expect to be subject to strengthened public supervision concerning urban development projects. As the land-centred model of growth receives increasing scrutiny within the wider society, the sustainability of the current mode of cooperation between local governments and developers has also come under challenge. Such societal demands are intrinsically linked to debates about social justice, citizenship and the right to the city, and can translate into broader social movements (Bobbette, 2014; Rolnik, 2014). How, and whether, the increase in public discontent and debates will bring forth a shift in state-capital-society relations will have important implications not just for the future of foreign real estate investment but also the coming shape of urbanisation in China.

Acknowledgements

The author would like to thank Sin Yee Koh, Dallas Rogers and the reviewers for their comments on earlier drafts of this paper. The research assistance of Oriana Cheung, Peggy Ip and Ian Ho is greatly appreciated.

Disclosure statement

No potential conflict of interest was reported by the author.

Funding

This research was supported in part by a research grant at Centennial College, Hong Kong [grant number CRG/14/01].

Notes

1. See the Global Family Business Index compiled by the Center for Family Business at the University of St. Gallen, Switzerland, at http://familybusinessindex.com/#table-info

2. There are three categories of government budget in China, namely budgetary, extra-budget, and off-budget revenues. Prior to the 1994 tax reform, a fiscal revenue-sharing system was enforced where local governments were allowed to retain extra-budgetary revenues upon remitting the requisite amount of 'central fixed revenue' to the centre. This arrangement greatly strengthened the financial power of local governments, which prompted the central leadership to push forward a series of fiscal policies to re-establish its position in 1994. The reform readjusted central-local apportionments of tax revenues with the outcome of radically downsizing local revenues. The paucity of municipal finances led to the rapid growth of off-budget financing. Since off-budget revenues can be wholly retained, local governments had high incentive in raising and collecting off-budget funds (Wong, 1998).

3. In 1999, the Ministry of Land and Resources introduced *Rules on the Disposal of Idle Land* to prohibit developers from stockpiling land without commencing development. Measures introduced in 2005 gave local governments the power to take action on land parcels left idle for two years, and a State Council notice issued in 2008 further granted local governments the authority to impose tax, of 20 per cent of land grant premium, on sites left idle for a year, as well as the power to seize lots left idle for two years without compensating the developer.

4. See the corporate profile of New World China Land, updated as of 31 December 2014, at http://www.nwcl.com.hk/html/eng/corporate/nwcl_intro.aspx.

5. See the interactive news webpage at http://gz.house.163.com/special/gz_gztd/.

6. Closely following the incident, the central government produced an action plan that tightened rules on idle land and increased the responsibility of local governments in supervising all development projects. The action plan obligates land and resources bureaus at all levels to closely monitor the development progress of land parcels under its jurisdiction. Provincial-level departments are made responsible for reporting cases of idle land to financial regulators at the same level. The policy tightening of 2010 culminated in the release of a revised *Rules on the Disposal of Idle Land*, which came into effect in 2012. The new amendments formally incorporated the aforementioned measures and corrected loopholes in the 1999 version by refining the definition of idle land, specifying the procedures by which idle land should be determined and disposed of, and clarifying the responsibilities of the local government in enforcing the provisions.

References

Baum, R. (1999). Enter the dragon: China's courtship of Hong Kong, 1982–1999. *Communist and Post-Communist Studies, 32*(4), 417–436.

Bobbette, A. (2014, September 25). Occupy central is really a battle over the idea of the city. *South China Morning Post*. Retrieved from http://www.scmp.com/comment/article/1600289/occupy-central-really-battle-over-idea-city

Broadman, H.G., & Sun, X. (1997). The distribution of foreign direct investment in China. *The World Economy, 20*(3), 339–361.

Cao, J.A. (2015). *The Chinese real estate market: Development, regulation and investment.* Abingdon: Taylor and Francis.

Cartier, C. (2005). Regional formations and transnational urbanism in south China. In J. Wang (Ed.), *Locating China: Place, space, and popular culture* (pp. 52–71). London: Routledge.

Chen, H., & Chen, T. (1998). Network linkages and location choice in foreign direct investment. *Journal of International Business Studies, 29*(3), 445–467.

Chen, L. (2015). GangAo jugu yu gaige kaifang zhi chu de Guangdong yang jiudian [Hong Kong and Macau magnates and the foreign hotels of Guangdong on the eve of reform]. *Guangdong Shizhi*. Retrieved from http://121.15.254.4:1980/SuniT/info.huizhou.gov.cn/shtml/guangdong/sqyj/shgc/2015/04/15/123309.shtml

Chen, X. (2000). Both glue and lubricant: Transnational ethnic social capital as a source of Asia-Pacific subregionalism. *Policy Sciences, 33*, 269–287.

China Business Review. (1992a). China's real estate revolution. *China Business Review, 19*(6), 44–51.

China Business Review. (1992b). The great China land rush. *China Business Review, 19*(6), 51–52.

China Business Review. (1993). Guangdong's Rockefeller. *China Business Review, 20*(1), 38.

China Daily. (2010, March 13). Former PCPD unit triggers Beijing land ban. Retrieved from http://www.chinadaily.com.cn/hkedition/2010–03/13/content_9583814.htm

China.org.cn. (2007, December 5). Chinese developers warned against land hoarding. Retrieved from http://www.china.org.cn/english/business/234441.htm

Chung, J. H. (2001). Reappraising central-local relations in Deng's China: Decentralization, dilemmas of control, and diluted effects of reform. In C. Chao & B.J. Dickson (Eds.), *Remaking the Chinese state: Strategies, society and security* (pp. 46–75). London and New York, NY: Routledge.

Crawford, D. (2000). Chinese capitalism: Cultures, the Southeast Asian region and economic globalization. *Third World Quarterly, 21*(1), 69–86.

Dittmer, J., & Dodds, K. (2008). Popular geopolitics past and future: Fandom, identities and audiences. *Geopolitics, 13*(3), 437–457.

Dittmer, J., & Gray, N. (2010). Popular geopolitics 2.0: Towards new methodologies of the everyday. *Geography Compass, 4*(11), 1664–1677.

Dittmer, J., & Sharp, J. (2014). General introduction. In J. Dittmer & J. Sharp (Eds.), *Geopolitics: An introductory reader* (pp. 1–9). London and New York: Routledge.

Fung, H.-G., Huang, A.G., Liu, Q.W., & Shen, M.X. (2006). The development of the real estate industry in China. *The Chinese Economy, 39*(1), 84–102.

Gaubatz, P. (2005). Globalization and the development of new central business districts in Beijing, Shanghai and Guangzhou. In L.J.C. Ma & F. Wu (Eds.) *Restructuring the Chinese city: Changing society, economy and space* (pp. 98–121). London: Routledge.

Goodstadt, L. (2009). *Uneasy partners: The conflict between public interest and private profit in Hong Kong*. Hong Kong: Hong Kong University Press.

Haila, A. (2000). Real estate in global cities: Singapore and Hong Kong as property states. *Urban Studies, 37*(12), 2241–2256.

He, C., Wang, J., & Cheng, S. (2011). What attracts foreign direct investment in China's real estate development? *The Annals of Regional Science, 46*(2), 267–293.

He, C., & Zhu, Y. (2010). Real estate FDI in Chinese cities: Local market conditions and regional institutions. *Eurasia Geography and Economics, 51*(3), 360–384.

He, S., & Wu, F. (2005). Property-led redevelopment in post-reform China: A case study of Xintiandi redevelopment project in Shanghai. *Journal of Urban Affairs, 27*(1), 1–23.

Hong Kong Trade and Development Council [HKTDC]. (2003a). CEPA: Shanghai and Hong Kong to cooperate on all fronts. *Business Alert – China, 11*. Retrieved from http://info.hktdc.com/alert/cba-e0311sp.htm

HKTDC. (2003b). CEPA signals new dawn of Beijing Hong Kong economic cooperation. *Business Alert – China, 12.* Retrieved from http://info.hktdc.com/alert/cba-e0312sp.htm

HKTDC. (2012). Prudence and pragmatism pay off for SHKP. Retrieved from http://econo mists-pick-research.hktdc.com/business-news/article/Success-Stories/Prudence-and-prag matism-pay-off-for-SHKP/ss/en/1/1X000000/1X09QLUF.htm

Hsing, Y. (1996). Blood, thicker than water: Interpersonal relations and Taiwanese invest- ment in southern China. *Environment and Planning A, 28,* 2241–2261.

Hsing, Y. (2006). Global capital and local land in China's urban real estate development. In F. Wu (Ed.), *Globalization and the Chinese city* (pp. 167–189). Abingdon: Routledge.

Hsing, Y. (2010). *The great urban transformation: Politics of land and property in China.* Oxford: Oxford University Press.

Huang, Y., & Yang, D. (1996). The political dynamics of regulatory change: Speculation and regulation in the real estate sector. *Journal of Contemporary China, 5*(12), 171–185.

Hubbard, P., & Hall, T. (1998). The entrepreneurial city and the 'new urban politics.' In T. Hall & P. Hubbard (Eds.), *The entrepreneurial city: Geographies of politics, regime and representation* (pp. 1–26). Chichester: John Wiley & Sons.

Hui, E.C.M., & Chan, K.K.K. (2014). Foreign direct investment in China's real estate mar- ket. *Habitat International, 43,* 231–239.

Jean, R.B., Tan, D., & Sinkovics, R.R. (2011). Ethnic ties, location choice, and firm perfor- mance in foreign direct investment: A study of Taiwanese business groups FDI in China. *International Business Review, 20,* 627–635.

Jessop, B. & Sum, N.-L. (2000). An entrepreneurial city in action: Hong Kong's emerging strategies in and for (inter-)urban competition. *Urban Studies, 37*(12), 2290–2315.

Jiang, D., Chen, J.J., & Isaac, D. (1998). The effect of foreign investment on the real estate industry in China. *Urban Studies, 35*(11), 2101–2110.

Kan, K. (2016). The transformation of the village collective in urbanizing China: A historical institutional analysis. *Journal of Rural Studies.* doi:10.1016/j.jrurstud.2016.07.016

Ley, D. (2010). *Millionaire Migrants: Trans-Pacific Life Lines.* West Sussex: Wiley- Blackwell.

Lin, G.C.S., & Ho, S.P.S. (2005). The state, land system, and land development processes in contemporary China. *Annals of the Association of American Geographers*, 95(2), 411– 436.

Ming Pao. (2009, November 19). Hubao zhi Li Jiacheng dunde [Shanghai newspapers accused Li Ka-shing of land hoarding]. Retrieved from http://www.mpfinance.com/htm/ finance/20091119/news/ec_eca1.htm

Nanfang Dushibao. (2013). Luo Kangrui de Xintiandi moshi buneng zai fuzhi [The Xintiandi model pioneered by Luo Kangrui cannot be copied]. Retrieved from http://epaper.oeeee. com/epaper/A/html/2013-06/03/content_2518017.htm?div=-1

Nanfang Ribao. (2013, June 20). Jinglingtai fengbo zheshe dachai dajian shidai luanxiang [The destruction of Jinlingtai reflects the problems of demolition-for-development]. Retrieved from http://news.dayoo.com/guangzhou/201306/20/73437_31210227.htm

Netease. (2015, March 24). Xianggang dichan moshi de jintou [The demise of the Hong Kong real estate model]. Retrieved from http://bj.house.163.com/15/0324/09/ALFBR B6E00073SD3.html

Nonni, D., & Ong, A. (1997). Chinese transnationalism as an alternative modernity. In A. Ong & D. Nonni (Eds.), *Ungrounded empires: The cultural politics of modern Chinese transnationalism* (pp. 171–203). London: Routledge.

Ó Tuathail, G., & Dalby, S. (1998). Rethinking geopolitics: Towards a critical geopolitics. In G. Ó Tuathail & S. Dalby (Eds.), *Rethinking Geopolitics* (pp. 1–15). London and New York: Routledge.

Ong, A. (2004). The Chinese axis: Zoning technologies and variegated sovereignty. *Journal of East Asian Studies, 4*, 69–96.

Poon, A. (2010). *Land and the ruling class in Hong Kong.* Hong Kong: Enrich Professional Publishing.

Rauche, J.E., & Trindade, V. (2002). Ethnic Chinese networks in international trade. *The Review of Economics and Statistics, 84*(1), 116–130.

Rogers, D. (2016). *The geopolitics of real estate: Reconfiguring property, capital and rights.* London: Rowman & Littlefield.

Rogers, D., & Dufty-Jones, R. (2015). 21st-century Australian housing: New frontiers in the Asia-Pacific. In R. Dufty-Jones & D. Rogers (Eds.), *Housing in 21st century Australia: People, practices and policies* (pp. 221–236). Aldershot: Ashgate.

Rogers, D., Lee, C.L. & Yan, D. (2015). The politics of foreign investment in Australian housing: Chinese investors, translocal sales agents and local resistance. *Housing Studies, 30*(5), 730–748.

Rolnik, R. (2014). Place, inhabitance and citizenship: The right to housing and the right to the city in the contemporary urban world. *International Journal of Housing Policy, 14*(3), 293–300.

Rowen, I. (2016). The geopolitics of tourism: Mobilities, territory and protest in China, Taiwan, and Hong Kong. *Annals of the American Association of Geographers, 106*(2), 385–393.

Shen, J. (2003). Cross-border connection between Hong Kong and mainland China under 'two systems' before and beyond 1997. *Geografiska Annaler, 85B*(1), 1–17.

Sit, V. (1998). Hong Kong's 'transferred' industrialization and industrial geography. *Asian Survey, 38*(9), 880–904.

Sit, V., & Yang, C. (1997). Foreign-investment-induced exo-urbanization in the Pearl River Delta, China. *Urban Studies, 34*, 647–677.

Siu, H.F. (1993). Cultural identity and the politics of difference. *Daedalus, 122*(2), 19–43.

Smart, A., & Hsu, J. (2004). The Chinese diaspora, foreign investment and economic development in China. *The Review of International Affairs, 3*(4), 544–566.

Smart, A., & Smart, J. (1998). Transnational social networks and negotiated identities in interactions between Hong Kong and China. In M.P. Smith & L.E. Guarnizo (Eds.), *Transnationalism from below* (pp. 103–129). New Brunswick: Transaction Publishers.

Smart, J., & Smart, A. (1991). Personal relations and divergent economies: A case study of Hong Kong investment in south China. *International Journal of Urban and Regional Research, 15*(2), 216–233.

Smith, N. (1996). *The new urban frontier: Gentrification and the revanchist city.* London: Routledge.

South China Morning Post. (2013, June 17). Tycoon's firm razes home of opera legend.

Time Weekly. (2014, August 7). ChangHeji cheng meiyou dunde yitao [Cheung Kong group says it has no intention to hoard land]. Retrieved from http://www.time-weekly.com/html/20140807/25949_1.html

Tseng, Y.-F. (2002). From "us" to "them": Diasporic linkages and identity politics. *Identities: Global Studies in Culture and Power, 9*, 383–404.

Wall Street Journal. (2010, March 13). Li envoys to probe Beijing land block. Retrieved from http://www.wsj.com/articles/SB10001424052748703780204575119151989729276

Wang, H. (2000). Informal institutions and foreign investment in China. *The Pacific Review, 13*(4), 525–556.

Wang, L. (2011a). *Foreign direct investment and urban growth in China.* Surrey: Ashgate.

Wang, S.W.-H. (2011b). The evolution of housing renewal in Shanghai, 1990–2010: A 'Socially Conscious' entrepreneurial city? *International Journal of Housing Policy, 11*(1), 51–69.

Wong, C. (1998). Fiscal dualism in China: Gradualist reform and the growth of off-budget finance. In D.J.S. Brean (Ed.), *Taxation in modern China* (pp. 187–208). New York, NY, and London: Routledge.

Wong, J. (1999). Southeast Asian ethnic Chinese investing in China. *Global Economic Review: Perspectives on East Asian Economies and Industries, 28*(1), 3–27.

Wong, S. H. (2015). Real estate elite, economic development, and political conflicts in post-colonial Hong Kong. *China Review, 15*(1), 1–38.

Wu, F. (2000). The global and local dimension of place-making: Rethinking Shanghai as a world city. *Urban Studies, 37*(8), 1359–1377.

Wu, F. (2002). Real estate development and the transformation of urban space in Chinese transitional economy: With special reference to Shanghai. In J.R. Logan (Ed.) *The new Chinese city: Globalization and market reform* (pp. 151–166). New York, NY: Blackwell.

Wu, F. (2003). The (post-)socialist entrepreneurial city as a state project: Shanghai's reglobalisation in question. *Urban Studies, 40*(9), 1673–1698.

Wu, F. (2015). Commodification and housing market cycles in Chinese cities. *International Journal of Housing Policy, 15*(1), 6–26.

Yang, D. (2006). Economic transformation and its political discontents in China: Authoritarianism, unequal growth, and the dilemma of political development. *Annual Review of Political Science, 9*, 143–164.

Yangcheng Wanbao. (2013, June 15). Miandui kaifashang de qianghan zhengfu yao geng yingqi [The government should take a stronger stance towards developers]. Retrieved from http://www.ycwb.com/ePaper/ycwb/html/2013-06/15/content_179137.htm?div=-1

Ye, J.P., Song, J.N., & Tian, C.G. (2010). An analysis of housing policy during economic transition in China. *International Journal of Housing Policy, 10*(3), 273–300.

Ye, M. (2014). *Diasporas and foreign direct investment in China and India.* New York, NY: Cambridge University Press.

Yeh, A., & Wu, F. (1999). The transformation of the urban planning system in China from a centrally-planned to transitional economy. *Progress in Planning, 51*(3), 167–252.

Yeung, H.W. (2000). Local politics and foreign ventures in China's transitional economy: The political economy of Singaporean investments in China. *Political Geography, 19*, 809–840.

Zhang, K.H. (2005). Why does so much FDI from Hong Kong and Taiwan go to mainland China? *China Economic Review, 16*, 293–307.

Zhang, T. (2002). Urban development and a socialist pro-growth coalition in Shanghai. *Urban Affairs Review, 37*(4), 475–499.

Zhongguo Jingying Bao. (2012, May 7). Hengji chude shengjin yu zhengce jinguzhou [Henderson's land banking model met with policy tightening]. Retrieved from http://gz.house.163.com/12/0507/11/80TAA2O000873C6D.html

Zhu, J. (1999). Local growth coalition: The context and implications of China's gradualist urban land reforms. *International Journal of Urban and Regional Research, 23*(3), 534–548.

Zhu, J., Sim, L., & Zhang, X. (2006). Global real estate investments and local cultural capital in the making of Shanghai's new office locations. *Habitat International, 30*, 462–481.

Courting the 'rich and restless': globalisation of real estate and the new spatial fixities of the super-rich in Singapore

C.P. Pow

How have the globalisation of real estate and the rise of a transnational class of super-rich homebuyers challenged conventional analyses of local residential property markets? What analytical tools and concepts can we deploy to understand the dialectical tensions between the local and global; fixity and motion as well as the deterritorialisation and reterritorialisation of real estate by the super-rich? Drawing on Singapore as a case study, this paper interrogates the new 'spatial fixities' of the super-rich housing market at two inter-related scales of analysis. At the national scale, this spatial fixity could be interpreted in terms of the attempts by the Singapore 'property state' to attract high net-worth individuals to reside and invest in the country as a 'quick fix' way to boost national capital. At the global scale, this new spatial fixity of highly mobile super-rich can be seen in their territorialisation strategies to constantly seek out new safe havens to physically 'park' and grow their wealth beyond the traditional confines of national boundaries. Insofar as these two kinds of spatial fixes both complement and feed off one another via conspicuous real estate development, they also risk colliding and generating social contradictions that may potentially threaten their symbiotic relations.

Introduction

Until recently, housing has often been treated as a highly localised form of consumption that is bound up in the interests of local urban growth coalitions and shaped by indigenous forces of 'homegrown' real estate markets. As Paris (2013, p. 95) noted: housing researchers have hitherto 'largely ignored the impact of globalisation and typically conceive housing markets as sets of interactions contained by national boundaries'. More specifically, what has also been ignored thus far is the emergence of super-rich transnational housing investors whose property portfolio reportedly span several 'hotspot' locations in cities such as Vancouver, London, Sydney, Hong Kong, Singapore, etc. This paper fills the gaps in the housing studies literature by critically examining how the recent globalisation of real estate and rise of a transnational class of super-rich housing investors have disrupted nationally bounded understanding of the housing market. To be sure, since the 1990s, there has already been considerable internationalisation of the property market bolstered in part by the securitisation of housing finance and the liberalisation of property ownership regulations (see, for example Ley, 2015 on the internationalisation of real estate in Vancouver). Rogers (2016) further argued how global real estate tech companies and Internet technologies have also helped to rearticulate the boundaries between the nation-state and global real estate.

Nevertheless, it would be overstating the case to suggest that the housing market is now wholly shaped by global processes. To a large extent, the housing market remains spatially 'fixed' and embedded in particular locations and is constituted by place-specific forms of local political-economic processes. Housing, after all, is a physically immobile *real* asset that needs to be spatially grounded in a specific geographical locale (even though it can now be bought and sold with relative ease in the virtual global market place). What then needs to be disentangled here are complex scalar processes relating to global financial flows and the variety of investment strategies of (super-rich) housing consumers as well as the local urban/national governments that are constantly seeking to attract mobile capital investments and 'fix' them in space.

Drawing on the case study of Singapore, this paper interrogates the 'spatial fixities' of the super-rich housing market at two dialectical scales of analysis. At the national scale, this spatial fixity could be interpreted in terms of the attempts by the local nation-state to attract the high net-worth to reside and invest in the country as a 'quick fix' way to boost national capital. At the global scale, the spatial fixity of the highly mobile super-rich can be seen in their deterritorialisation strategies to constantly seek out safe havens to park and grow their wealth. Such deterritorialisation processes may entail the physical relocation of individuals and the disembedding of their social relations and political-economic ties *away* from their native land into global 'spaces of flows' that are seen to render national territorial borders porous (Brenner, 2004). Yet deterritorialisation does not signal the 'hollowing out' of local places as 'cities and states are also being reconfigured, reterritorialised and re-scaled in conjunction with the capitalist globalisation' and 'remain essential forms of territorial organisation upon which the world-scale circulation of capital is premised' (Brenner, 2004, p. 433). As this paper will demonstrate, city-states such as Singapore have attempted to reterritorialise the global circulation of mobile capital by enacting various 'spatial fix' strategies in order to attract and ground super-rich investment albeit with mixed results and consequences.

It is worth noting that the term 'spatial fix' is often associated with the Marxist geographer David Harvey (2001, pp. 25–26) who alluded to the territorial imperatives of capitalism – namely that in order to survive and resolve its internal crisis of capital over-accumulation, capital (and the state) needs to constantly seek out new spatial fixes that coalesce around territorially based class interests and factions. In this respect, this paper extends the notion of spatial fix by examining the dialectical tensions and contradictions associated with the spatial fixities of the super-rich and the Singapore state through investments in the secondary circuit of capital via prime real estate properties.[1] Here, the concept of the 'property state' (Haila, 2000, 2015) is instructive in highlighting how governments in city-states such as Singapore (and Hong Kong) capitalise on land rent as an important source of state revenue by mobilising real estate as a channel to spatially fix footloose capital flows. In particular, Haila (2015, p 16) pointed to three ways in which public land has been harnessed by the Singapore property state as a means to secure national economic growth: 'state land in Singapore is treated as a use value (public housing and industrial space), as exchange value (leased for private developers) and as a source of public revenue (land leases and property tax)'. This paper further extends the argument on the Singapore property state by showing how the state actively mobilises land as a form of spatial fix strategy to capture mobile super-rich capital.

By critically unpacking the Singapore government's spatial fix strategy to remake Singapore as an investment and lifestyle hub of 'high net worth individuals' (HNWIs), this paper makes a distinct contribution to the theorisation on the role of the (property) state in the globalisation of real estate and the spatial reproduction super-rich capital. To substantiate the arguments, this paper will be organised in four main sections. Following this introduction, the paper will briefly review the literature on the globalisation of housing and highlight the dialectical relations between the local state dynamics and global processes. In particular, the paper will elaborate how the idea of spatial fix can be deployed as a useful analytical tool to analyse the relationship between the property state and the globalisation of super-rich housing investments. Following this, the third section proceeds to profile how the Singapore state benchmarks itself as a global wealth centre and lifestyle hub for the super-rich by rolling out a series of urban economic 'spatial fix' strategies that are aimed to attract HNWIs to live and bank in the city-state. However, as the final section will argue, insofar as these spatial fix strategies are aimed to produce highly spatialised forms of capital investment and conspicuous real estate consumption, they also risk colliding and generating serious social contradictions and tensions that may potentially threaten their symbiotic relations (Harvey, 2001, p. 28).

Globalisation of housing and the new spatial fix of super-rich capital

Housing provisions and housing markets, as Forrest (2003, p. 5) stated, 'are inherently local in nature in terms of who provides the housing, how it is marketed and how we access or buy it. They require, in the main, local knowledge on the part of both agents and consumers, providers and clients'. As Bardhan and Kroll (2007, p. 1) further suggested, real estate is among the 'least tradable of products' by virtue of the fact that it is often considered a physically immobile asset even though it can be bought and sold both domestically and internationally.

It is hardly surprising that the real estate industry has largely been bypassed in globalisation research until recently (see, for example Bardhan, Edelstein, & Leung, 2004; Nijman, 2000; Rogers, Lee, & Yan, 2015; Zhu, Sim, & Zhang, 2006). Why real estate has now been taken seriously by globalisation scholars could be attributed to a number of factors such as the growing internationalisation of non-manufacturing services sectors including various sub-sectors of the real estate industry ranging from brokerage firms, consulting and services firms, real estate finance firms and investors who have 'extended their area of operations beyond local markets to a world-wide base' (Bardhan and Kroll, 2007, p. 1). Most remarkably, real estate is now increasingly entrenched and implicated in global financial flows due in part to the financialisation and securitisation of the real estate market through the introduction of various financial tools that allow for greater levels of liquidity and tradability in real estate equity and mortgage financing.

On the consumption side, the profile of home buyers has also become increasingly global and 'cosmopolitan' as multinational companies relocate worldwide and drive up demand for local real estate especially in emerging markets of the Global South. In tandem, affluent global elites are also extending their property portfolio and list of 'trophy homes' to virtually every part of the world. Paris (2013, p. 96) for example observed that 'unlike the super-rich of the pre-industrial era, their contemporary counterparts have almost unlimited mobility, typically in their own or chartered planes or luxury yachts'. What all of this means for housing researchers is the need to pay greater attention to how transnational forces (global property investors, firms and institutions) are reconfiguring and (re)constituting local housing dynamics and interacting with local state forces in ever more complex ways. As Brenner (2004, p. 452) argued: 'state spatial process under global capitalism is not a thing, a container or a platform but a socially produced, conflictual and dynamically evolving matrix of sociospatial interaction'. In much the same way, housing researchers need to move beyond the 'territorial trap' (Agnew, 1994) of a purely state-centric view by considering how local housing markets are being shaped and constituted through dialectical global and local processes. For Forrest (2003, p. 7), home-ownership now 'embodies the juxtaposition of both the local and the global as a use value (locally rooted lived experience) and as something to be traded (exchange value) on the international financial market'. Ley (2015) for example has shown how the Canadian governments tried to 'reboot' the beleaguered regional economy with the introduction of a Business Immigration Programme (BIP) that encourages wealthy BIP migrants from the Asia Pacific to invest in Vancouver property at or before their arrival in Canada.

Notwithstanding the challenges posed by globalisation, the state remains an important force to reckon with, not least because nation states are 'reasserting control over major subnational political-economic spaces by integrating them(selves) within operationally rescaled but still nationally coordinated, accumulation strategies' (Brenner, 2004, p. 481). Furthermore, housing investors and real estate professionals do not operate in an abstract global space but rather 'in specific local sites that have been networked together by electronic technologies and global real estate events' (Rogers et al., 2015, p. 10). In this context, Haila's (2000, 2015) notion of the 'property state' is useful in highlighting the role of the state in coordinating and mobilising global real estate for local economic development. At the root of the concept of the property state is the monopolisation of land and the active interventionist role of the state in managing real estate for certain desired national goals or outcome. For Haila, Singapore proves to be an exemplary property state that possesses several key characteristics such as extensive public land ownership (up to 87% of total land in Singapore is publicly owned) which allow the state to determine what are deemed appropriate or strategic land-use plans while at the same time curtailing the speculative power of private property developers; and the importance of real estate as a pillar of economic growth where land rent serves as an important source of revenue and profit that contributes to a substantial portion of overall national economic growth.[2] In short, the property state is a highly territorial entity that banks on the value of 'fixed capital embedded in the land' (primarily in the form of the built environment) that is 'therefore fixed in place' (Harvey, 2001, p. 27).

While Haila does not explicitly invoke the Marxist concept of spatial fix, the property state arguably operates through various forms of spatial fix strategies by capitalising on immobile land rent. As Haila (2000, p. 2249) observed: '...expensive expatriate housing is a channel to fix part of the profit produced by MNCs locating in Singapore...'. Harvey, in particular, has suggested that the word 'fix' could refer to something that is territorially rooted such as physically immobile real estate properties that are fixed in space. But the word 'fix' could also refer to a certain fixation or even an addiction to something (Harvey, 2001, p. 24). Combining these multiple meanings, the term spatial fix used in this paper can thus refer to the fixation of the property state that is constantly on the look out to capture the capital of the mobile super-rich in order to spatially fix them in national space. In the most literal sense, such a spatial fix can be read as efforts to (temporarily) 'halt' and 'ground' the highly mobile super-rich in specific places through investments in the secondary circuit of capital via real estate properties.

Not surprisingly, nation states and cities are often compelled to pursue and capture such footloose HNWIs. For Paris (2013, p. 106), there is a 'distinctively *new* geography of the super-rich in terms of their spatial reach' with their homes increasingly spread across the globe in a complex network. Thus what sets the contemporary super-rich apart from their older counterparts is their greater sense of mobility to travel *further and faster* as well as the new urban/housing regimes that cater *to and for* them. Arguably, what is also qualitatively new about the spatial fixities of the super-rich in the contemporary world (as opposed to earlier forms of industrial capitalism) is not just the new geographical destinations where such wealth is now being parked but also the allure and lifestyle appeal of these cities or what Florida (2008) termed as the 'buzz' and 'fun factor'. If industrial towns and cities were considered the geographical anchors of industrial capitalism, 'tax-friendly' urban regimes and lifestyle destinations are now the new spatial fix of the super-rich capital in the contemporary age. As Harvey (2001, p. 28) reminded us, in order for places to function effectively as a spatial fix, they must also 'serve as attractive sites for the convergence of commodities, people, ideas, information, cultural activities, and the like'. In short, spatial fixity must also rely on aggressive urban place-marketing and the lifestyle appeal of cities.

With this in mind, the next section will now profile how the Singapore property state actively courts super-rich capital by benchmarking itself as a global wealth-centre and rolling out a series of urban economic 'spatial fix' strategies that are aimed to attract HNWIs to live and bank in the city-state. In addition to a host of 'tax-friendly' policies, Singapore has also (re)branded itself in the recent decade as a 'lifestyle haven' for the global super-rich with place-marketing campaigns that centre on the production of spectacular urban landscapes and conspicuous real estate projects.

Courting the 'rich and restless': marketing Singapore as Asia's lifestyle capital for the super-rich

If the latest Knight Frank (2016) 'Global Wealth Report' is anything to go by, the world according to the global super-rich does not exist as a flat isotopic plane but one that is highly differentiated geographically according to 'cities that matter' – where the world's wealthy apparently prefer to 'live, invest, educate their children, grow their businesses, network and spend their leisure time' (Knight Frank, 2016, p. 36). In this vaunted list of cities that matter (at least for the super-rich), while London and New York have emerged as clear favourites, cities such as Shanghai, Dubai, Hong Kong and Singapore have emerged as leading contenders, each vying for the attention of the 'rich and restless' class of wealthy investors. In Singapore, the Knight Frank (2016) Global Wealth Report estimated that there are 2360 'ultra-high net worth individuals' (UHNWI) (defined as those with a net worth of more than US$30 million) residing in the city-state although this figure is marginally lower than in previous years due to the global economic downturn. Notwithstanding that, Singapore's private bankers now reportedly manage S$634.5 billion (approximately US$470 billion)[3] worth of private assets, making the city-state Asia's second-largest offshore centre by assets after Hong Kong (Business Times, 2015). Overall, Singapore was placed in the sixth position globally in terms of the number of ultra-super rich, behind New York (5,600), London (4905), Hong Kong (3854), Moscow (3457) and Los Angeles (2820) and it was further projected that over the next 10 years, the UHNWI population in Singapore will increase a further 48%

(Channel News Asia, 2016). Beyond such superlative claims and city boosterism, what need to be further scrutinised here are the territorial strategies of these super-rich investors and the state's role in facilitating such 'policy-led wealth migration' as well as the resultant effects (Ley, 2015, p. 3).

While growing in numbers in selected cities around the world, the spatial fixity of these supposedly highly mobile super-rich[4] can be seen in their territorial strategies to constantly seek out safe havens to park and grow their wealth beyond the traditional confines of national boundaries. These strategies often entail perpetual rounds of deterritorialisation and reterritorialisation of capital. A case in point here is Eduardo Saverin, one of the co-founders of Facebook who had relocated from the USA to Singapore in 2009. As was widely reported, Saverin had strategically renounced his US citizenship in 2011 (shortly before the public offering of Facebook) in exchange for a Singapore permanent residency and in the process saving himself up to US$700 million in terms of capital gain tax and estate tax (Wall Street Journal, 2012). Notably, Singapore was chosen by Saverin because the city-state does not have capital gain tax and has a relatively low personal income and corporate tax capped at 20% and 17%, respectively. Over the years, the Singapore government has also progressively reduced corporate tax from 20% in 2005 to a flat rate or 17% from 2010 onwards irrespective of whether the company is local or foreign owned. In addition, companies are also granted 30% corporate income tax rebate (capped at S$20,000).

To be sure, it is not just the low tax regime that supposedly made Singapore attractive for the super-rich. As part of its spatial fix strategy to attract HNWIs to 'live and bank' in Singapore, the government is also rebranding the city-state as Asia's new 'capital of fun and creativity'. As Harvey (2001, p. 28) has pointed out, the infrastructure of urbanisation serves not only as crucial foci of investment to absorb surpluses of capital and labour but also as a way to physically tie up and pin down large amounts of capital in place through the production of fixed and immobile capital in the built environment. To this end, spectacular urban development projects such as the brand new downtown at Marina Bay complete with six-star hotels, casinos, luxurious waterfront housing have all been designed as a spatial sponge to soak up super-rich capital. Built entirely on state reclaimed land, the Marina Bay downtown has been projected to house global headquarters of leading financial institutions and other advanced producer services, ultra-luxurious residences and hotels as well as entertainment retail complexes (Pow, 2010). Amongst some of the landmark developments in the area are the Marina Bay Sands Integrated Resorts (designed by celebrity 'starchitect' Moshe Safdie) and iconic cultural infrastructure such as the Esplanade Theatres on the Bay. At the centre of the downtown development is a 3.55 hectare Business and Financial Centre (BFC) comprising state-of-the-art office towers, luxurious hotels and 6-star residential developments such as The Sail @ Marina Bay.

To the extent that the spatial fix strategy of the Singapore property state hinges on such spectacular urban development and luxurious real estate projects, Paris (2013) has warned of the growing disconnect as a result of the 'decoupling' of prime residential districts from the rest of the city/country. For example, the prime real estate in inner west London is increasingly de-coupled from wider developments in the UK housing market and in the process, squeezing those 'merely-rich' British families out of some of the attractive areas in Mayfair, Bishops Avenue in Hampstead or Kensington Palace Gardens in Knightsbridge (Paris, 2013, p. 106). To be certain, this process of 'super-rich gentrification' is as much driven by wealthy global investors as at the behest of landowners (e.g. the Duke of Westminster in the case of London) and the local government. As will be shown in the next section, with a near monopoly of land ownership, the property state in Singapore plays a pivotal role in regulating and promoting luxury housing as part of its spatial fix strategy to attract HNWIs.

'Storing wealth in bricks and mortar': Singapore's luxury property market

According to the *Savills'* index of prime 'global billionaire' property, the homes of the super-rich in the top 10 cities worldwide (Hong Kong, London, Moscow, Mumbai, New York, Paris, Singapore, Shanghai, Sydney and Tokyo) rose by an average 10% in value in the first six months of 2011. In particular, price growth of ultra-high value homes since 2005 has been the highest in the emerging 'new world' economies of Singapore (+144%), Mumbai (+138%), Moscow (+110%) and Hong Kong (+83%). Going by the 2015 Global Luxury Residential Real Estate Report released by Wealth-X and Sotheby, the typical UHNWI homebuyer in Singapore tends to be about 59 years of age on average with a median net worth of around US$105 million. Eighty-five percentage of them are based locally in Singapore and the top foreign owners of Singapore's luxury properties hail from Indonesia, China and India.[5] As the CEO of Sotheby's pointed out, for this group of luxury housing buyers, Singapore is often thought to be an attractive market due to its thriving economy and international marketplace and has been ranked the seventh 'hottest spot' by the UHNWIs for buying overseas properties, after New York, London, Hong Kong, Los Angeles, San Francisco and Washington DC. In 2014, a *Savills* report further estimated that five cities – Hong Kong, London, Moscow, Singapore and New York – collectively accounted for 40%, or $2.2 trillion, of all global UHNWI real estate holdings with Hong Kong taking the lead followed by London.

To be sure, foreigners have been investing in Singapore's prime real estate market as early as the late 1980s and early 1990s. As Haila (2015, p.170) noted, these foreign real estate investors hail from neighbouring countries such as Malaysia, Indonesia, Brunei, Hong Kong and Taiwan but also further afield in Japan, Kuwait, England and the USA. While foreign real estate investments are concentrated primarily in the city-state's commercial properties in the central business districts and the Orchard Road shopping belt, there has been a more targeted shift since 2000 towards high-end luxury property developments such as The Sail @ Marina Bay where 40% of the units were bought by foreigners and the Sentosa Cove where over half of the luxury homes were sold to well-heeled foreigners (see Haila, 2015, p. 170).

In Singapore, luxury properties (typically priced above S$4 million) include many of the upscale condominiums located in the Orchard Road belt and the new Marina Bay downtown area as well as 'good class bungalows' in the central districts 10 and 11. The latter, often considered to be the most exclusive and prestigious form of landed property in land-scarce Singapore, are single- to two-storey bungalow houses occupying a land plot area of 1400 m^2 and are only found in approximately 39 residential areas designated as Good Class Bungalow areas by the URA. The local newspaper *The Straits Times* (Ong, 2013) further echoed such buoyant real estate market sentiments with its headline article 'Marina Bay project attracts the well-heeled':

> New residential and office developments like V on Shenton that have been springing up in the vicinity are magnets for the well-heeled buyers. Tenants with cash to spend like the area as well, not just for the proximity to work but also to attractions such as the Marina Bay Sands integrated resort, Gardens by the Bay and the city centre.

The Singapore state has been instrumental in the development of the luxury property market in the new downtown area and had committed S$1 billion in infrastructure work in Marina Bay to support the growth of the bay area. Clearly, the property state in Singapore plays a pivotal role in regulating and promoting luxury housing as part of its spatial fix strategy to attract HNWIs. Fundamentally, the private housing market is *not* what lies outside of 'public' state control. Rather in the context of Singapore, the private housing market is often determined and shaped directly by the state as in the case of the Sentosa Cove, a luxury master planned community that was spearheaded by Sentosa Development Corporation (a statutory board under the Ministry of Trade and Industry) alongside other private developers (see Pow 2011). According to the developers, the residents of Sentosa Cove comprise not only affluent locals who bought their property as a second 'holiday home' but also HNWIs and expatriates working in global banking and financial industries in Singapore and the Asia Pacific region (over 60% of Sentosa Cove's homeowners are foreigners). At its peak, a detached house in Sentosa Cove costs between S$16 and $20 million whereas non-landed property such as a condominium apartment unit goes for over S$21,500 per m^2 (Rashiwala, 2015). In an unprecedented move to spatially 'fix' super-rich capital, the Singapore government had also liberalised home ownership rules by lifting the long-standing restriction on foreign ownership of landed property in Sentosa Cove. According to the property ownership laws in

Singapore, foreigners are effectively barred from buying and owning landed properties to prevent land speculation in the land-scarce city-state. Sentosa Cove is, however, established as a special zone where residents who own a landed property on
the island can qualify for special Long Term Social Visit Pass (LTSV) of up to
3 years which allows them multiple entries into Singapore without restriction. Like
Vancouver's Business Immigration Programme (BIP) (see Ley, 2015) and other
'golden visas' schemes, the Singapore government also rolled out a fast track application for Permanent Residency under the 'Financial Investor Scheme' (FIS) for
residents who own bungalow units in Sentosa Cove and have S$5 million worth of
total assets held in Singapore. But insofar as the recent developments such as the
Marina Bay downtown and Sentosa Cove are targeted to attract the super-rich, these
landscapes of opulent wealth and excesses also raise the spectre of an increasingly
polarised society that breeds politics of discontent as will be discussed in the next
section.

Super-rich and the politics of discontent

In the preceding sections, the paper has elaborated on the twin spatial fixities of the
property state in Singapore and the global super-rich who resided in the country's
prime residential districts. However, insofar as these two kinds of spatial fixes both
complement and feed off one another to generate spatialised forms of capital investment via conspicuous real estate development, they also risk colliding and generating serious contradictions and social tensions that may potentially threaten their
symbiotic relations (Harvey, 2001, p. 28). One clear sign of this is how the gap
between the median and the mean income earners in Singapore has become one of
the largest amongst the developed economies around the world. According to a
Credit Suisse report, the top 1% of Singapore's wealthiest holds more than a quarter
of the country's wealth (Chan, 2014). Figures released by the Singapore Department of Statistics however presented a less stark scenario with the Gini coefficient
for income inequality in Singapore at 0.464 in 2014 (or 0.412 after adjusting for
government aid, transfers and tax rebates) (Department of Statistics, 2014).

Clearly, the state's logic of spatial fix to transform Singapore into an investment
and lifestyle hub for the super-rich is not a fool-proof one and runs the risk of generating several unintended social consequences. Indeed, if the political legitimacy of
the Singapore property state rests squarely on its ability to generate national revenue and provide for affordable universal public housing (see Chua, 1997), such a
social compact that has existed in Singapore for the past five decades may be desta-
bilised by increasingly salient forms of social inequalities. Most notably, these
social disparities are spatially marked in the urban landscape with the juxtaposition
of highly valorised global spaces of consumption (such as the Marina Bay downtown, luxurious shopping malls in the Orchard shopping district and exclusive gated
communities like Sentosa Cove) that are in stark contrast to pockets of low income

and ageing neighbourhoods with predominantly one-room rental flats in the HDB heartlands. As an editorial report in *The Straits Times* (Chua, 2014) noted, low-income workers are now found living further away from the city centre and public housing estates such as those in Jurong West have a disproportionately higher concentration of low-income people (about 31,382) with monthly income below S$1500 compared to prime residential estates such as Tanglin near the city centre (with only 479 low-income individuals).

The social-spatial polarisation of income groups is also becoming increasingly pronounced in the newly drafted 2013 master plan released by the URA where prime central areas in the Marina South downtown and the Kampong Bugis area have been designated by the state planning authorities for upscale private housing only, prompting critics to ask why was public housing not included in the area, despite that around 9000 new private homes have been slated to be constructed in the 21.5 hectare Marina South land and 4000 private homes in the 18 hectare Kampong Bugis area. In a gesture towards 'inclusive' planning, the URA was reported to have stated that the new private housing developments in the Marina and Bugis areas will not be 'gated communities' for the rich but 'fenceless precincts' and pedestrian-friendly zones for 'everyone' (Tan, 2013). Yet it is questionable just how truly inclusive these new residential projects are, given that the entire area has been reserved for private condominium projects. If there is any indication, public opinion on whether to build HDB flats in the prime Marina South district is divided, with proponents of public flats arguing that the social benefits of promoting greater inclusiveness and social diversity in the area will far outweigh its economic costs whereas detractors warned that building public flats in the prime district does not maximise land revenue and may even lower the land value of the surrounding areas (Tan, 2013).

Be that as it may, the polarising tendencies of Singapore's 'rich-poor' divide (whether perceived or real) is now becoming increasingly evident and the 'decoupling' of prime private residential projects from the rest of the country can be gleaned from recent studies on housing affordability in Singapore. According to the indicators released by the 11th Annual Demographia International Housing Affordability Survey 2015, housing in Singapore remains 'seriously unaffordable' with a score of 5.0.[6] In particular, Abeysinghe and Gu (2013) have argued that private housing affordability in Singapore has shown a general deteriorating trend across all income groups with median priced private units being only affordable to the top 20% income groups. As Figure 1 illustrates, since 2012 median priced private units have fallen outside the accessible range (i.e. ratio of 1.0) even for the households in the 80th income percentile. In particular, landed properties (terrace houses and semi-detached houses) are the most inaccessible with a ratio of above 2.0 and 3.0, respectively. By contrast, public housing in the median priced range is in general relatively more affordable for the majority of the Singaporean population

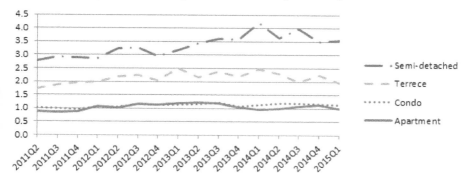

Figure 1.   Private housing accessibility in Singapore from 2012 to 2015. Note: Housing is accessible if the accessibility ratio ≤1.0.
Source: http://www.fas.nus.edu.sg/ecs/scape/recenttrend.html

except for the bottom 20% of income groups (Abeysinghe and Gu, 2013, p. 23; see also Phang, 2015).

Clearly, Singapore's housing market is bifurcated between public and private housing where the latter is increasingly out of reach except for the affluent top one-fifth of income groups.[7] In the recent years, however, in response to growing public sentiments against rising housing costs and fear of an emerging property bubble, the Singapore state had introduced a slew of housing cooling measures including the imposition of an Additional Buyer's Stamp Duty (ABSD) on private properties. In the revised rules, private homebuyers now have to pay a stamp duty of about 3% for all home purchases and an additional 7% for their second properties and an additional 10% for third and subsequent properties. Foreign buyers will also need to pay an additional 15% stamp duty on all private home purchases. As a result, prime residential property prices in Singapore went down by almost 8% in mid-2014 with the city state's prime property prices registering the sharpest decline out of the 32 cities tracked by global property consultancy firm Knight Frank's Prime Global Cities Index (Holliday, 2014). In particular, landed properties such as the Good Class Bungalows (GCB) have fallen in demand which is reflected in the drastic drop in rental prices by as much as 40%.

In tandem with global economic slowdown, vacancy rates for Singapore's private housing stock have also risen from 4% at the end of 2010 to over 8% at the end of 2015 (see Figure 2), prompting the *Business Times* to commission a photo essay that profiles several 'dark condos' (unlit and presumably vacant condominium homes) in several prime districts in the city including those in upscale Marina Bay and Sentosa Cove (Rashiwala, 2014). These unoccupied upscale homes point not only to the dampening demands of expensive private homes but also reflect the

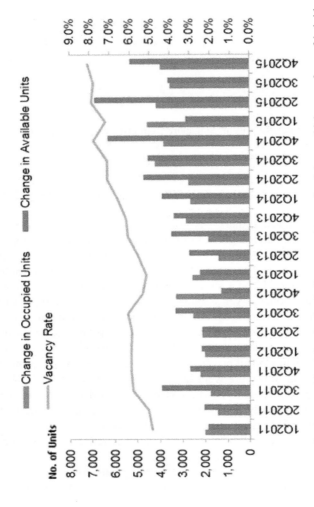

Figure 2. Vacancy rate of private residential units (excluding executive condominiums which are a form of hybrid government-built condominium with a minimum occupancy period of 5 years before they can be sold in the private housing market). Source: Urban Redevelopment Authority, https://www.ura.gov.sg/uol/media-room/news/2016/jan/pr16-06.aspx

supposedly highly mobile nature of its inhabitants. As the chief executive of real estate consultancy firm DTZ (Southeast Asia) pointed out: 'Roving expats and rich foreigners occupying condos only part of the time could be seen as contributing to the sub-optimal use of Singapore's real estate...(but this is) the price you pay for being a global city' (quoted in Rashiwala, 2015).

Overall, while the spatial fix strategies adopted by the Singapore property state have purportedly transformed the island (at least on the surface) into a global real estate and lifestyle hub for the HNWIs, these strategies clearly risk generating serious social contradictions and tensions. While it is beyond the scope of this paper to enumerate in detail the socio-economic consequences and societal conflicts associated with the presence of the super-rich in Singapore, there are rising concerns about the social alienation between the 'rich' and the 'rest' as well as how the hyper-consumption by the super-rich may have a knock-on effect on everyone by raising overall cost of living and property prices (Mahtani, 2013). Between 2006 and 2015, even though the Consumer Price Index (CPI) grew moderately by 2.79%, consumer prices in housing and utilities, transport, education and food have all shown above-average inflation with accommodation registering high growth rates of 4.94% from 2006 to 2015 (Bhaskaran and Ng, 2016).

Notwithstanding this, it is unlikely that the Singapore government will be unduly concerned about the need to contain the high prices of private housing because of the 'safety buffer' provided by the relatively more affordable public housing market that accommodates well over 80% of the Singapore population. Not least, the Singapore property state also derives substantial revenue from land/property-related transactions. According to the Singapore budget statement, revenues from property tax on private properties alone have risen by 2.9% to almost S$3.5 billion in 2012 to an estimated S$4 billion in 2014. Sale of land has also generated a receipt of between S$18 billion in 2013 and S$16 billion in 2014 (Ministry of Finance, 2014). As Ley (2015, p. 16) argued, provincial and local governments in Vancouver who value the revenues of high property prices and BIP fees are often unwilling to 'harm the goose that lays the golden egg' through any forms of active intervention in the property market despite rising public discontent over the alleged role of foreign investors in boosting local house prices. Just as Vancouver had used the residential property market to 'reboot' its troubled regional economy, the Singapore state had similarly mobilised valuable land resources to shore up the country's fledgling ambition as a global hub for HNWI capital. But unlike Vancouver (and arguably elsewhere), the near monopoly of land ownership by the Singapore property state meant that practically all national/urban development is shaped and regulated by the government although, as Haila (2015, p.16) qualified, this often entails 'a delicate balancing act between maximising rent revenue and using its landed property for the provision and funding of public goods including public housing as well as for industrial uses'.

To return to Haila's (2015) argument on the Singapore property state, state land in the city-state serves a threefold purpose as both use value (e.g. for developing public housing and industrial facilities), exchange value (leased to private developers) and as an important source of public revenue. This paper further extends the argument on the Singapore property state by showing how the government also actively mobilises land as a spatial fix strategy to capture purportedly highly mobile super-rich capital. But, even in the case of a dominant property state like Singapore, such spatial fix strategies are certainly not fool-proof.

Conclusion

Drawing on Singapore as a case study, this paper has focused on how transnational forces such as super-rich capital interact with state power and in the process transform the local housing landscape. Using the analytical insights on the spatial fixity of capital, this paper went on to critically interrogate the spatial fixities of the super-rich housing market at two dialectical scales of analysis. To briefly reiterate the arguments, this spatial fixity at the national scale is evident in the attempts by the Singapore property state to attract the high networth to reside and invest the country as a 'quick fix' way to boost national capital. Specifically, spectacular landscapes of consumption such as luxurious housing found in various prime districts in Singapore have been carefully designed and built to soak up the 'surplus' capital and excesses of the super-rich. At the global scale, the spatial fixity of the highly mobile super-rich can be seen in their territorialisation strategies to constantly seek out safe havens to physically 'park' and grow their wealth beyond the traditional confines of national boundaries. Notwithstanding the purported hyper-mobility of the global super-rich, their housing investment decisions do not occur in an abstract transnational space but are territorially conditioned and 'fixed' in specific local sites that have been networked together by local state dynamics as much as global real estate events and technologies (Rogers et al., 2015).

However, as the paper has demonstrated, insofar as these spatial fixes complement and feed off one another to generate spatialised forms of capital investment via conspicuous real estate development, they also risk colliding and generating serious contradictions and social tensions that may potentially threaten their symbiotic relations. Indeed, if home-ownership now embodies the critical juxtaposition of locally rooted lived experience versus globally traded exchange value (Forrest, 2003, p. 7), then it will be imperative for housing researchers to pay critical attention to how the new spatial fixities of the global super-rich intersect with local state power and real estate interests in the production of contested housing landscapes.

70

Notes

1. 'Prime property' often refers to the most desirable and expensive properties listed in a city such as the 'alpha territories' of super-rich neighbourhoods in Belgravia, Knightsbridge and Kensington in west London.
2. In practically every aspect of national/urban development from the provision of public housing to the planning of business and industrial infrastructures, the Singapore property state wields an enormous power by its sheer ability to command and control scarce land resources (Klublall and Yuen, 1991; Chua, 1997; Dale, 1999; Kong and Yeoh, 2003; Seek, Sing, & Yu, 2016). By invoking the Land Acquisition Act (1966), the state was able to acquire loose land parcels that were subsequently assembled and sold to the private developers through the highly profitable Sale of Sites programme (between 2013 and 2014, land sales alone generated revenues of more than S$35 billion for the state (Ministry of Finance, 2014)). Through this system, the state was able to own, directly or indirectly through government agencies and statutory boards, up to 87% of the land in Singapore. Currently, the state owns up to 58% of the land in Singapore, with another 29% held by statutory boards, while only 13% is under private ownership.
3. US$1 is approximately equivalent to S$1.35.
4. It is debatable just how footloose and physically mobile the super-rich truly are. As Ley (2010) reminds us, transnational elites no matter how financially well-endowed and global savvy are no 'masters of the universe' as their everyday family lives remain quite localised. While their business investment strategies may be highly mobile, their everyday lives are relatively more grounded and spatially fixed in particular cities or places over a period of time.
5. It needs to be qualified that super-rich homebuyers in Singapore include both foreigners as well as wealthy local Singaporeans. In the ultra-rich Sentosa Cove development for example, local Singaporeans make up as much as 40% of the homeowners (though some of these Singaporean-owned units may be rented out to wealthy foreigners). Many of these local super-rich are also expanding their property portfolio to cities in Australia, New Zealand, the UK and China (Haila, 2015, p. 172). In 2013, Singaporean investors were the largest overseas buyers of new homes constructed by Berkeley, London's largest housing developer. Wealthy Singaporean housing investors also comprised 3.8% of all buyers in London's prime districts before dropping to 1.7% recently as the result of the capping of bank borrowing limits imposed by the Singapore government as a domestic property cooling measure (The Straits Times, 2015).
6. The Demographia report (2015) uses the 'median multiple' measurement (i.e. the median house price divided by gross annual median household income) to rate housing affordability across 378 cities in nine countries. Accordingly, a grade of 3.0 and below is considered to be affordable, 3.1−4.0 moderately unaffordable, 4.1−5.0 seriously unaffordable and 5.1 and above severely unaffordable.
7. It should also be noted that while the Singapore state intervenes in the pricing of new flats sold directly by the Housing Development Board, the resale of public housing flats in the property market is left largely to market forces. Since the 2009, the transacted prices of resale HDB flats have risen beyond the median average household income, prompting the government to impose several indirect market 'cooling' measures such as the introduction of higher stamp duties and changes to the resale process of HDB flats (Cheam, 2011).

Disclosure statement

No potential conflict of interest was reported by the author.

References

Abeysinghe, T., & Gu, J. (2013, February). *Estimating bubbles and affordable housing price trends: A study based on Singapore* (SCAPE Working Paper Series Paper No. 2013/01). Department of Economics. Retrieved from http://www.fas.nus.edu.sg/ecs/pub/wp-scape/1301.pdf

Agnew, J. (1994). The territorial trap: The geographical assumptions of international relations theory. *Review of International Political Economy, 1*(1), 53–80.

Bardhan, A., & Kroll, C. (2007). *Globalization and the real estate industry: Issues, implications, opportunities*, Sloan Industry Studies Working Paper, Number WP-2007-04. Retrieved from http://web.mit.edu/sis07/www/kroll.pdf

Bardhan, A.D., Edelstein, R.H., & Leung, C. (2004). A note on globalization and urban residential rents. *Journal of Urban Economics*, 56:505–513.

Bhaskaran, M., & Ng, Y.H. (2016). Grappling with rising costs in Singapore. Retrieved from http://www.ipscommons.sg/grappling-with-rising-costs-in-singapore/

Brenner, N. (2004). Urban governance and the production of new state spaces in western Europe, 1960–2000. *Review of International Political Economy*, 11(3):447–488.

Business Times. (2015, August 18). Singapore bankers rattled by Asian moves to chase undeclared wealth. Retrieved from http://www.businesstimes.com.sg/banking-finance/singapore-bankers-rattled-by-asian-moves-to-chase-undeclared-wealth.

Channel News Asia. (2016, March 2). Fall in number of Singapore's ultra-high net worth individuals: Survey. Retrieved from http://www.channelnewsasia.com/news/business/singapore/fall-in-number-of/2565348.html

Chan, R. (2014, February 11). Income + wealth inequality = More trouble for society. *The Straits Times*. Retrieved from http://www.straitstimes.com/singapore/income-wealth-inequality-more-trouble-for-society

Cheam, J. (2011, July 23). Resale flat market hots up again. *The Straits Times*. Retrieved from http://www.stproperty.sg/articles-property/singapore-property-news/resale-flat-market-hots-up-again/a/17118

Chua, B.H. (1997). *Political legitimacy and housing: Stakeholding in Singapore*. London: Routledge.

Chua, M. H. (2014, April 2). Watch out for emerging fault lines rising from ideological and regional rifts. *The Straits Times*. Retrieved from http://www.straitstimes.com/opinion/watch-out-for-emerging-faultlines-rising-from-ideological-and-regional-rifts

Dale, J. (1999). *Urban planning in Singapore: The transformation of a city*. Singapore: Oxford University Press.

Demographia. (2015). *Eleventh annual Demographia international housing affordability survey: 2015*. Belleville, IL: Demographia. Retrieved from http://www.demographia.com/dhi.pdf

Department of Statistics. (2014). Key Household Income Trends. Retrieved from http://www.singstat.gov.sg/docs/default-source/def3ault-document-library/publications/publications_and_papers/household_income_and_expenditure/pp-s21.pdf

Florida, R. (2008). *Who's your city? How the creative economy is making where to live the most important decision of your life*. New York: Basic Books.

Forrest, R. (2003). Some reflections on the housing question. In R. Forrest & J. Lee (Eds.), *Housing and social change east–west perspectives* (pp. 1–19). London: Routledge.

Haila, A. (2000). Real estate in global cities: Singapore and Hong Kong as property states. *Urban Studies*, 37(12): 2241−2256.

Haila, A. (2015). *Urban land rent: Singapore as a property state*. London: Wiley-Blackwell.

Harvey, D. (2001). Globalization and the 'spatial fix'. *Geographische Revue*, 2: 23−30.

Holliday, K. (2014). Slump in Singapore prime property worst globally. Retrieved from http://www.cnbc.com/id/101905114#

Klublall, N., & Yuen, K.P. (1991). *Development control and planning law in Singapore*. Singapore: Longman.

Knight Frank. (2016). *The wealth report*. Retrieved from: http://content.knightfrank.com/research/83/documents/en/wealth-report-2016-3579.pdf

Kong, L., & Yeoh, B.S.A. (2003). *The politics of landscapes in Singapore: Constructions of 'Nation'*. Syracuse, NY: Syracuse University Press.

Ley, D. (2010). *Millionaire migrants: Trans-pacific life lines*. London: Wiley-Blackwell.

Ley, D. (2015). Global China and the making of Vancouver's residential property market. *International Journal of Housing Policy*. Advance online publication. doi:10.1080/14616718.2015.1119776

Mahtani, S. (2013). *Wealth over the edge: Singapore*. Retrieved from http://www.wsj.com/articles/SB10001424127887324662404578334330162556670

Ministry of Finance. (2014). *Total estimated receipts for FY2014 by object class*. Retrieved from http://www.singaporebudget.gov.sg/data/budget_2014/download/4%20Government%20Revenue%202014.pdf

Nijman, J. (2000). Mumbai's real estate market in 1990s − De-regulation, global money and casino capitalism. *Economic and Political Weekly*, 35(7), 575−582.

Ong, C. (2013, April 27). Marina Bay project attracts the well-heeled. *The Straits Times*. Retrieved from http://www.stproperty.sg/articles-property/singapore-property-news/marina-bay-projects-attract-the-well-heeled/a/116471

Paris, C. (2013). The homes of the super-rich: multiple residences, hyper-mobility and decoupling of prime residential housing in global cities. In I. Hay (Ed.), *Geographies of the super-rich* (pp. 94−109). Cheltenham: Edward Elgar.

Phang, S.Y. (2015, April 3). Home prices and inequality: Singapore versus other global superstar cities. *The Straits Times*. Retrieved from: http://works.bepress.com/sockyong_phang/79

Pow, C.P. (2010). Recovering from the 'promethean hangover'? Critical reflections on the remaking of Singapore as a global city. In K. Kesavapany & T. Chong (Eds.), *The management of Singapore revisited: A critical survey of modern Singapore* (pp. 400−416). Singapore: Institute of Southeast Asian Studies.

Pow, C.P. (2011). Living it up: Super-rich enclave and elite urbanism in Singapore. *Geoforum*, 42(3), 382−393.

Rashiwala, K. (2014, June 10). Let there be light. *Business Times*. Retrieved from http://www.businesstimes.com.sg/bt_files/infographics/Let-there-be-light.pdf

Rashiwala, K. (2015, June 25). Dark condos point to supply overhang. *Business Times*. Retrieved from http://www.businesstimes.com.sg/real-estate/dark-condos-point-to-supply-overhang.

Rogers, D. (2016). Uploading real estate: Home as a digital global commodity. In N. Cook, A. Davison, & L. Crabtree (Eds.), *Housing and home unbound: Intersections in economics, environment and politics in Australia*. London: Routledge.

Rogers, D., Lee, C., and Yan, D. (2015). The politics of foreign investment in Australian Housing: Chinese investors, translocal sales agents and local resistance. *Housing Studies*. Advance online publication. doi:10.1080/02673037.2015.1006185

Seek, N.H., Sing, T.F., & Yu, S.M. (Eds.). (2016). *Singapore's real estate: 50 years of transformation*. Singapore: World Scientific.

Tan, M. (2013, December 12). HDB Flats in Marina South? *The Straits Times*. Retrieved from http://www.straitstimes.com/singapore/hdb-flats-in-marina-south

The Straits Times. (2015, June 22). Fewer Singaporeans buying prime homes in London. Retrieved from http://www.straitstimes.com/business/property/fewer-singaporeans-buying-prime-homes-in-london

Wall Street Journal. (2012, May 18). So how much did he really save? Retrieved from http://www.wsj.com/articles/SB10001424052702303360504577410571011995562

Zhu, J.M., Sim, L.L., & Zhang, X.Q. (2006). Global real estate investments and local cultural capital in the making of Shanghai's new office locations. *Habitat International, 30*, 462−481.

The geopolitics of real estate: assembling soft power via property markets

Mirjam Büdenbender ⓘ and Oleg Golubchikov ⓘ

The article problematises the role of real estate in geopolitical circulations. The internationalisation of real estate increases mutual dependencies and vulnerabilities between nation states and, therefore, calls for a better appreciation of the geopolitical externalities and exteriorities of real estate. The article brings together disjoint bodies of literature on real estate globalisation, assemblage theory, and international relations to show how real estate is a case of the geopolitics of the multiple – geopolitics that is being assembled by diverse and distributed actors, discourses, and materialities representing the contingent and emergent formation of connections and considerations, which affect the ways how foreign relations are negotiated today. The argument is substantiated by considering several dimensions of the real estate/geopolitics nexus: (1) external influences over domestic real estate markets; (2) the implications of outward real estate investment; and (3) state-led mega-projects conveying externally the power of the state. These dimensions are considered empirically in the context of the renewed geopolitical tensions between a resurgent Russia and the West. Overall, the article calls for a better positioning of real estate in the conceptualisations of soft power, state power, and geopolitics.

Introduction

Real estate is increasingly internationalised. Ever more property actors penetrate markets beyond their area of origin, drawing on multiple networks and sources of knowledge, finance and materials. A growing body of research investigates aspects of this process, ranging from cross-border property investment, the transfer of knowledge to the transformation of real estate into liquid financial assets. Yet, this literature hardly explores how the internationalisation of real estate affects geopolitics, that is, 'struggles over territories for the purpose of political control over space'

(Lacoste, 1993, p. 696). And yet, as newspapers write on an almost daily basis about the 'invasion' of global cities by foreign property investors, there is a growing awareness that the geopolitical relations of property internationalisation warrant academic investigation (Rogers, Lee, & Yan, 2015).

Setting out from this (lack of) recognition, the present article seeks to explore some of the venues that may expose the 'geopolitics of real estate' (Büdenbender & Golubchikov, 2016; Golubchikov, 2013): that is, how the internationalisation of real estate interplays with, and redefines, contemporary geopolitics and how the latter is made more complex as a result, involving actors and discourses that can sit inside but also outside formal state institutions. Indeed, owing to its multi-scalar and distributed nature, the realm of real estate fits well both into those conceptualisations of state authority that see the latter as de-territorialised and diffused (Agnew, 2005) and into the new conceptions of geopolitics, which, as Moisio and Paasi (2013, p. 257, drawing on Reuber, 2009) suggest, 'refers to a complex assemblage of phenomena and agency, such as geopolitical discourses as representation of space and power, or the geo-policymaking of political actors, scientists, consultant, and the media...'. What this also alludes to is an increasing messiness in the construction of international relations (IR) in the era of globalisation, giving rise to what we call here the 'geopolitics of the multiple'.

In the following, we discuss the extant literature and its inattention to the geopolitical intricacies of real estate. We explain this as a lack of dialogue between bodies of relevant literatures. On the one hand, work on real estate internationalisation focuses on private actors, which are not commonly associated with IR or geopolitics. On the other hand, the state-centrism of traditional IR has weakened this discipline's ability to account for non-state actors and their multi-scalar and interpenetrating relations. We take inspirations from political geography, the idea of 'soft power' and assemblage thinking to account for the complex actors and channels making up states' interrelationships in the global political economy. We argue that real estate is a case of 'the geopolitics of the multiple' – that is, increased international influences and dependencies that emerge not simply through the conscious actions of institutionalised authority but also circuitously, via the wider assemblages of actors, practices, discourses and materialities.

We explore our propositions empirically through the instance of Russia. The case is interesting given the renewed geopolitical tensions between a resurgent Russian state and the West. The internationalisation of real estate, driven both by foreign actors in Russia and by Russian interests abroad, has created interdependencies, which contribute complexity to the ways international relations between Russia and Europe are negotiated today. We first outline the internationalisation of property within Russia, and show how this process is shaped by competition between institutions and organisations representing different nationally specific interests. We explore the ways in which these dynamics have defined and affected geopolitical considerations. Second, we turn our attention to the opposite directions of internationalisation, that is, Russian real estate activities abroad; here, we focus on both property investments in the so-called safe tax havens and Russians' property acquisitions in Southern Europe as examples of non-state-driven geopolitical assemblages. Third, we consider the overseas expansion of the Russian Church via property acquisition and the realisation of mega real estate projects within Russia (Sochi Olympics) as domains that are more commonly associated with Russian soft power and international influence. These varied cases will help us illustrate how real estate is charged with geopolitical symbolism and soft power corollaries.

Seeking the geopolitical in real estate globalisation

Following Clark and Lund (2000, p. 468) the globalisation of real estate implies a growing number of actors 'at increasing distances from the market area, involved in the production, ownership, maintenance, use and reproduction of the built environment'. This process is not only driven by the international expansion of property investors and consultants but also by the increasing integration of all types of real estate, from housing to infrastructure, into global financial flows (Aalbers, 2016; Weber, 2010). Indeed, financial de- and re- regulation, innovation and the rise of institutional investors have facilitated the transformation of spatially fixed and idiosyncratic properties into 'just another asset' that can be traded like any other financial product (van Loon and Aalbers, 2016).

While real estate internationalisation is driven by economic interests, the scale and scope of this process creates vulnerabilities and leverage that those girded with state power, and other actors, may consider when negotiating their states' position in the international political economy. Yet, the literature exploring the internationalisation of real estate does little in the way of addressing the potential geopolitical implications of this process. If considered at all, geopolitics is used descriptively, as a *context* in which business is conducted (e.g. Maier, Kaufman, & Baroian, 2014), not as a *process* that may well involve real estate itself as one of its ingredients and that needs to be problematised as such. In other words, there are no explicit attempts to consider the co-production of real estate and geopolitics – i.e. seeing geopolitics not merely *conditioning*, but also *conditioned by*, real estate production and circulation.

One reason for this inattention to the role of real estate in the production of geopolitics lies with this literature's predominant focus on private actors, such as households (Cook, Smith, & Searle, 2013; Montgomerie & Büdenbender, 2014), real estate businesses (De Magalhães, 2001) and foreign investors (Rogers et al., 2015) – as opposed to nation states and international relations. This is further complicated by two other factors. First, the use of geopolitics in this literature is somewhat bounded by state-centrism of IR that has traditionally shaped geopolitical imaginaries even well beyond its own discipline (Flint and Taylor, 2011). In traditional IR studies, state sovereignty is considered contingent on territorially bounded state spaces; domestic and foreign affairs are seen as separate; state power is performed by formal state structures. It is not surprising then that the networks of private real estate actors are not considered as agents of international relations and of geopolitical relevance, while state power is seen tangentially, as external to real estate circulations. Second, even when rejecting the crude idea of state capture, the literature on real estate internationalisation nevertheless tends to emphasise a weak state vis-à-vis international real estate interests and to see regulatory changes as the outcome of the seductive powers of private markets (e.g. Aalbers, Engelen, & Glasmacher, 2011). The interplay of state power and real estate internationalisation is consequently seen as producing 'downward' effects for state power, while the potential for the 'upward' effects, such as consolidating, circulating and discharging state power via real estate processes, remains beyond the explanatory nets of this literature.

Recent advances in political geography and IR studies, however, challenge state-centrism and the view of the state as necessarily weak; they offer conceptual tools to better account for the multiple actors and spaces of modern statecraft, which can also enrich the real estate internationalisation literature. For example, state-space theory, exploring the relationships between economic globalisation and the spatial organisation of the state, rejects the notion of the nation state being hollowed-out; it instead highlights a shift in state spatial priorities from the all-national territorial development to selected subnational locations as strategic sites and scales for state regulation and accumulation (Brenner 2003, 2009). In conjunction with an increasing openness of national economies and a greater regulatory power of supranational agencies, this process is conceptualised as 'glocalisation' (Brenner, 2004; Swyngedouw, 2004). It also considers 'glocalised' real estate projects and processes as a way of making states externally competitive – although the focus here is on *geo-economic*, not geopolitical competitiveness, as well as on a purposeful agenda setting by state agents (Cowen and Smith, 2009; also Moisio & Paasi, 2013). However, despite its advances, the literature preserves a hierarchical, scalar language and imagery, which makes it difficult to capture non-hierarchical (and oft-unintended) embodiments and entanglements of state power (Allen & Cocharane, 2010).

What is more, Agnew (1994, 2004) argued that conventional IR theory has led to a 'territorial trap' and that territorially bounded 'container' perspective of the state is insufficient to account for the diverse spheres, actors, and materialities that make up the infrastructure of state power and geopolitics. Nye's (1990, 2004) concept of 'soft power' may address these criticisms, at least to some extent, as it opens up conceptual space to account for alternative, benevolent and non-coercive means of state power, such as cultural diplomacy, economic links, and co-option. Nye's writings have been particularly directed at analysing the role of soft power in promoting US interests in the contemporary world. As such, the origin and the use of this concept are inherently geopolitical. Indeed, it has been quickly adopted in writings on geopolitics, informing, *inter alia*, the distinction between 'hard' and 'soft' geopolitics (Gritsch, 2005). While the boundary between soft and hard power – and between soft and hard geopolitics for that matter – is open to interpretation, the key value of the idea lies particularly in its recognition that non-state actors can be (and are) part of the production of geopolitical landscapes.

The above-discussed works can elucidate our understanding of the different scales, domains and agents of state power under globalisation. What is still missing, however, for the purpose of our analysis is a unifying framework that would capture how exactly multi-scalar and distributed places, actors and relations can come together to perform '*the geopolitics of the multiple*', and the role of real estate within it. Thinking geopolitics through assemblage theory is an apposite strategy to address this gap.

Assemblage theory, while admittedly representing diverse and not always consistent arrays of ideas, draws on philosophical traditions that emphasise the heterogeneity and relationality of things, people and the broader world of substance, material being and experience (Deleuze & Guattari, 1988). This provides the foundation for analyses of the co-combination and mutual constitution of what is often ontologically divided: material things and bodies, social representations, and subjective experiences (Robbins & Marks, 2009, p. 197). DeLanda (2006) proposes assemblage as a theory of 'relations of exteriority'; in other words, a whole (e.g. a state or company) is made up of component parts, material and immaterial, which are themselves not reducible to their function within it, nor to a single logic, but can simultaneously be part of other wholes or reassembled into other relationships (Dittmer, 2014; Ong & Collier, 2005). A particular focus here lies on emergence, contingence, performance and events rather than on formations and permanencies (McFarlane, 2009). From this perspective, the state appears not as a territorially closed and internally coherent unit, but rather as fickle performative assemblage of heterogeneous and continuously transforming components.

A number of scholars have applied elements of assemblage thinking to the realm of state territory and power. Sassen (2008), for example, conceptualises modern state power in terms of assemblages of distributed authority, which are constituted and continuously renegotiated by state hierarchies, private actors, partnerships and supranational institutions. Following Allen and Cochrane (2010, p. 1078), such assemblages 'perform a key role in effectively unbundling what were formerly seen as exclusive territories such as the nation state, but in ways that produce partial formations of private and public authority operating according to their own rhythms and spatial practices'. In addition to accounting for the role of different actors and materialities in making up assemblages of state authority, the perspective repudiates the oppositions between territorial and relational, macro and micro, domestic and foreign. It also emphasises the contingence of state power on the dynamics of its constituent elements.

Turning to geopolitics more directly, Dittmer (2014, p. 386) argues that 'assemblage embeds a relational ontology that dissolves the macro/micro scalar tensions at the heart of geopolitics'. Indeed, geopolitics emerges here as a domain of *the multiple* – as emergent and diffused, performed by a multiplicity of agencies that produce dynamic narratives, subjectivities, actions and routines that interplay with the more formal spheres of international relations. From this perspective, geopolitics may well also appear *within* and *through* the worlds of real estate.

Of course, there are still copious debates with respect to assemblage theory per se, including critiques of its ability to conceptualise the forces that hold assemblages together, account for underpinning motives of actors, as well as for the more persistent and hegemonic tendencies and causalities (Fuller, 2013). However, our take on assemblages is more tactical than ontological. Assemblage thinking equips us with a more integrative and interpretive apparatus that mediates between the perspectives offered by the works on real estate internationalisation, state spaces and soft power, thus facilitating proper initial accounts of conceptualising the geopolitics of real estate as the geopolitics of the multiple.

In order to specify and substantiate this perspective, we will now turn to different dimensions of the real estate/geopolitics nexus. We structure our discussions with attention to the following themes: (1) external influences and objectives shaping Russia's domestic real estate markets; (2) the geopolitical implications of Russia's property investments abroad; and (3) mega-projects that externally convey the power of the state.

The internationalisation of real estate from the outside in

Real estate as a marketable and profit-making good emerged during Russia's transition from state socialism to capitalism. During late socialism most properties, including land, buildings, infrastructure, were state owned or collectivised. In 1990 before privatisation began, 67% of the national housing stock was state-owned. In urban areas, state ownership was even higher with 79% of the housing stock in state hands. In rural areas housing tenure was more balanced with only 37% state- and 54% private home ownership (Kosareva, 1993, p. 202).[1] In the 1990s, large-scale privatisation and liberalisation programmes transferred a sizeable portion of real estate to private hands, opening opportunities not only for local but also for international advisors and investors.

Indeed, national and multinational bodies 'emerged en masse at the end of the Cold War, at the end of history, marching out of American and Europe to teach the rest of the world to be like them' (Pomerantsev, 2014, p. 36). Sweden, for instance, played a key role in the development of Russia's land registration and cadastral system (Volovich & Nikitina, 2012), while German experts and state institutions provided expertise in the field of spatial planning (Wende et al., 2014). While they were all 'missionaries of democratic capitalism' (Pomerantsev, 2014, p. 36), ideological differences concerning the specific financial, legal and institutional systems they promoted remained. The development trajectory Russia or other transition countries would take mattered internationally as it was thought to determine which countries would be able to extend political influence and benefit most from the newly created markets.

The choice of the national housing finance model is a case in point. The adoption of a housing finance system in Russia was shaped by the competition between institutions representing different national models (Stephens, Lux, & Sunega, 2015). For example, even though German Bausparkassen[2] offered advantages in the Russian context (which was characterised by the undeveloped banking system, few institutional investors, and the absence of personal credit histories), they were not able to dominate the expert discourse (Khmelnitskaya, 2014, p. 161). US-based actors spearheaded by the US Agency for International Development, who lobbied for mortgage-backed securitisation[3] (Zavisca, 2012, p. 49), decried the Bauspar system for not being 'modern' and side tracking savings 'out of the normal financial system' (Diamond, 2002, p. 4). They succeeded, and between 1993 and 1998, the legal foundations for a secondary mortgage market were put in place and the Agency for Housing Mortgage Lending, modelled after US Fannie Mae, was established.

America's ability to promote financial globalisation to enhance its own 'soft power' has been widely researched (Panitch & Konings, 2008; Seabrooke, 2001). Focussing on the globalisation of real estate, Gotham (2006) showed that the United States actively steers this process by promoting the adoption of financial tools, standardised legislation and best practices. Yet, it is evident that the United States was only partially successful in incorporating Russia into an US-dominated system. In the early years of transition, the development of the primary mortgage market – not to speak of securitisation – was inhibited by a dysfunctional banking system, high inflation and interest rates (World Bank, 2003). In the 2000s, when Russia experienced economic growth, mortgages began to take off; yet, lending was primarily financed by state-owned banks and government subsidies. Even though securitisation grew rapidly in particularly 2006–2007, its share of overall mortgages remained around 5% (IFR Russia, 2008).[4,5] Regardless of these limitations, the United States has succeeded in extending its ideological hegemony. Despite the blatant anti-Americanism in Russia's present-day politics, Russian policy-makers do not question the superiority of long-term debt over saving models in housing finance. The US-backed institutions have firmly determined all key parameters in which housing-related policy reforms are pursued. Furthermore, the institutional and legal infrastructures are in place to kick-start fully-fledged securitisation at an appropriate time, in this respect making the extension of US financial power an imminent possibility in the future.

It is not only via the institutions and mechanism of housing finance that the geopolitics of real estate has been demonstrated. The permeation of property by foreign capital and expertise as well as the acquisition of land and real estate abroad are key sites through which (multi-scalar) international relations unfold. Already in Soviet times, a few foreign real estate companies operated in the Soviet territory as part of specific bilateral trade agreements. Turkish Enka and Finish YIT, for instance, were involved in infrastructure projects and participated in the reconstruction of historic buildings (Enka, 2016; YIT, 2012). When the Soviet Union collapsed, these companies continued to operate in Russia. Yet, it was not until the early 2000s when Vladimir Putin was elected President that the internationalisation of property gained a wider momentum. Upon his arrival in power, Putin reformed political institutions and the tax system, putting an end to the previous decade of institutional chaos. Coupled with rising oil-prices these reforms initiated a period of economic growth, which translated into rising salaries and growing consumer appetite, giving rise to a boom in office and retail construction (Rutland, 2008).

This expansion in development activities was heavily financed by foreign capital. Indeed, in the context of notoriously high inflation in Russia and a liquidity glut globally, foreign capital readily replaced domestic sources of funding (Arakelyan & Nestmann, 2011). Not only were all real estate banks operating in Russia foreign owned, but Russian banks themselves increasingly financed their lending activities on international capital markets (Egorov & Kovalenko, 2013). What is more, foreign investors began to enter the Russian market directly. According to the estimations of leading real estate consultancies, the share of foreign investors in commercial real estate transactions reached over 60% between 2004 and 2008 (Cushman and Wakefield, 2016, p. 14; JLL, 2014, p. 4). While this number should be treated with caution, as it is likely to over-represent more transparent transactions involving foreign capital as well as to reflect an offshore structure of Russian business, it is unquestionable that the share of foreign capital and investors engaging in commercial real estate transactions in Russia increased dramatically.

The presence of foreign property actors, dependence on external capital and offshores not only made Russia vulnerable to global economic shocks but also opened up a new stage for its geopolitical relations. Foreign businesses, especially those owning extensive real estate in Russia, are naturally interested in its political and economic stability. This has become visible in the context of the Russo-Ukrainian conflict and the ensuing sanctions that were levied by the West against Russia in 2014. Calls by German companies (such as retailer Metro) to end the sanctions were so loud and persistent that the German lobbying association BDI felt pressured to send a disciplinary letter to more than 1000 of its members (Deutsche Wirtschafts Nachrichten, 2015). Even diplomats acknowledged that business interests put the German government under pressure to avoid potentially tougher sanctions on Russia (Karnitschnig, 2014; The Economist, 2014a). While property-related companies are not the only ones to lobby against sanctions, they have good reasons to be particularly concerned. As real estate is fixed and capital intensive, making market-exit difficult and expensive, property-holding companies are particularly vulnerable to any lasting disruptions of international relations.

As we have shown above, the internationalisation of real estate through the entrance of foreign knowledge, actors and capital creates complex assemblages of distributed authority. Internationalisation can be part of a soft geopolitics agenda, as in the case of US financial power. Alternatively, as in the case of foreign real estate interests in Russia, internationalisation generates new interdependencies. Furthermore, the geopolitics of real estate is not only shaped by engagement with external influences, but can equally be assembled by outward-oriented activities. In the next section, we will examine how the 'export' of Russia's private and public capital creates an infrastructure through which geopolitical relations are further negotiated.

Going global: the geopolitics of outward real estate investment

The uneven and at times contradictory assemblages of state power through real estate internationalisation become apparent in the outflow of Russian capital into properties abroad. Russia is a major outward investing country, with its only officially registered stock of cumulative outward foreign direct investment (OFDI) having risen from US$2 billion in 1993 to $479 billion by 2014, although then shrinking to $336 billion by 2016 (CBR, 2016). This makes Russia second largest foreign direct investor among emerging economies (Panibratov 2010).[6]

Real estate makes up a major part of this, exceeding 20% of all OFDI according to some estimates (Kuznetsov, 2011, p. 7). Whilst the international expansion of Russian companies constitutes part of foreign real estate investments (Panibratov, 2010), property purchases by Russian households also plays a role. In 2014–2015, there were 114 Russian dollar billionaires (Wealth-X & Sotheby's, 2015) and 242,000 millionaire households (BCG, 2015) for whom a terraced house in Chelsea or a penthouse in Manhattan was the most direct entry ticket to the West and a 'safe deposit box' (Fernandez, Hoffman, & Aalbers, forthcoming). In 2013 5.2% of all new-built homes in central London were sold to Russians (Knight Frank, 2013, p. 4), and in 2014 Russians owned 20% of 'super prime' properties in London – those with asking prices of £10 million or more (Barrett, 2014). Even though already impressive, these numbers may actually understate the true total, as they do not capture offshore structures fronted by nominees, of which Russians are particularly fond (The Economist, 2014b).

The resulting formation of vested interests and trans-border interdependencies produces an unstable assemblage of regulation, business interests, built environment and financial flows that can both facilitate and constrain geopolitical interests. On the one hand, the case of Russia's elite seeking to place their wealth outside the country, can be considered an indicator of a vulnerable Russia where 'even those who have done well [...] prefer to store at least a portion of their wealth in countries with strong legal safeguards and a history of political stability' (Scott Cooper, 2015). This means that the basis for Russia's current strengths and future prospects – tax revenues, investments but also an educated workforce – is eroded (Boltenko

& Gaydarova, 2015; Reznik, Galouchko, & Arkhipov, 2015). On the other hand, the large-scale capital flight from Russia and its 'materialisation' in overseas property also equips the Russian state with certain leverage. This is exemplified by a confidential report that was famously photographed when delivered to UK Prime Minister David Cameron in the wake of the Crimea crisis, which suggested that Britain should 'not support, for now, trade sanctions' or 'close London's financial center to Russians'(Judah, 2014, p. A19). It has been mentioned more than once that London's thorough permeation with Russian wealth contributes to Britain's reluctance to take a policy stance towards Russia as strong as some of its political fractions demanded (The Economist, 2014b).

Yet, the geopolitical significance of property investment abroad is not limited to the super rich. Whilst Russia's wealth elite invests in real estate in London, New York and other world cities, the country's middle class buys secondary properties as holiday homes in Russia's neighbouring countries and Southern Europe (Lipkina, 2013). This also has implications for geopolitical relations. Montenegro, a popular holiday destination for Russians, is a case in point. The country of only 260,000 inhabitants produces around one quarter of its GDP through tourism (WTTC, 2015). Russians not only make up the largest share of it, but are also the biggest foreign investors (SEEbiz, 2014). According to the Central Bank of Montenegro, the biggest share of Russia's annual investments in 2013 went to the real estate sector (EUR 108.3 million), with intercompany debt (EUR 25.1 million) and investments in companies and banks (EUR 3.0 million) lagging far behind (Intellinews, 2014). Russian newspaper *Novaya Gazeta* and the Organized Crime and Corruption Reporting Project (OCCRP), who gained access to Montenegro's state cadastral record, reported that as much as 40% of Montenegrin real estate is Russian-owned (Anin, Suchotin, Kobylkina, & Burskaya, 2011; OCCRP, 2011). In addition to middle class owners, Russian oligarchs have purchased large land plots for commercial purposes (Anin et al., 2011).

Russia's presence in Montenegro's real estate market not only creates economic dependencies but also a rather vocal political constituency. This became visible in the context of Montenegro's accession to NATO and its eventual support of the European Union (EU) sanction regime against Russia – to which pro-Russian groups responded by organising protests and calling for the resignation of Montenegro's Prime Minister (Gramer, 2015; Radio Free Europe, 2015). Yet, at the same time as the current geopolitical tensions have highlighted the leverage Russia has in Montenegro, they may also contribute to the eclipse of this very influence. The devaluation of the ruble – the effect of sanctions and low global oil prices, as well as anger amongst Russians about Montenegro's geopolitical alliance have led to a decline in tourism with many Russians trying to sell their properties and leave that country (Rujevic, 2015). It remains to be seen to what extent this will have an impact on the country's economy, but it has already created difficulties for the Montenegrin government in finding a political balance between EU and Russia.

Properties in Greece in contrast have experienced a constant inflow of Russian capital, with the number of luxury villas bought by Russians doubling in 2015. This can be partially explained by the dramatic decline of real estate prices – by approximately 50% for luxury properties since 2009 (Barzilay, 2015). What is more, however, in contrast to Montenegro, Greece's Syriza government condemned the sanctions against Russia and has done much to strengthen Greek-Russian relations. Greek real estate therefore not only offers investment opportunities, but the close relations between the two countries simultaneously present some sort of protection from possible asset seizures as part of the EU sanction regime (Khan, 2015). At the same time, the increasing share of Russian property interests in Greece will likely create a new level of interdependencies between the two countries.

The geopolitical relevance and sensitivity of foreign property ownership also affects everyday life discourses. For instance, a Financial Times article (Hope, 2014) about the growing presence of Russians in Bulgaria – an estimated 400,000 Russians own properties in the country – invoked heated debates amongst its readers online. Some readers complained that Bulgaria is turning into a backdoor to the EU through which Russians can influence European political agendas. Such discourses echo posters such as 'Yesterday Russian tanks, today Russia banks' used in Prague during the commemoration of the 45th anniversary of the Prague Spring in 2013, soon after the Russian state-owned Sberbank acquired Austria's Volksbank International, which operates across Eastern Europe (Sputnik, 2012). While admittedly anecdotally, this 'everyday geopolitics' nonetheless highlights an acute awareness of the complex interdependencies and (geo)political sensitivities produced by foreign real estate ownership.

The internationalisation of real estate also creates new vulnerabilities that competing states can exploit. The sanctions the EU and United States imposed on Russia in 2014, for example, restricted transactions with a number of major Russian companies, some of which owned properties abroad. The heavy presence of Russian capital in Ukraine has also increased Russia's vulnerability. For example, radicals have regularly attacked street offices of Russian retail banks in Ukraine (AP, 2016). This has led major Russian banks to seek strategies to sell off their branches in Ukraine (Dement'yeva & Lokshina, 2016).

The geopolitics of state-led projects

In the previous sections, we outlined some cases of dependencies that characterise trans-border real estate links and their implications for international relations. However, discursive geopolitics can also be generated by symbolic, rather than commercial real estate projects. The construction of a large state-funded project on foreign land (the Russian Orthodox Church in Paris) and the state-led mega-project achieved domestically (the Sochi Winter Olympics) are two examples, which we want to finally discuss here.

Since the 2000s, the Russian Orthodox Church (ROC) has expanded its structures globally and undergone a process of conscious internationalisation. Building on its already dense network of properties, ROC acquired new land and built churches across the globe (Blitt 2011 p. 415). Although ROC is formally separated from the Russian state, it has traditionally played a part in assembling the 'Russian world' (*russkiy mir*). Thus, even in the absence of the formal state institutions, churches and parishes in Russia's both locally and abroad provide the material infrastructure for the Russian state to additionally exert its geographic reach if not influence (Suslov, 2014, p. 46).

The geopolitics of ROC's international expansion is well illustrated by the project of the state-financed Russian Orthodox Spiritual and Cultural Centre in Paris (*Centre Spirituel et Culturel Orthodoxe Russe*). The plan to build a large orthodox centre by the Seine dates back to 2007 and was supported by Russia's highest authorities (Gauthier-Villars, 2013). The cathedral, called Sainte-Trinité, which is part of the Russian centre, will have diplomatic immunity and has become a key stage on which the complex relations between Russia and France and their respective position vis-à-vis the EU and United States are played out. President Hollande has been repeatedly criticised by the United States for supporting the project despite the EU sanction regime (Gauthier-Villars 2013). What is more, the project is not only a proxy in EU-Russian relations, but also served as lever in the international negotiation of Russian domestic power struggles. In 2014, an international arbitration court in The Hague ruled that Russia should pay Yukos shareholders $50 billion as compensation for bankrupting the oil company. Lawyers of Hulley Enterprises Limited, a Cyprus registered company, representing former Yukos shareholders, consequently requested the seizure of the Church in Paris, albeit unsuccessfully (BBC, 2015; Tass, 2016).

The multiple levels of contestation surrounding Sainte-Trinité highlight the assembled nature of authority and the resulting difficulty in differentiating between outward oriented functions of power projection and introspective objectives of identity building. On the one hand, the cathedral is an outpost of the Russian state, providing a material and discursive space for the Russian presence in France. On the other hand the church may be seen as an attempt to 'gain hold over Russian émigré communities' (Herpen, 2015, p. 251). This supports the narrative of the 'Russian World', which includes all members of the Russian civilisation, even beyond the country's current territorial borders. Putin, for example, has spoken about the 'multimillion Russian world which is, of course, much larger than Russia' (Putin, 2007). This narrative is part of Russia's attempt to bolster its authority through a shared national, or indeed civilisational, consciousness; in Benedict Anderson's terminology, to create an imagined community (2006), which does not unfold along territorial borders but cuts across them and draws new borderings in the process (Moisio & Paasi, 2013).

However, it is not only the trans-border presence of foreign actors that can render the domain of real estate geopolitically relevant; the geopolitics of real estate can take place even in the absence of extra-territorial presence. Like strategic military weapons, which do not necessarily need to cross borders to make a hard power statement in international relations, specific real estate projects can send certain messages internationally (even if of a more subtle, soft power nature). Such external geo-political effects of real estate can be enabled by symbolically significant domestic projects. Historically, these effects were performed by powerful monuments and buildings with a particular 'statement' – be those the Egyptian pyramids or Dubai skyscrapers. For example, ever since Soviet times, Russians have played a game of building the tallest skyscrapers in Europe (i.e. the main building of Moscow State University in 1953-1990 and a range of skyscrapers at the Moscow International Business Centre more recently). Soviet national and regional capital cities also sought to play the role of 'model socialist cities' to showcase, through their planning and built environment a superior socialist, pro-workers way of life. In these examples, inherently domestic projects involve extra-domestic, and arguably geopolitical, dimensions – such as bidding for extra-territorial recognition, respect, and influence.

The neoliberal competitive state has only heightened the soft geopolitics of real estate. Here, we can draw again on Brenner's (2004) account of the rescaling of state spaces under neoliberalism, which he describes as the attempt of the nation-state to rearticulate its economic power via privileging certain territories as 'strategic' and promoting them internationally on behalf of the whole state. This conceptualisation of state space restructuring can be extended to account for many instances of the geopolitics of real estate. First, the 'glocalisation' of states' territorial priorities can be embodied in real estate projects, which may, secondly, underpin not only the geo-economic competitiveness of the state, as Brenner suggests, but also its soft power and geopolitical standing.

Among such glocalised real estate projects with extra-territorial reach are mega-projects, such as the Olympic Games. Indeed, mega-events have long been recognised as some of the key strategies that shape contemporary territorial governance (Essex & Chalkey, 2004; Gold & Gold, 2010; Hiller, 2006). They are powerful marketing tools, which provide opportunities to boost the image of not only specific cities, but also a whole country. The Olympic Games specifically are widely acknowledged for their soft power implications, which also explain why countries are so keen to host them despite records of the chronic financial problems the Games create for public budgets. The 2008 Beijing Olympics, for example, provided the opportunity to demonstrate China's rapid economic growth and increasing global dominance (Dimopoulou, 2009; Sun & Ye, 2010). Many commentators have argued that much like the Beijing Olympics, the Sochi Winter Games, which took place in 2014, also were an attempt to project an image of a re-emerging Russia (e.g. Persson & Petersson, 2014; for a more differentiated discussion see:

Golubchikov & Slepukhina, 2014). Indeed, after the loss of its superpower status during the Soviet era in the 'humiliating' decade of the 1990s, Putin's Russia has sought to regain its place among the world's most powerful nations. Russia's renewed national consciousness has meant the abandonment of the non-ideological, interest-based foreign policy of the 1990s (Morozova, 2009, p. 668), and a 'a noisy and confrontational return to the international scene' as of the early 2000s (Krastev, 2008, p. 49). The Sochi Winter Olympics represented the soft power dimension of Russia's resurgent international ambitions.

It is significant that the international impact of the Olympics is importantly leveraged via particular real estate projects, including sport stadia, but also urban regeneration and infrastructure. In the case of Sochi, these were overwhelmingly state-sponsored. The Sochi Winter Olympics made the world news as the most expensive event in history, with the total costs of investment in the city's preparation for the Games of around $50 billion. The project was designated as one of Russia's national priorities, turning Sochi into 'one of the largest construction sites in the world' (Fox Sports, 2012). The main sponsors of the Olympics were large, often government-controlled corporations such as Gazprom, and Rosneft, and companies that received loans from state-owned banks, mainly VEB and Sberbank.

It is conceptually important that investing a large amount of state resources in localised projects with a global reach like Sochi also involves states' spatial priorities, where particular locations are represented as internationally (and geopolitically) significant (Golubchikov, 2010). Sochi has been identified as one such place. While the 2014 Winter Olympic event was the cornerstone of this strategy, 80% of the costs Sochi's redevelopment accrued were unrelated to sport (Golubchikov, 2016). This means that even 'more mundane' urban regeneration, real estate creation (including hotels and housing), and urban infrastructure became part of the complex geopolitical assemblages centred on the event of the Olympics.

Taken together, the examples of Paris and Sochi further demonstrate that the urban, the national and the geopolitical are not necessarily autonomous from each other as the domains of different spatial scales and territories, but rather interpenetrate each other through the assemblages of meanings, practices and processes involved in the production of politically and geopolitically significant real estate.

Conclusions

In 2014 *Foreign Affairs* announced that old-fashioned geopolitics is back, and with it Russia as a central player (Mead, 2014). It is true that we are witnessing a new wave of struggles over territory. Yet, this 'old-fashioned' or 'hard' geopolitics is intermingled with new forms of 'soft' geopolitical power offered by economic globalisation. The internationalisation of real estate interests represents this. Nation states (as institutionalised authority) create regulatory conditions that allow real estate business to take place across national borders; while doing so, nation states make room, intentionally or unintentionally, for the interplay of geopolitical interests – effectively inserting real estate more eloquently as a component into the fluid geopolitical assemblages.

Russia is just one example of a state that experiences the geopolitical implications of the internationalisation of real estate – in terms of both promoting its own soft power and exposing itself to other states' influences. We reviewed several entanglements of real estate internationalisation and its specific geopolitical constitutions and implications. Firstly, the case of Russia's housing finance system showed how the export of institutionalised norms and legislation presents lasting influence over foreign territory. Secondly, the cross-border capital flows through real estate have circuitous yet potent effects on making international relations: property built or purchased abroad becomes a conduit of geopolitical influences and dependencies. Thirdly, real estate can also be an arena for performing state soft power more directly – if embodied in edifices that are designed to project a certain image of the state beyond national boundaries or that are 'read' as such by international communities.

This is of course not to overstate the power of real estate in influencing foreign policy and international relations; real estate is simply one of many spheres that assemble international politics and geopolitics and deserves to be studied as such. Yet real estate importantly runs like a red thread through diverse aspects of our contemporary reality, often connecting them in unexpected ways. This pervasiveness is already well reflected in the multiple streams of research that varyingly highlight the role of real estate for global finance, everyday life and as a dominant sector of the economy. However, the geopolitical consequences of real estate globalisation remain less researched. The ontological and epistemological imaginaries in the related bodies of literatures have so far precluded investigations of the role of real estate in the production of geopolitics.

With this paper, we invite further research on the geopolitical implications emanating from real estate. In this way the scope of the literature on real estate internationalisation can be extended, for example, to problematise the role of real estate in geopolitics and the understanding of real estate circulations as geopolitical circulations. Similarly, studies in IR, geopolitics, political geography and the like can also be enriched through a better appreciation of the political externalities (and exteriorities) of real estate, as well as more inclusive conceptualisations of the constitution of state power and soft power. Indeed, we consider the geopolitics of real estate not simply as a politico-economic or regulatory context important for the operation of real estate markets, but rather as a case of the geopolitics of the multiple: that is, multi-actor and distributed material and discursive assemblages that represent the contingent and emergent formation of connections and considerations, which affect the ways in which formal and informal inter-state relations are being negotiated and how formal and informal political geographies are being made and remade.

Disclosure statement

No potential conflict of interest was reported by the authors.

Funding

European Research Council [grant number ERC-2012-StG_20111124], [grant number 313376].

Notes

1. The higher share of privately owned housing in rural areas can be explained with the urban bias of socialist policies, which often left rural dwellers to their own devices, including the provision of housing (Harloe, 1996; for an overview of Soviet housing policies see Sillince, 2014).
2. The system of Bausparkassen is a comprehensive instrument for financing homeownership. It is based on a loan-savings collective that is independent from the capital market. Housing loans are financed by the savings of ongoing members and redemption payments of those who have already been given a loan.
3. In the process of securitisation, lenders move mortgage loans off-balance and sell them as financial asset to investors. The role of securitisers is taken by so-called special purpose vehicles. They are the market makers who buy mortgage portfolios from lenders ('originators'), package them and resell them as mortgage-backed securities (MBS) to investors (Aalbers, 2008, p. 152).
4. To put this into perspective, mortgage securitisation in the United States amounted to more than 50% of the mortgage market in 2009 (Federal Reserve, 2009).
5. It is important to note that the failure of the US model of securitisation did not leave a complete vacuum in the provision of housing finance. On the contrary, since the early 2000s, the Russian state has actively promoted mortgage financing by offering subsidised housing loans to different sectors of society, e.g. families (through maternity capital) and state employees (subsidised mortgages for teachers and housing vouchers for military families) (Khmelnitskaya, 2015; Zavisca, 2012).
6. It should be noted, however, that as per 2015, more than half of Russia's OFDI was attributed to just three countries – Cyprus (37%), Netherlands (13%), and British Virgin Islands (12%) (CBR, 2016). These are not genuine investments but attempts to take capital 'off-shore' to protect it from the Russian state or to evade domestic taxation.

ORCID

Mirjam Büdenbender http://orcid.org/0000-0002-6240-0865
Oleg Golubchikov http://orcid.org/0000-0002-7355-0447

References

Aalbers, M.B. (2008). The financialization of home and the mortgage market crisis. *Competition & Change, 12*(2), 148–166.
Aalbers, M.B. (2016). *The financialization of housing: A political economy approach.* London: Taylor & Francis Group.

Aalbers, M.B., Engelen, E., & Glasmacher, A. (2011). "Cognitive closure" in the Nether-lands: Mortgage securitization in a hybrid European political economy. *Environment and Planning A, 43*(8), 1779–1795.

Agnew, J. (1994). The territorial trap: The geographical assumptions of international rela-tions theory. *Review of International Political Economy, 1*(1): 53–80.

Agnew, J. (2004). *Geopolitics: Re-visioning world politics*. London: Routledge.

Agnew, J. (2005). Sovereignty regimes: Territoriality and state authority in contemporary world politics. *Annals of the Association of American Geographers, 95*(2), 437–461.

Allen, J., & Cochrane, A. (2010). Assemblages of state power: Topological shifts in the orga-nization of government and politics. *Antipode, 42*(5), 1071–1089.

Anderson, B. (2006). *Imagined communities: Reflections on the origin and spread of nation-alism* (revised ed.). London, NY: Verso.

Anin, R., Suchotin, A., Kobylkina, D., & Burskaya, Z. (2011, January 11). Russian money buried in Montenegro. Retrieved April 18, 2016, from http://en.novayagazeta.ru/investi gations/49509.html

Arakelyan, M., & Nestmann, T. (2011). *Russia's quasi-sovereign debt – A sizeable contin-gent liability* (current issues). Frankfurt am Main: Deutsche Bank Research.

AP. (2016, February 20). Ukraine demonstrators attack Russian banks in kiev. *Wall Street Journal*. Retrieved April 14, 2016, from http://www.wsj.com/articles/kiev-demonstra tors-attack-russian-banks-1455977173

Barrett, C. (2014, November 25). Sales of £10m-plus London homes "up by a third". Retrieved June 7, 2016, from http://www.ft.com/intl/cms/s/0/a3fccca8-7485-11e4-8321-00144feabdc0.html#axzz3oLNh4EPg

Barzilay, M. (2015, October 19). Russians are buying up real estate in Greece, should you? Retrieved April 18, 2016, from http://www.forbes.com/sites/omribarzilay/2015/10/19/russians-are-buying-up-real-estate-in-greece-should-you/

BBC. (2015, June 19). Russian fury at Belgium asset seizure in Yukos oil case. Retrieved April 15, 2016, from http://www.bbc.com/news/world-europe-33197782

BCG. (2015). *GLobal wealth 2014 – Riding a wave of growth* (Global Wealth Report). Bos-ton, MA: Boston Consulting Group.

Blitt, R. (2011). Russia's "orthodox" foreign policy: The growing influence of the Russian orthodox Church in shaping Russia's policies abroad. *University of Pennsylvania Jour-nal of International Law, 33*, 363–460.

Boltenko, O., & Gaydarova, A. (2015). Russia's "de-offshorization" rules and the new taxa-tion of controlled foreign companies. *Trusts & Trustees, 21*(6), 605–609.

Brenner, N. (2003). Metropolitan institutional reform and the rescaling of state space in con-temporary Western Europe. *European Urban and Regional Studies, 10*(4), 297–324.

Brenner, N. (2004). Urban governance and the production of new state spaces in western Europe, 1960–2000. *Review of International Political Economy, 11*(3), 447–488.

Brenner, N. (2009). Open questions on state rescaling. *Cambridge Journal of Regions, Econ-omy and Society, 2*(1), 123–139.

Büdenbender, M., & Golubchikov, O. (2016, May 4). The geopolitics of real estate: How Russia learned the political value of property. Retrieved October 4, 2016, from http://the conversation.com/the-geopolitics-of-real-estate-how-russia-learned-the-political-value-of-property-55793

CBR. (2016). Statistika | Statistika vneshnego sektora | Bank Rossii [Statistics | Statistics of the external sector | Bank of Russia]. Retrieved. June 7, 2016, from http://www.cbr.ru/sta tistics/?Prtid=svs

Clark, E., & Lund, A. (2000). Globalization of a commercial property market: The case of Copenhagen. *Geoforum, 31*(4), 467–475.

Cook, N., Smith, S.J., & Searle, B.A. (2013). Debted objects: Homemaking in an era of mortgage-enabled consumption. *Housing, Theory and Society, 30*(3), 293–311.

Cowen, D., & Smith, N. (2009). After geopolitics? From the geopolitical social to geoeconomics. *Antipode, 41*(1), 22–48.

Cushman and Wakefield. (2016). *Marketbeat Q4 2015*. Moscow: Author.

DeLanda, M. (2006). *A new philosophy of society: Assemblage theory and social complexity* (annotated edition edition). London, NY: Continuum.

Deleuze, G., & Guattari, F. (1988). *A thousand plateaus: Capitalism and schizophrenia*. (B. Massumi, Trans.). Minneapolis, MN: University of Minnesota Press.

De Magalhães, C. (2001). International property consultants and the transformation of local markets. *Journal of Property Research, 18*(2), 1–23.

Dement'yeva, K., Bakaleyko, B., & Lokshina, Y. (2016). Ukrainskiye "dochki" na vydan'ye [Ukrainian "daughters" ready to get married]. *Kommersant, (85)*, 1.

Deutsche Wirtschafts Nachrichten. (2015, July 4). Deutsche Industrie rebelliert gegen Russland-Sanktionen [German industry rebeling against Russia sanctions]. Retrieved April 12, 2016, from http://deutsche-wirtschafts-nachrichten.de/2015/04/07/deutsche-indus trie-rebelliert-gegen-russland-sanktionen/

Diamond, D.B. (2002). *Comments on the bauspar system and porposal for Lithuania*. Presented at the Round table discussion on the Bauspar system, Vilnius.

Dimopoulou, E. (2009). *Mega events as an opportunity for urban regeneration. Impact on a host Greek city*. Presented at the International Workshop on Spatial Information for Sustainable Management of Urban Areas, Mainz.

Dittmer, J. (2014). Geopolitical assemblages and complexity. *Progress in Human Geography, 38*(3), 385–401.

Egorov, A., & Kovalenko, O. (2013). *Structural features and interest-rate dynamics of Russia's interbank lending market* (Discussion Paper No. 23). Helsinki: Bank of Finland, BOFIT Institute for Economies in Transition.

Enka. (2016). History. Retrieved from http://www.enka.com/about-us/history/

Essex, S., & Chalkey, B. (2004). Mega–sporting events in urban and regional policy: A history of the Winter Olympics. *Planning Perspectives, 19*(2), 201–204.

Federal Reserve. (2009). FRB: Mortgage debt outstanding, first quarter 2009. Retrieved April 12, 2016, from http://www.federalreserve.gov/econresdata/releases/mortoutstand/mor toutstand20090331.htm

Fernandez, R., Hoffman, A., & Aalbers, M.B. (2016). London and New York as safe deposit box for the transnational wealth elite. *Journal: Environment and Planning A*. Advance online publication. doi: 10.1177/0308518X16659479

Flint, C., & Taylor, P. (2011). *Political geography: World-economy, nation-state and locality* (6th ed.). Abingdon: Routledge.

Fox Sports. (2012). A baby boom starts in the Russian city of Sochi thanks to the impending 2014 Winter Olympics. Retrieved November 9, 2015, from http://www.foxsports.com. au/more-sports/winter-olympics/a-baby-boom-starts-in-the-russian-city-of-sochi-thanks-to-the-impending-2014-winter-olympics/story-e6frf61c-1226513895191

Fuller, C. (2013). 'Urban politics and the social practices of critique and justification: Conceptual insights from French pragmatism'. *Progress in Human Geography, 37*(5), 639–657.

Gauthier-Villars, D. (2013, June 8). Russian church creates Paris furor. *Wall Street Journal*. Retrieved from http://www.wsj.com/articles/SB100014241278873238448045785312540 33340238

Gold, J.R., & Gold, M.M. (2010). *Olympic cities: City agendas, planning, and the world's games, 1896*–2016 (2nd ed.). London: Routledge.

Golubchikov, O. (2010). World-city-entrepreneurialism: Globalist imaginaries, neoliberal geographies, and the production of new St Petersburg. *Environment and Planning A, 42*(3), 626–643.

Golubchikov, O. (2013, December 2). The urbanisation of transition and the geo-politics of real estate. *Friction Spaces guest lecture.* Retrieved from https://set.kuleuven.be/phd/dopl/archief/13-14/Friction3.pdf

Golubchikov, O. (2016). The 2014 Sochi Winter Olympics: who stands to gain? In Global Corruption Report: Sport (Ed.), *Transparency international*, pp. 183–191. Abingdon: Routledge.

Golubchikov, O., & Slepukhina, I. (2014). Russia: Showcasing a "re-emerging" state? In J. Grix (Ed.), *Leveraging legacies from sports mega-events: Concepts and cases* (pp. 166–177). London: Palgrave Macmillan.

Gotham, K.F. (2006). The secondary circuit of capital reconsidered: Globalization and the U.S. real estate sector. *American Journal of Sociology, 112*(1), 231–275.

Gramer, R. (2015, December 22). The new thorn in Russia's side. Retrieved April 14, 2016, from https://www.foreignaffairs.com/articles/yugoslavia-montenegro/2015-12-24/new-thorn-russias-side

Gritsch, M. (2005). The nation-state and economic globalization: Soft geo-politics and increased state autonomy? *Review of International Political Economy, 12*(1), 1–25.

Harloe, M. (1996). Cities in the transition. In G. Andrusz, M. Harloe, & I. Szelenyi (Eds.), *Cities after socialism – Urban and regional change and conflict in post-socialist societies* (pp. 1–30). Oxford: Blackwell.

Herpen, M.H.v. (2015). *Putin's propaganda machine: Soft power and Russian foreign policy.* Lanham, MD: Rowman & Littlefield.

Hiller, H. H. (2006). Post-event outcomes and the post-modern turn: The Olympics and urban transformations. *European Sport Management Quarterly, 6*(4), 317–332.

Hope, K. (2014, November 30). Russians find the good life in Bulgaria. *Financial Times.* Retrieved April 15, 2016, from http://www.ft.com/intl/cms/s/0/2deb249e-76f9-11e4-944f-00144feabdc0.html#axzz466H23Bq8

IFR Russia. (2008). Safe and securitised. Retrieved March 10, 2015, from http://www.ifre.com/safe-and-securitised/559721.article

Intellinews. (2014, April 10). Russia tops list of Montenegro's largest investors in 2013. Retrieved April 15, 2016, from http://www.intellinews.com/russia-tops-list-of-montenegro-s-largest-investors-in-2013-34208/

JLL. (2014). *Russia's real estate investment market" main drivers, trends and implications.* Moscow: Author.

Judah, B. (2014, March 7). London's laundry business. *The New York Times.* Retrieved April 15, 2016, from http://www.nytimes.com/2014/03/08/opinion/londons-laundry-business.html

Khan, M. (2015, April 6). Isolated Greece pivots east to Russia, China and Iran. But will it work? Retrieved April 15, 2016, from http://www.telegraph.co.uk/finance/economics/11511653/Isolated-Greece-pivots-east-to-Russia-China-and-Iran.-But-will-it-work.html

Karnitschnig, M. (2014, May 2). German businesses urge halt on sanctions against Russia. *Wall Street Journal.* Retrieved April 15, 2016, from http://www.wsj.com/articles/SB10001424052702303948104579535983960826054

Khmelnitskaya, M. (2014). Russian housing finance policy: State-led institutional evolution. *Post-Communist Economies, 26*(2), 149–175.

Khmelnitskaya, M. (2015). The tools of government for the development of the Russian housing sphere. *Public Administration Issues, Journal of the National Research*

University Higher School of Economics, Special Issue, (5), 96–111. Retrieved from http://vgmu.hse.ru/en/2014-5.html

Knight Frank. (2013). *International residential investment in London* (International Project Marketing). London: Author.

Kosareva, N.B. (1993). Housing reforms in Russia. *Cities, 10*(3), 198–207.

Krastev, I. (2008). What Russia wants. *Foreign Policy,* (166), 48–51. Retrieved from http://www.jstor.org/stable/25462293

Kuznetsov, A. (2011). *Outward FDI from Russia and its policy context, update 2011* (Columbia FDI Profiles). New York, NY: Vale Columbia Center on Sustainable International Investment.

Lacoste, Y. (1993). *Dictionnaire de géopolitique* [Dictionary of Geopolitics]. Paris: Flammarion.

Lipkina, O. (2013). Motives for Russian second home ownership in Finland. *Scandinavian Journal of Hospitality and Tourism, 13*(4), 299–316.

Maier, G., Kaufman, P., & Baroian, E. (2014). Geopolitical changes in Vienna's real estate market. In F. Nozeman & A.J. Van der Vlist (Eds.), *European metropolitan commercial real estate markets* (pp. 523–561). Heidelberg: Springer.

McFarlane, C. (2009). Translocal assemblages: Space, power and social movements. *Geoforum, 40*(4), 561–567.

Mead, W.R. (2014, May). The return of geopolitics. *Foreign Affairs, 93*(3). Retrieved April 15, 2016, from https://www.foreignaffairs.com/articles/china/2014-04-17/return-geopolitics

Moisio, S., & Paasi, A. (2013). Beyond state-centricity: Geopolitics of changing state spaces. *Geopolitics, 18*(2), 255–266.

Montgomerie, J., & Büdenbender, M. (2014). Round the houses: Homeownership and failures of asset-based welfare in the United Kingdom. *New Political Economy, 20*(3), 386–405.

Morozova, N. (2009). Geopolitics, Eurasianism and Russian foreign policy under Putin. *Geopolitics, 14*(4), 667–686.

OCCRP. (2011, November 30). Russian elites pay millions for real estate in Montenegro. Retrieved April 18, 2016, from https://www.occrp.org/en/daily/1250-russian-elites-pay-millions-for-real-estate-in-montenegro

Nye, J. (1990). *Bound to lead: The changing nature of American power.* New York, NY: Basic Books.

Nye, J. (2004). *Soft power: The means to success in world politics.* New York, NY: Public Affairs.

Ong, A., & Collier, S.J. (eds.) (2005). *Global assemblages: Technology, politics and ethics as anthropological problems.* Oxford: Blackwell.

Panibratov, A. (2010). *Russian multinationals: Entry strategies and post-entry operations* (No. 15). Turku: Pan-European Institute.

Panitch, L., & Konings, M. (2008). *American empire and the political economy of global finance.* London: Palgrave Macmillan.

Persson, E., & Petersson, B. (2014). Political mythmaking and the 2014 Winter Olympics in Sochi: Olympism and the Russian great power myth. *East European Politics, 30*(2), 192–209.

Pomerantsev, P. (2014). *Nothing is true and everything is possible: The surreal heart of the New Russia* (1st ed.). New York, NY: PublicAffairs.

Putin, V. (2007). Poslanie Federal'nomu Sobraniyu Rossiiskoi Federatsii [Message to the Federal Assembly of the Russian Federation] Moscow. Retrieved October 21, 2016, from https://rg.ru/2007/04/27/poslanie.html

Radio Free Europe. (2015, December 13). Thousands in Montenegro protest against NATO membership. *Radio Free Europe/Radio Liberty*. Retrieved from http://www.rferl.org/con tent/thousands-montenegro-protest-against-nato-membership/27423524.html.

Reuber, P. (2009). Geopolitics. In R. Kitchin & N. Thrift (Eds.), *International encyclopedia of human geography* (pp. 441–452). London: Elsevier.

Reznik, I., Galouchko, K., & Arkhipov, I. (2015, September 21). Putin faces growing exodus as Russia's banking, tech pros flee. Retrieved September 22, 2015, from http://www. bloomberg.com/news/articles/2015-09-21/putin-faces-growing-exodus-as-russia-s-bank ing-tech-pros-flee

Robbins, P., & Marks, B. (2009). Assemblage geographies. In S.J. Smith, R. Pain, S.A. Marston, & J.-P. J. III (Eds.), *The SAGE handbook of social geographies* (pp. 176–195). Los Angeles, CA: SAGE Publications.

Rogers, D., Lee, C.L., & Yan, D. (2015). The politics of foreign investment in Australian housing: Chinese investors, translocal sales agents and local resistance. *Housing Studies, 30*(5), 730–748.

Rujevic, N. (2015, November 18). Rückzug der Russen von der Adriaküste | Europa | DW.COM | 18.11.2015 [Retreat of Russians from the Adriatic coast]. Retrieved April 13, 2016, from http://www.dw.com/de/r%C3%BCckzug-der-russen-von-der-adriak%C3%BCste/a-18860616

Rutland, P. (2008). Putin's economic record: Is the oil boom sustainable? *Europe-Asia Studies, 60*(6), 1051–1072.

Sassen, S. (2008). *Territory, authority, rights: From medieval to global assemblages*. Princeton, NJ: Princeton University Press.

Scott Cooper, A. (2015, November 2). Is Putin's demise spelled out in New York's real estate listings? Retrieved April 15, 2016, from http://foreignpolicy.com/2015/02/11/is-putins-demise-spelled-out-in-new-yorks-real-estate-listings/

Seabrooke, L. (2001). *US power in international finance. The victory of dividends*. Basingstoke: Palgrave.

Sillince, J.A.A. (2014). *Housing policies in Eastern Europe and the Soviet Union*. London: Routledge.

SEEbiz.eu. (2014, March 20). *Kriza na Krimu smanjuje ruske investicije u Crnu Goru* [The crisis in the Crimea decreases Russian investments in Montenegro]. Retrieved April 15, 2016, from http://www.seebiz.eu/kriza-na-krimu-smanjuje-ruske-investicije-u-crnu-goru/ar-84097/

Sputnik. (2012, February 16). Sberbank buys Volksbank International for 505 Mln Euros. Retrieved June 7, 2016, from http://sputniknews.com/business/20120216/171341558. html

Stephens, M., Lux, M., & Sunega, P. (2015). Post-socialist housing systems in Europe: Housing welfare regimes by default? *Housing Studies, 30*(8), 1210–1234.

Sun, J., & Ye, L. (2010). Mega-events, local economies, and global status: What happened before the 2008 olympics in beijing and the 2010 world expo in Shanghai. *Journal of Current Chinese Affairs, 39*(2), 133–165.

Suslov, M.D. (2014). "Holy Rus": The geopolitical imagination in the contemporary Russian orthodox church. *Russian Politics & Law, 52*(3), 67–86.

Swyngedouw, E. (2004). Globalization or "glocalisation"? Networks, territories and rescaling. *Cambridge Review of International Affairs, 17*(1), 25–48.

Tass. (2016, January 31). Paris court rejects claim of former Yukos shareholders on construction of Russian center. Retrieved April 15, 2016, from http://tass.ru/en/economy/853411

The Economist. (2014a, March 15). Lovers, not fighters. *The Economist*. Retrieved from http://www.economist.com/news/business/21599034-german-exporters-are-pushing-back-against-economic-sanctions-russia-lovers-not-fighters

The Economist. (2014b, March 22). Honey trapped. *The Economist*. Retrieved from http:// www.economist.com/news/briefing/21599408-london-has-more-lose-most-when-it-comes-scaring-oligarchs-honey-trapped

van Loon, J., & Aalbers, M.B. (2016). *How real estate became 'just another asset class': The financialization of the investment strategies of Dutch institutional investors* (Working paper). Leuven: KU Leuven.

Volovich, N., & Nikitina, E. (2012). The conflicts between the systems of public and private land law in Russia. In E. Hepperle, R.W. Dixon-Gough, V. Maliene, R. Mansberger, J. Paulsson, & A. Pödör (Eds.), *Land management: Potential, problems and stumbling blocks* (pp. 195–209). Zürich: vdf Hochschulverlag AG.

Wealth-X, & Sotheby's. (2015). *The global luxury residential real estate report 2015*. London: Sotheby's.

Weber, R. (2010). Selling city futures: The financialization of urban redevelopment policy. *Economic Geography, 86*(3), 251–274.

Wende, W., Wirth, P., Albrecht, J., Közle, E., Magel, A., Maz, A., & Neumann, A. (2014). *Integrating ecological concerns into Russia's territorial planning*. Dresden: Leibniz Institute of Ecological Urban and Regional Development.

World Bank. (2003). *Developing residential mortgage markets in the Russian Federation: Final report* (No. 29014). Washington, DC: Author.

WTTC. (2015). *Travel & tourism economic impact 2015 – Montenegro*. London: World Travel & Tourism Council.

YIT. (2012). YIT history – YIT group. Retrieved April 11, 2016, from http://www.yitgroup. com/YIT_GROUP/about-us/YIT-in-brief/history

Zavisca, J.R. (2012). *Housing the New Russia*. New York, NY: Cornell University Press.

Transnational real estate in Australia: new Chinese diaspora, media representation and urban transformation in Sydney's Chinatown

Alexandra Wong

Foreign real estate investment, especially from Asia, is growing rapidly in many global cities. Whilst transnational real estate has recently been highlighted in various media coverage, its actual process is still relatively under researched by housing scholars. This paper fills this research gap by framing transnational real estate in the broader context of intensified globalisation and increased transnational mobility of people, capital and information and by grounding it within the case study of Sydney's Chinatown in Australia which focuses on three dimensions of the process, namely the role of Chinese diaspora in shaping transnational real estate practices, the locality characteristics of Chinatown which contribute to Chinese capital accumulation and urban transformation in the area, and the manner in which transnational real estate investment practices have been reshaped, due to misrepresentation of the issue in public media. Based on in-depth interviews, content analysis of newspapers and analysis of official statistics, this paper demonstrates the global–local nexus of transnational real estate process in Australia which is constituted, and shaped, by various global forces and local factors, including social actors' motives and practices, geographical settings and cultural politics.

Introduction

In the past few years, there has been concern in the media about the growing number of foreign investors purchasing property in Australia. According to a report by the National Australia Bank (NAB), in the first quarter of 2015, foreign investors accounted for 15.6% of the new property demand in Australia (NAB, 2015), which means that almost one in six new homes were sold to overseas buyers. In fact, Australia is not alone in attracting foreign real estate investment. Many global cities such as London, New York, Vancouver, Singapore and Hong Kong have also seen an influx of foreign investors, especially buyers from Asia, in their real estate markets (Warren, 2010).

In spite of this, the subject of transnational real estate is still neglected by housing scholars. On the one hand, most of the previous research on the topic was conducted at the national or regional/state level, based on quantitative methods, with the aim of identifying the different economic drivers, or variables, of foreign real estate investment (Fereidouni & Masron, 2013; Ross, 2011). On the other hand, many studies adopted an a priori approach and focused on the impact of foreign real estate investment on the host country, in areas such as property prices (Gholipour, Al-mulali, & Mohammed, 2014), neighbourhood transformation (Ley 2010; Lin, 1998) and racially based tensions between foreign investors and local residents (Hajdu, 1999; Rogers, Lee, & Yan, 2015). However, many questions about the actual process of transnational real estate remain unanswered.

This paper attempts to fill this research gap by grounding it within an in-depth case study of Chinese foreign real estate investment in Sydney's Chinatown. Strategically located in the south of Sydney's CBD, Chinatown has long been seen as a 'natural place' for doing business with Chinese people and an important 'transnational hub for economic and cultural exchange and flow' between Australia and China/Asia (Ang, 2015, p. 1). In the past few years, Sydney's Chinatown has emerged as a 'hub' for real estate services and one of the most popular locations for property investment in Sydney for local and offshore Chinese buyers. To address some of the problems associated with quantitative data such as their inabilities to capture abstract concepts like ethnic networks and cultural capital, when trying to understand the complexities of transnational real estate, the data for this paper were collected through multiple methods. These included in-depth interviews with eight real estate agents, four migration agents, one lending manager and two Chinese migrants from Chinatown, participant observation at two property exhibitions in Chinatown, statistical data from the Australian Bureau of Statistics (ABS[1]) and content analysis of 86 articles about foreign property investment from broadsheet newspaper *Sydney Morning Herald* between 2013 and 2014. Although the Chinese community in Australia has diverse ethnic origins, class and cultural backgrounds, the scope of this paper is limited to the discussion of recent migrants from mainland China with a view to illuminating their relations with transnational real estate activity in Sydney.

New mobility paradigm, global cities and transnational urbanism

Housing used to be seen as a national issue. However, the intensified globalisation and enhanced mobility of people, capital and information under the 'new mobility paradigm' (Sheller & Urry, 2006) have disrupted this conventional understanding. The movement of a wide range of human and non-human agents has intensified and quickened, whilst places are tied into networks which stretch beyond their spatial boundaries, facilitated by the development of modern transportation and communication technologies. As a result, the housing market has become part of the 'distanciated economy' (Amin & Thrift, 2002) which is increasingly affected by the flow of people, capital and information beyond a country's national borders.

However, this 'new mobility' is a spatially uneven process, as most international immigration and investment tend to target 'global cities' (Sassen, 2001) or 'gateway cities' (Ley & Murphy, 2001). In particular, neo-liberalisation of the economy (Harvey, 2007) has led to greater demand for international investment and knowledge workers in global cities. In turn, the economic and socio-cultural landscapes of these cities are constantly shaped by immigrants and their connections with their country of origin.

The implications of contemporary diasporas and their interactions with multiple places have been widely studied in the field of transnationalism. Glick-Schiller, Basch, and Blanc-Szanton (1992, pp. 1−2) have defined transnationalism as

> the process by which immigrants build social fields that link together their country of origin and their country of settlement…transmigrants develop and maintain multiple relations—familial, economic, social, organisational, religious and political that span borders. Transmigrants take actions, make decisions and feel concerns and develop identities within social networks that connect them to two or more societies simultaneously.

This transnational social field relates to Castells' (1996) concept of 'spaces of flows' which are created by diasporas through 'compressed time and space'. They are made up of three elements: the things that flow, the medium through which they flow and the nodes which circulate the flows (Stalder, 2002).

As a crucial medium for the transnational space of flow, many contemporary migrants, especially those in business and professional occupations, with their super mobility and flexible citizenship (Ong, 1999), are often highly valued by host countries for their economic contribution. These so-called 'middle class' migrants actively take advantage of their cultural capital and social ties, as well as their knowledge and information across two or more places, to engage in various forms of entrepreneurial business activity (Collins, 2002). Many scholars attributed the success of such ethnic businesses to migrants' social ties which help to build trust and minimise transaction costs (Ouchi, 1980; Waldinger et al., 1990). A node of a transnational space is usually exemplified in a city characterised by high concentration of migrants and strong transnational connections. In contrast to most migration studies that cities are treated as a 'static' place, Glick-Schiller and Caglar (2010) saw them as a dynamic space embedded within distinctive local production system, networks and milieu (Camagni, 1991; Scott, 1998; Storper, 1995). They proposed an analytical framework focusing on the active role of migrants as place/scale-makers to show how cities which are embedded within different power hierarchies 'shape and are shaped by different forms of migrant incorporation' (Glick-Schiller & Caglar, 2009, p. 182).

Glick-Schiller and Caglar's (2009, 2010) framework resonates Smith's (2001, 2005) concept of 'transnational urbanism' which is a bottom-up approach to studying the global−local nexus of transnational social processes within which agencies and localities play crucial roles. First, he saw social agencies as 'socially and spatially situated subjects' (Smith, 2005, p. 243) who can act upon economic and social structures, via their transnational practices, and also shape locality characteristics. Second, he emphasised that a place, embedded within its historical and geographical context, in which transnational practices of social agencies take place, has the power to mediate the global forces in the process of neo-liberal restructuring. Sometimes, this power may be exercised through social agencies' local politics or social movements (Guarnizo & Smith, 2009).

The above literature shows that when studying transnational real estate, it is necessary to take into account the global forces behind the transnational networks and practices of major actors, in particular, the contemporary migrants who become essential buyers or brokers in the transnational social fields. Besides, we need to consider place not only as a backdrop for transnational real estate processes, but also as having the power to shape those processes through its local particularities. Finally, we need to look at the contestations on transnational real estate as resistance from social actors can reshape the transnational process from 'below'.

The context: Sydney as a global city and middle-class Chinese immigrants

'As we look at globalisation in the housing market, we are engaging not just anonymous distant capitalists, but also immigrants, who are both buyers and neighbours' (Ley & Tutchener, 2001, p. 200). The close relations between transnational real estate and immigration is evidenced in Ley (2010)'s book, in which he presented the cases of wealthy Hong Kong business migrants who supported transnational real estate investments in Canada in the 1980s. As in Canada, migrants from mainland China also played crucial roles in Australia's recent transnational housing market.

Although the history of mainland Chinese immigration to Australia can be traced back to the gold rush in the 1850s, the rapid increase of mainland Chinese population took place in the 1990s. Many scholars attributed this to the change of Australia's immigration rules in favour of skilled migrants and the existence of a migration pathway for international students in Australia since the mid-1990s (Hugo, 2008; Robertson, 2013). Largely motived by this migration pathway, the number of Chinese international students in Australia has jumped from 5673 in 1994 to 150,116 in 2013 (Australian Education International (AEI), 2001, 2013).

Many of them went on to apply for migration through the skilled scheme and obtained permanent residency in Australia. By 2013, there were 427,590 China-born people in Australia, an increase of 70% since 2006, accounting for 1.8% of Australia's total population (Department of Immigration and Border Protection (DIBP), 2015).

Among all the places in Australia, Sydney is by far the most popular place for mainland Chinese settlement, with the 2011 census showing that 46.6% of the mainland Chinese migrants were residing in greater Sydney (ABS, 2011). As Australia's global city, Sydney is a popular destination for international finance, businesses, migrants, students and tourists, and 40% of top 500 Australian corporations have headquarters in Sydney (City of Sydney, 2015). The knowledge-based economy of Sydney, which is evidenced in the high concentration of finance, creative and business services industries in its central business district (CBD), has attracted a high number of skilled migrants from mainland China. As the 2011 census showed, these new Chinese diasporas are relatively well educated, 35.8% of them had a degree or higher qualification, over 60% of them are fluent in English and 13.1% of them were employed in professional occupations. The census data also suggest that more and more Chinese migrants, especially those younger professional workers, prefer to live in the city. The China-born population in the Sydney local government area (LGA) has increased 64% between 2006 and 2011, making them the fastest growing ethnic group in the city (ABS, 2011).

The pull and push factors of Chinese foreign real estate investment

Asians' interest in Australian real estate market can be seen in a number of studies (e.g. Adrian & Stimson, 1986; Hajdu, 2005). In 2009–2010, China overtook Singapore as the largest Asian foreign investor in Australia's real estate sector with the total investment approval worth over A$2.4 billion[2] (Foreign Investment Review Board (FIRB), 2010). In 2013–2014, the amount has jumped dramatically to A$12.4 billion, representing a 416% growth in five years (FIRB, 2014). According to Andrew Taylor, co-founder of Juwai.com, a popular online platform for mainland Chinese to purchase overseas properties, Australia is ranked second among US, UK, Canada and Singapore in the top five markets for Chinese property buyers in 2014,[3] as Chinese buyers saw them as safe, highly regulated housing markets with robust growth potential (Bloomberg, 2014). Our interviewee #11 explained the reasons why Australia is attractive to Chinese property buyers:

> When we talk about the Chinese investors, they choose us—number one, it's close, only eight to ten hours flight. Number two, the education system is okay, the climate is good and the environment is much cleaner. And in terms of our political system, it's fairly stable or relatively stable compared to other countries. So I think that contributes a lot to the reason why Australia is so attractive to investors (Interviewee #11, real estate agent and property expo organiser).

Regarding the motives for Chinese investment in foreign real estate, the Annual Report on Chinese International Migration 2014 revealed that the top three reasons were planning for overseas migration, children's education and wealth security (e.g. investment diversification) (Centre for China and Globalisation, 2014). This has been confirmed by our interviewee #11 that offshore Chinese property buyers in Sydney can be roughly divided into three types, ranging from would-be migrants, who purchase houses for their own use, parents buying houses for children, who are studying in Sydney, and investors who have no desire to migrate but are interested in capital gains or rental income. However, in reality, the differentiation of these three types of buyers is not so clear-cut, due mainly to their high level of mobility. For example, many middle-class Chinese send their children to study abroad or buy investment properties overseas prior to their eventual migration. The blurred boundary between different types of buyers and the lack of official record on property buyers' citizenships (Standing Committee on Economics, 2014) also mean that it is difficult to estimate the number of Chinese foreign investors in Australia's housing market.

According to our interviewee #13, who is a senior lending manager of a local bank in Chinatown, large-scale Chinese foreign investment in Sydney's housing market started about five years ago. He attributed this to the changes of Australia's foreign investment policy in 2008. After the global financial crisis, in an attempt to stimulate the economy, the government relaxed the rules to allow developers to sell up to 100% of their products to overseas buyers and to obtain foreign investment pre-approval for non-residents.[4] This has made overseas property purchases much easier as the developers can take their already-approved product to sell directly in the overseas markets.

Apart from the pull factors stated above, the push factors from China also contributed to the situation. According to the China Private Wealth Report in 2012, the number of China's high net worth individuals, with an investable asset of RMB 10 million, has reached 700,000, and their aggregated investable assets were equal to RMB 22 trillion (China Merchants Bank & Bain & Company, 2013). However, the growing wealth of Chinese people coincided with the government tightening its control of the real estate market. With the aim of cooling down the over-heated real estate market in China, caused partly by the government's policy of supporting housing prices after the global financial crisis, a number of controlling measures have been put in place since late 2009. For instance, in order to control property speculation, a tax of 5.5% was introduced for anyone selling a second-hand property within five years (Anderlini, 2009). From 2010 to 2013, the government further stepped up its effort to contain the surge of housing prices by: imposing restrictions on the number of purchases; ordering stricter enforcement of 20% capital gains tax on home sale profit; and demanding 60% down payment and higher interest rate on second-home mortgages in most tier 1 and tier 2 cities (Bloomberg, 2013). As a result, property prices fell in 70 major Chinese cities and increased uncertainty in the housing market, which encouraged private buyers and developers to seek alternative investment in overseas property markets (Knight Frank, 2015).

Chinatown as a 'node' for diasporic transnational real estate networks

In view of the growing demand of Chinese buyers in Sydney's housing market, major national real estate agents such as Ray White, LJ Hooker and McGrath have set up China/Asian divisions, headed by Chinese diaspora staff, and have recruited members of the Chinese diaspora, who are fluent in Cantonese and/or Mandarin, as sales people. Interviewee #1, who is also a migrant from China, explained that his bilingual skills were essential for reaching Chinese buyers 'because I can help them better in talking in their language' (Interviewee #1, real estate agent, head of Asian division).

A growing number of Chinese migrants have set up real estate agencies and professional firms in Chinatown to provide a wide range of real estate related information and services to co-ethnic customers; these include property conveyancing, migration and education advice, accounting and financial planning. Statistics from the City of Sydney showed that there were over 160 professional and property services companies aggregated in the core Chinatown precinct, an increase of 22% between 2007 and 2012 (City of Sydney, 2012). Moreover, nine major banks, including international banks such as Bank of China and HSBC, have opened branches in Chinatown. Home loan services were available at these banks for both local and overseas property buyers. Our interviewee #13, who is a senior lending manager in Chinatown, admitted that non-resident loans have been 'creeping up to 60 or 70%' of his branch's mortgage business in the last few years.

More recently, these Chinese diasporas began to leverage their transnational ethnic networks to organise large-scale property exhibitions in Sydney for Chinese customers. For instance, in 2012 and 2013, two property exhibitions entitled 'Chinese Sydney Property Expo' were held in Dixon Street at Chinatown and Lower Town Hall in Sydney CBD. Organised by Window to China, a property service company founded by Chinese migrants based in Chinatown, each event has attracted over 20 exhibitors and 3000 customers. At the two property expos, a large number of relatively new Chinese developers, such as Longton, Springfield, and War Hing, and Chinese real estate agents, such as Property Investors Alliance and BE100, were exhibiting their property projects alongside major national property developers and real estate agents who saw the expo as an opportunity for them to penetrate into the Asian market. Most of the properties exhibited at the Expo were off-the-plan apartment buildings located in places with high concentrations of Chinese population, such as Sydney South (Haymarket), Inner city (Surry Hill, Zetland, Rosebery), Hurstville, Chatswood and Parramatta. To facilitate communications with Chinese customers, Chinese-speaking interpreters were hired, and property brochures were published in Chinese.

Major local banks, including ANZ Bank & St George Bank, headed by Chinese-speaking lending managers and professional firms, such as mortgage brokers, investment consultants, migration agents and legal agencies run by Chinese migrants, also set up booths there to provide *one-stop-shop* advice and services for Chinese buyers. In 2013, with support from China Eastern Airlines, one of the expo's sponsors, 150,000 invitations were sent to the members of the Airline's frequent flyer programme, and a business-class discount was offered to those who attended the expo after flying from China. Both property expos were endorsed by then Australian Prime Minister Julia Gillard, who sent a congratulatory message reiterating the support of the Australian Government for Chinese foreign investment, which was in line with the objectives stated in the government's 2012 'Australia in the Asian Century' White Paper:

> I welcome the Sydney Chinese Property Expo, which presents a valuable opportunity for home-buyers, investors, property developers and real estate agents to explore opportunities in Australia's vibrant property sector and for Australian firms to build stronger ties abroad. The 'Asian Century' is a time of immense opportunity for our two countries and I urge businesses and entrepreneurs on both sides to take advantage of this remarkable moment in history (Window to China, 2012, p. 3).

Apart from attending property expo, interviewee #1 confirmed that buying properties on the Internet is increasingly commonplace. As he observed: 'They [the customers]'re on the website, I give them information, they just buy it, and afterwards, they don't even look at their properties, what they look like...' (Interviewee #1, real estate agent, head of Asian division). The launch of online platforms, such as Juwai.com in 2011, has greatly enhanced the information exchange between China and overseas markets. Many Australian real estate agents, such as LJ Hooker and Ray White, have registered with Juwai.com's multiple listing services, which enables potential buyers in China to obtain real-time information about properties listed in Australia.

Chinese capital and Chinatown's transnational real estate

Chinatown is also an important residential space for many Chinese migrants. The latest census revealed that over 35% of the population residing in Chinatown (Haymarket) had Chinese ancestry (ABS, 2011). In the past few years, Chinatown and its surrounding areas have undergone rapid urban transformation. Data showed that Chinatown and CBD South have one of the largest housing stocks in the Sydney LGA in 2012–2013, with 804 units completed, and over 4000 units at the stages of development, approval and construction (City of Sydney, 2013). Many of these residential developments were supported by transnational capital from China. Table 1 lists the apartment buildings funded by Chinese capital in Chinatown and CBD South.

Table 1. Examples of residential buildings funded or developed by Chinese capital in Chinatown and CBD South (City of Sydney, 2013–2015).

Address	Building name	Developer	Country of origin	No. of unit	Land cost* (million)	Construction cost** (million)
Building status: completed						
61–79 Quay Street, Haymarket	The Quay	Ausbao	China	286	$38	$105
Building status: commenced						
115–119 Bathurst Street, Sydney	Greenland Centre	Greenland Group	China	490	$110	$355
141–149 Bathurst Street, Sydney	The Castlereagh	Lenland Property	China	66	$20	$16
49–53 Dixon Street, Haymarket	Hing Loong	War Hing	Local Chinese company	47	Unknown	$20
Building status: development application lodged						
130–134 Elizabeth Street, Sydney		Aoyuan & Ecove	China & Australia joint venture	148	$121	$106
9–25 Commonwealth Street, Sydney		Private Chinese developer	Local Chinese company	52	$45	$67

*Data compiled from various newspaper and property websites such as *Sydney Morning Herald*, *The Telegraph*, my-property-report.com
**Data compiled from City of Sydney development approval applications documents on estimated construction cost only.

One of the high-profile residential developments in Chinatown was the 'The Quay' apartment on 61–79 Quay Street. The site was the former poultry section of Paddy's Market and had been vacant for 20 years before it was sold to Ausbao Pty Ltd., a subsidiary of China's fourth largest developer, Beijing Capital Development, in 2009. The Quay has about 270 units, with a selling price from A$390,000 to over A$1.7 million each (Wilmot & Thistleton, 2012). Chinese buyers showed great interests in the launch of the off-the-plan units in April 2012. The buying activities were reportedly 'frenzied' with 'about 35 apartments sold each hour'. During the launch weekend, 200 out of 270 apartments were sold and the rest of the stock was marketed to overseas buyers in Hong Kong (Knowlton, 2012). The construction of this development was completed in 2014 and a news report revealed that buyers had already achieved 20% capital gains from their properties in January 2015 (Anderson, 2015).

Another example is the development of Sydney's tallest residential tower 'Greenland Centre' near Chinatown by China's state-owned developer Greenland Group, a company currently ranked 359th in the global Fortune 500 list. This development is located on 115 Bathurst Street of Sydney's CBD, which includes a 66-storey residential tower with over 400 units and a five star hotel converted from the former Sydney Water Board building. Similar to The Quay, the first stage launch of Greenland Centre's off-the-plan apartments in December 2013 received a very good response from the Chinese buyers. Apart from Australia, the apartments also went on sale simultaneously in Shanghai, Hong Kong and Singapore. News reports revealed that 214, out of the 250, apartments were sold in the first morning. Of these, 95% went to Chinese buyers; half of them were from overseas (Macken, 2013). The construction work in this development began in 2014 and is expected to be completed in 2016.

The geography of Chinatown and Chinese transnational real estate practices

Chinatown's distinctive geographical characteristics have encouraged Chinese buyers to take a strong interest in local properties. As shown in Figure 1, Chinatown is centrally located within walking distance of the Town Hall and the central CBD, the major business and commercial hub, in the north and Darling Harbour, a world famous tourist spot, in the west. It is also well connected with various suburban areas through the railway at Central Station in the south. Besides, Chinatown is surrounded by a number of universities, technical colleges and language schools, which has attracted a large number of international students residing in this area.

According to our interviewee #13, who is a senior lending manager, Chinatown's location, within Sydney's CBD, was seen as the primary advantage by many Chinese property buyers. He said that 'for some reason they [Asians] love being closer to the city'. Chinatown's city location is also particularly attractive to new Chinese migrants, many of whom regard Chinatown as an 'entry point' or 'gateway' for them into Sydney. As interviewee #5 explained:

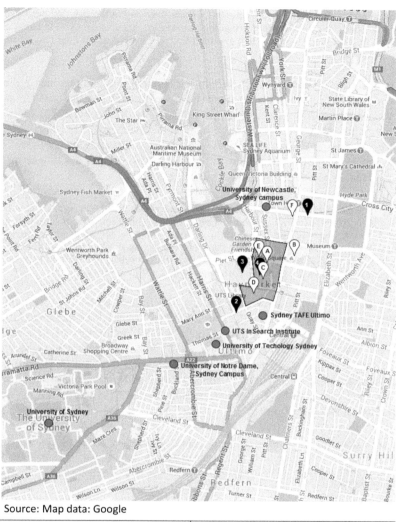

Source: Map data: Google

Major shopping malls near Chinatown	Apartment buildings popular among Chinese investors near Chinatown
A. Sussex Centre B. World Square C. Dixon House D. Market City E. Number 1 Dixon Shopping Centre F. Regent Place	1. Sydney Greenland Centre 2. The Quay Apartment 3. Darling Square 4. Hing Loong Apartment

Figure 1.   Location of Chinatown in the city centre. *Source*: Map data: Google.

New migrants coming here we find a lot of cases they stay in the city first before they have decided which suburb they are going to move to...they usually would buy a unit in the city as a place they can live and then keep it for investment later (Interviewee #5, real estate agent).

The local milieu of Chinatown, which is a distinctive Asian precinct in the city, has been perceived favourably by many Chinese migrants. In the core Chinatown area, there are over 200 Asian ethnic restaurants (City of Sydney, 2012) and several large shopping malls, housing a large number of Asian style shops. A variety of Chinese-speaking professional services, ranging from Chinese doctors to real estate agents, are available in Chinatown. Interviewee #14, who is a Chinese migrant, explained the socio-cultural reasons for settling in Chinatown:

The language is our first consideration. When we newly arrived in Sydney, if everything is so different [from our home country], or if we have settled in an Anglo-dominated suburb, we may find it difficult to adapt to the new environment. However in Chinatown, people speak our mother language and have a similar culture [as our home country]. This gives us a sense of security, as we know that if we come across any problems, we can easily find help (Interviewee #14, Chinese migrant).

The residential rental market in Sydney also influenced Chinese migrants and investors' purchasing decisions. Research by CoreLogic RP Data showed that the weekly average price of renting an apartment is $592, an increase of 3.9% annually in the last five years (CoreLogic RP Data, 2015). Instead of paying expensive rents, many Chinese migrants, or parents who have children studying in Sydney, opt to buy an apartment instead. The high rental returns and potential capital growth of properties in Chinatown have attracted investors to purchase apartments in the area, as interviewee #4 pointed out:

To them it's a safe investment...firstly location is good you will never lose a tenant, and when the location is good the rental can increase yearly at least 3-4% that is added value already. Once the rental increases, the property value increases (Interviewee #4, real estate agent).

The lucrative market for property investment in Sydney further promoted more 'aggressive' investment behaviours by Chinese property buyers, as interviewee #13 indicated when talking about his experience of dealing with Asian customers:

In terms of the property, if they like it, they will buy it, they will buy even it is more expensive than what people think and they will still buy it and they will buy one, two, three, four. They will keep buying. Australians tend to buy one and then if they want to upgrade, they will sell and buy a second one, they will have one or two properties. Unlike the Asians, it's like a collection (Interviewee #13, senior lending manager).

Racialised media representation of Sydney's transnational real estate

As expected, in Sydney where property prices were ranked the second 'least affordable' in the world (Demographia, 2016), news stories about 'Chinese' real estate investment have regularly appeared in public media since 2010. Research by Ley and Murphy (2001) and Ray, Halseth, and Johnson (1997), showed that misrepresentation of ethnic minorities in the media may reinforce negative ethnic stereotypes of migrants in their host countries. This is also the case with media representations of 'Chinese' property buyers in Sydney, as 'Chinese buyers' are often singled out in the news reports. Table 2 summarised the results of the content analysis of 86 articles from *Sydney Morning Herald*, Sydney's major newspaper with over 5 million readers, between 2013 and 2014 about foreign property investment in Sydney,[5] 33 of which (38%) used the word 'Chinese' or 'China' in their headlines. In comparison, the more general word 'foreign' or 'overseas' has only been used in the headlines of 21 articles (24%).

Besides this, many of these news reports did not accurately represent the Chinese investment in properties. For instance, the news coverage about Chinese property buyers between 2013 and 2014 mainly fell into two categories. First, 'cashed-up' or 'super-rich' Chinese have bought trophy homes in affluent suburbs in Sydney. Second, foreign investors, particularly 'Chinese' buyers, have 'pushed up' property prices in Sydney and 'crowded out' local buyers. Some of these press anecdotes were not backed up with statistics. For example, NAB's data showed that only 5% of all properties bought by foreign buyers were valued over A$5 million (NAB, 2015). Besides, interviewee #10 pointed out that the wealth of the Chinese migrants has been exaggerated. She said:

> What we end up getting is they either export a couple of containers of red wine here and there just to meet the [visa] requirement, or to buy a 7-Eleven, a laundromat and most of them, I would say, are not substantial type of businesses (Interviewee #10, migration agent).

Another shortcoming of this type of media reporting was the tendency to emphasise the racial origin of property buyers as if it was the cause of the housing problem. An example of this was an article by a columnist with the headline 'Cashed-up Chinese are pricing the young out of the property market' (Sheelhan, 2014). However, the author did not clarify who these 'Chinese' buyers were, nor did he explain the complicated economic context, which includes increased competition from local property investors and upgraders as a result of favourable tax regimes and low interest rates. In other cases, the media tended to equate 'Chinese' buyers with 'foreign' buyers, ignoring the fact that there was a large Chinese diaspora community in Sydney. As the cases of The Quay and Greenland Centre showed, many property buyers of Chinese appearance were Australian residents or citizens with a Chinese heritage. Also, many 'foreign' Chinese buyers were, in fact,

Table 2. Content analysis of 86 articles from *Sydney Morning Herald* between 2013 and 2014 by number of articles in different sections.

Section	Content with Chinese/China	Content with foreign/overseas/ offshore	Content with Asia/names of Asian countries	Headline with Chinese/China	Headline with foreign/offshore/ overseas	Headline with Asia/names of Asian countries
1 January 2013–31 December 2013 (38 samples)						
News	1	0	0		0	0
Business	3	0	0	2	0	0
Property (domain)	24	5	3	15	4	0
Opinion/comment	2	0				0
1 January 2014–31 December 2014 (48 samples)						
News	4	4	0	3	3	0
Business	6	12		6	8	0
Property (domain)	9	5	2	5	3	0
Opinion/comment	2	4		2	3	0
Total 2013–2014 (86 samples)	51	30	5	33	21	0

'would-be' migrants who are purchasing their future homes in Australia. The treatment of media in generalising all Chinese home buyers into 'foreigners' not only reflects the difficulties in distinguishing 'local' and 'foreign' Chinese buyers, but also implies that Australia's cultural identity of Australia is still dominated by the 'white' imaginary, despite the multicultural policies pursued since the 1970s (Ang, Band, Noble, & Wilding, 2002).

Moreover, the frequency of reporting about Chinese property investments in public media also unintentionally exaggerated the magnitude of the issue. Despite that there are no official statistics on the number of Chinese foreign property buyers, drawing on data from ABS and FIRB, Hendrischke and Li (2015) estimated that off-shore Chinese residential investment in 2013–2014 amounted to approximately $5 billion, accounting for about 2% of the total $250 billion of the residential property market in Australia (Hendrischke & Li, 2015).[6] However, the media's treatment of the issue has stirred up hostility towards Chinese people. Scornful remarks about Chinese property buyers can be found in many newspapers' comment sections or discussion boards. For example:

> There are a lot of wealthy Chinese trying to protect their assets at the moment. Most wealthy Chinese would have benefited from graft and corruption somewhere along the line and there are good reasons for them to hide their money. Buying Australian property ticks all the boxes (comment by With Cheese on Whirlpool, 2013).

> Australia will become a place that is totally foreign owned, not only in property but the food bowl if the government does nothing and continues to pander to the Chinese. Very short sighted (comment by Keyo, on Sheelhan, 2014).

In May 2015, a protest against Chinese real estate investment was initiated by a group called the 'Party for Freedom', who distributed brochures, with the title 'Stop the Chinese invasion', to the residents in Sydney's lower north shore (Browne, 2015). Whilst most local Australians disagreed with this campaign,[7] it nevertheless reflected the growing concern about foreign property investment and ever-increasing housing prices in Sydney.

In response to the public concern, the government announced a parliamentary inquiry on foreign investment in Australia's real estate in March 2014. The report of the inquiry, which came out in November 2014, confirmed that foreign investment was only a small driver of housing prices, but reiterated that foreign real estate was highly beneficial to the local economy. Other factors, such as low interest rates, shortage of land, underdevelopment and problems with state and local council planning, were also involved in driving up prices (Standing Committee on Economics, 2014). In spite of this, the report did admit that the government did not have detailed data on foreign buyers and proposed a proper system to register property buyers' residency. Subsequently, new application fees for foreign residential purchases ($5000 for property valued below $1 million and $10,000 for every $1 million in the property price) were introduced in December 2015. Foreign investors who breach the rules will also face a maximum fine up to 25% of the market value of the property (FIRB, 2015). Although FIRB stressed that the new measures are intended to reinforce existing rules instead of curbing foreign investment, it is expected that these measures will slow down the inflow of Chinese residential investments in Australia, as has been the case in places, such as Hong Kong and Singapore, where higher property taxes were imposed on foreign buyers.

Conclusion

This paper demonstrates the relation between the rapid increase of contemporary Chinese diaspora in Sydney and the growing internationalisation of Sydney's residential property market, which was partly attributable to the increasing mobility and transnationality of this community. As the case study showed, the Chinese diaspora's transnational space of flow (Glick-Schiller, Basch, & Blanc-Szanton, 1992) has become more sophisticated and has evolved to involve a much wider range of human actors, and non-human factors. The types of elements involved in the transnational social field in the case of Chinese overseas property investment in Sydney are summarised in Table 3.

Table 3. Elements involved in the transnational social field of property purchase by offshore Chinese.

Micro level	Macro level
Non-human actors	*Local Institutional elements*
Capital	Immigration policy (e.g. visa schemes)
Local knowledge & information	Foreign Investment Review Board
Information technology (e.g. Internet)	Federal government fiscal policy (e.g.
Cultural capital (e.g. language &	interest rate, tax policy)
cultural knowledge)	State & local government (e.g. urban
Diaspora social & information network	planning, building approval)
	Education policy and education
	institutions
	Foreign policy (e.g. 'Asian Century'
	strategy)
Individual human actors	*International institutional elements*
Chinese diaspora in Australia	Emigration policy in China
Overseas Chinese buyers	Education policy in China
Real estate agents	Economic growth in China
Property developers	Political stability in China
Financiers (e.g. banks or mortgage	Environmental policy in China
companies)	Housing policy in China (national and
Solicitors & accountants	provincial)
Migration & education agents	Banking sector in China (currency
	exchange & transfer)
	Foreign investment policy in China

As discussed in this paper, two macro factors set the context for transnational real estate in Sydney. First, immigration policy in Australia favours skilled and wealthy migrants. Second, China's emigration and education policies allow citizens to live and study abroad. Transnational real estate in Sydney is impacted by a number of special circumstances in the two countries. In China, spectacular economic growth has generated a large wealthy middle class, but restrictions on housing purchase have caused them to look for housing investment overseas. Growing concerns over China's political and economic stabilities and environmental problems drive Chinese people to migrate to another country or send their children abroad. They are keen to buy houses for themselves or their children in Sydney. Although the Chinese government has set a limit of transferring $US50,000 overseas per person a year, Chinese people sometimes use 'grey-channels' such as underground banks to send money abroad for their property purchase.

In Australia, national policies such as 'Asian Century' strategy and relaxation of foreign investment rules after the global financial crisis encouraged transnational property investment. Universities and education institutions are keen to recruit international students from China after the Australian government's successive funding cuts. Chinese diaspora are acting as bridges or brokers for transnational real estate, leveraging their bilingual skills and understanding of the cross-cultural context. The development of online property media, as well as ethnic networks formed by Chinese real estate agents, property developers, solicitors and migration agents further facilitated transnational property transactions from China.

The growing Chinese property investment has compounded the housing affordability problem in Sydney. This was partly caused by undersupply of housing due to slow the planning processes of the state and local governments and increased competition from domestic property investors driven by low interest rates and tax concessions. Whilst Chinese purchases made up a small proportion of overall property sales in Australia, they caused disproportionate impact in certain locations such as Sydney. Discontent among local residents has prompted FIRB to reform the rules for transnational real estate investment.

The expansion of this transnational space also means deeper integration and higher interdependency between the economies of Australia and China. However, the obverse side of this integration makes Australia's housing market more susceptible to policy and economic changes in China due to the effect of the 'distanciated economy' (Amin & Thrift, 2002). For example, the Chinese government's relaxation of its corporation rules to allow private individuals and enterprises to invest overseas and the anti-corruption campaign under the leadership of President Xi Jingping have caused more and more Chinese people to diversify their assets or hide their wealth in overseas countries. These circumstances have contributed to the growing offshore property investment in Australia from China in the past few years.

However, the latest figures from NAB showed that foreign investors were less active in the property market in the December quarter of 2015 (NAB, 2016). Key reasons behind this have been the weakening of the Chinese economy and the meltdown of its stock market. Moreover, China's tightening of controls over capital outflow and intensified crackdown on underground banks have made it more difficult for Chinese people to buy properties abroad (Grigg, 2016). This showed that transnational real estate in Sydney hinges not only on investment and housing regulations in Australia, but also on policies and economies in China.

Whilst transnational space has transcended national borders, it does not mean that 'locality' is no longer relevant. On the contrary, the case study showed that Chinatown's local milieu and location advantages have made it a popular 'gateway' for Chinese migrants. The place characteristics of Chinatown have influenced the types of Chinese migrants settled in this area, such as professional workers, international students and recent immigrants. This, in turn, attracted more developers to construct high-rise apartments in the area to meet the growing demand of this middle-class Chinese diaspora, which ultimately transformed the urban landscape in Chinatown. The Chinese diaspora also reshaped Chinatown's local economic structure over the years. For example, Chinese skilled migrants responded to local economic opportunities by setting up real estate services and professional companies. Together they mediated the information networks and facilitated local and transnational capital accumulation, helping to make Chinatown a hub/node (Castells, 1996) of Chinese transnational real estate activities in Sydney. The role of locality and the mutual shaping process between mobile subjects and local places to create transnational space of flow may deserve more study in future.

This paper also showed racialised anecdotes from the press have stirred up bitterness amongst local people towards Chinese investors and prompted the government to respond by imposing new regulations on foreign residential investments. However, it is worth noticing that despite the parliamentary inquiry confirming the benefits of foreign property investment to Australia, the racialised public discourse about 'Chinese driving out local home buyers' still prevails. The local resistance to Chinese property investment was partly due to the concerns over growing capital power of Chinese investment in Australia and the feeling of infringement of citizens' right (Guarnizo & Smith, 2009). Besides, there is a complicated historical, socio-economic (e.g. class), cultural and geopolitical context behind this. In Anderson (in press)'s words: '…significant cultural change, linked to the intensifying circulation of people and capital in the Asia-Pacific, is re-shaping Australian urbanism in ways that provoke a deepening unsettlement of the stale distinction-and hierarchy-between Australian "us" and an Asian "them"' (Anderson, in press). Nevertheless, this revealed a growing trend for government control over 'negative' transnationalism. For instance, Canada terminated its investor immigration scheme in February 2014 as a measure to control the influx of Chinese migrants and the rising house prices in its global city of Vancouver (Young, 2014). The governance of mobility and transnationalism may require further research in future.

Acknowledgements

This research has been carried out as part of an Australia Research Council Linkage Project entitled 'Sydney's Chinatown in the Asian Century: From ethnic enclave to transnational hub' at the Western Sydney University in partnership with the City of Sydney.

Disclosure statement

No potential conflict of interest was reported by the author.

Funding

This work is supported by Australian Research Council Linkage Grant [ARC LP 120200311], in partnership with the City of Sydney.

Notes

1. All the figures in this paper were complied with statistical data from the 2011 Census of Population and Housing by the Australian Bureau Statistics using Table Builder (Basic) software unless stated otherwise.
2. This amount included investments in both commercial and residential properties.
3. The ranking is simply based on the data flow through Juwai.com. Whilst it may reflect the broad trend of global real estate, it cannot be generalised to all real estate companies.
4. Under the Foreign Ownership Law, non-residents can only purchase brand new dwellings in Australia and they have to seek approval from the Foreign Investment Review Board. The policy changes in 2008 lifted the restriction that up to 50% of the dwellings can be sold to overseas buyers and streamlined the approval process by allowing developers to submit applications on behalf of buyers (Sydney Property Conveyancing, 2009).
5. The 86 articles from Sydney Morning Herald were collected via electronic newspaper database Factiva using key word search method. Key words used in the article search include 'Chinese/China and properties/real estate', 'foreign/overseas/offshore and properties/real estates' and 'Asia and properties/real estates'.
6. Urban Taskforce Australia, a lobby group representing property developers and equity financers also reached the same estimation that the total amount of Chinese foreign investment in residential properties was about $5 billion per annum (Urban Taskforce Australia, 2014)
7. It was reported that less than a dozen people attended the protest and they were outnumbered by the media and police (Newszulu, 2015). This implied that the dominant majority of local Australians objected to the 'racist' message of the group, but the massive media attention reflected that the housing problem is a matter of concern for the general public.

References

Australian Bureau of Statistics (ABS) (2011). *Census of population and housing*. Retrieved from http://www.abs.gov.au/websitedbs/censushome.nsf/home/data?opendocument#from-banner=LN

Adrian, C., & Stimson, R. (1986). Asian investment in Australian capital city property markets. *Environment and Planning A, 18*, 323–340.

Australian Education International (AEI) (2001). *Time series of student numbers by country 1994–2000*. Retrieved from https://internationaleducation.gov.au/research/International-Student-Data/Documents/INTERNATIONAL%20STUDENT%20DATA/2000/2000_02_pdf.pdf

AEI (2013). *AEI international student enrolment data 2013*. Retrieved from https://aei.gov.au/research/International-Student-Data/Documents/INTERNATIONAL%20STUDENT%20DATA/2013/2013Dec_0712.pdf

Amin, A., & Thrift, N. (2002). *Cities: Reimagining the urban*. Oxford, MA: Polity.

Anderlini, J. (2009, December 10). China revives property tax to avert bubble. *Financial Times*. Retrieved from http://www.ft.com/intl/cms/s/0/dfd473ec-e5a7-11de-b5d7-00144feab49a.html#axzz44LHMLVKq

Anderson, A. (2015, January 19). Investor reaps $16,500 windfall on Haymarket unit without even moving in. *Sydney Morning Herald*. Retrieved from http://news.domain.com.au/domain/real-estate-news/investor-reaps-165000-windfall-on-haymarket-unit-without-even-moving-in-20150115-12qtpi.html

Anderson, K. (in press). Chinatown unbound. In L. Wong (Ed.), *Chinese mobilities and Canada*. Vancouver: UBC Press.

Ang, I. (2015, May). *Chinatowns and the rise of China*. Paper presented at the Global China: New Approaches lecture series, University of Birmingham, UK.

Ang, I., Band, J., Noble, G., & Wilding, D. (2002). *Living diversity: Australia's multicultural future*. Artarmon: Special Broadcasting Services Corporation.

Bloomberg (2013, March 2). *China tightens mortgage rules as home prices keep rising*. Retrieved from http://www.bloomberg.com/news/articles/2013-03-01/china-tightens-mortgage-rules-as-home-price-increases-continue

Bloomberg (2014, November 12). *The top overseas markets for China's property investors*. Retrieved from http://www.bloomberg.com/news/videos/2014-11-12/the-top-markets-for-chinas-property-investors

Browne, R. (2015, May 29). Race hate flyers distributed in Sydney's north and inner city. *Sydney Morning Herald*. Retrieved from http://www.smh.com.au/nsw/race-hate-flyer-distributed-in-sydneys-north-shore-and-inner-city-20150529-ghayxq.html

Camagni, R. (Ed.) (1991). *Innovation networks: Spatial perspectives*. London: Belhaven Press.

Castells, M. (1996). *The rise of the network society*. Oxford: Wiley Blackwell.

Centre for China and Globalisation. (2014). 中国国际移民报告 [Annual report on Chinese international migration]. Beijing: Social Science Academic Press. Retrieved from http://www.scgti.org/zyx/中国国际移民报告2014-总报告.pdf

China Merchants Bank & Bain & Company (2013). *China private wealth report*. China Merchants Bank and Bain & Company. Retrieved from http://www.bain.com/Images/2013_China_Wealth_Report.pdf

City of Sydney (2012). *City of Sydney floor space and employment survey: Overview of core Chinatown precinct 2007–2012*. Unpublished data from City of Sydney.

City of Sydney (2013). *Residential monitor June 2013*. Retrieved from http://www.cityofsydney.nsw.gov.au/__data/assets/pdf_file/0005/189842/ResMonitorJun13web_Issue50.pdf

City of Sydney (2013–2015). *Development activity report* (various issues). Retrieved from http://www.cityofsydney.nsw.gov.au/development/development-applications/how-das-are-assessed/activity-reports

City of Sydney (2015). *Global Sydney*. Retrieved from http://www.cityofsydney.nsw.gov.au/learn/about-sydney/global-sydney

Collins, J. (2002). Chinese entrepreneurs: The Chinese diaspora in Australia. *International Journal of Entrepreneurial Behaviour & Research, 8*(1), 113–133.

CoreLogic RP Data (2015). *Weekly rents fall across most capital cities in September 2015*. Retrieved from http://www.corelogic.com.au/news/weekly-rents-fall-across-most-capital-cities-in-september-2015

Demographia (2016). *12th Demographia international housing affordability survey 2016*. Retrieved from http://www.demographia.com/dhi.pdf

Department of Immigration and Border Protection (DIBP) (2015). *Country profile: China*. Retrieved from http://www.border.gov.au/about/reports-publications/research-statistics/statistics/live-in-australia/country-profiles/peoples-republic-of-china

Fereidouni, H.G., & Masron, T.A. (2013). Real estate market factors and foreign real estate investment. *Journal of Economic Studies, 40*(4), 448–468.

Foreign Investment Review Board (FIRB) (2010). *Approvals by country of investor in 2009–10–industry sector*. Retrieved from. http://www.firb.gov.au/content/Publications/AnnualReports/2009-2010/_downloads/2009-10_FIRB_AR.pdf

FIRB (2014). *Approvals by country of investor by industry sector in 2013–2014*. Retrieved from http://www.firb.gov.au/content/Publications/AnnualReports/2013-2014/_downloads/FIRB-AR-2013-14.pdf

FIRB (2015). *Foreign investment reforms factsheet: Residential real estate*. Retrieved from https://firb.gov.au/files/2015/09/FIRB_fact_sheet_residential.pdf

Gholipour, H.F., Al-mulali, U., & Mohammed, A.H. (2014). Foreign investments in real estate, economic growth and property prices: Evidence from OECD countries. *Journal of Economic Policy Reform, 17*(1), 33–34.

Glick-Schiller, N.G., Basch, L., & Blanc-Szanton, C. (1992). Transnationalism: A new analytic framework for understanding migration. *Annals of the New York Academy of Science, 645*, 1–24.

Glick-Schiller, N.G., & Caglar, A. (2009). Towards a comparative theory of locality in migration studies: Migrant incorporation and city scale. *Journal of Ethnic and Migration Studies, 35*(2), 177–202.

Glick-Schiller, N.G., & Caglar, A. (Eds.). (2010). *Locating migration: Rescaling cities and migrants*. Ithaca, NY: Cornell University Press.

Grigg, A. (2016, January 21). Cash control on Chinese buyers to hit Sydney property. *Australian Financial Review*. Retrieved from http://www.afr.com/real-estate/residential/chinas-cash-controls-to-hit-sydney-property-20160120-gmagc9

Guarnizo, L., & Smith, M. (2009). The locations of transnationalism. In M. Smith & L. Guarnizo (Eds.), *Transnationalism from below* (pp. 3–34). New Brunswick: Transaction.

Hajdu, J. (1999). Japanese capital on Australia's Gold Coast as a catalyst of a localist–globalist conflict on national identity. *Global Society, 13*(3), 327–347.

Hajdu, J. (2005). *Samurai in the surf: The arrival of Japanese on the Gold Coast in the 1980s*. Canberra: Pandanus Books.

Harvey, D. (2007). Neo-liberalism as creative destruction. *Annals of the Academy of American Political and Social Science, 610*(1), 22–44.

Hendrischke, H., & Li, W. (2015). Chinese investment in residential real estate amounts to just 2%. *The Conversation*. Retrieved from https://theconversation.com/chinese-investment-in-residential-real-estate-amounts-to-just-2-47404

Hugo, G. (2008). A changing diaspora: Recent trends in migration between China and Australia. *Chinese Southern Diaspora Studies, 2*, 82–103.

Knight Frank (2015). *Chinese outward real estate investment globally and into Australia: Australian market insight April 2015*. Retrieved from http://www.knightfrank.com.au/resources/research/chinese-outward-investment-knight-frank-report.pdf

Knowlton, C. (2012, April 29). The quay development on long dormant Sydney Chinatown site sells well in first weekend. *Property Observer*. Retrieved from http://www.proper tyobserver.com.au/finding/residential-investment/new-developments/16203-the-quay-development-set-for-long-dormant-sydney-site.html

Ley, D. (2010). *Millionaire migrants: Transpacific life lines*. Chichester: Wiley Blackwell.

Ley, D., & Murphy, P. (2001). Immigration in gateway cities: Sydney and Vancouver in comparative perspective. *Progress in Planning, 55*(3), 119–194.

Ley, D., & Tutchener, J. (2001). Immigration, globalisation and house prices in Canada's gateway cities. *Housing Studies, 16*(2), 199–223.

Lin, J. (1998). *Restructuring Chinatown: Ethnic enclave, global change*. Minneapolis, MN: University of Minnesota Press.

Macken, L. (2013, December 14). From its harbour to its air, China is sold on Sydney real estate. *Sydney Morning Herald*. Retrieved from http://smh.domain.com.au/real-estate-news/from-its-harbour-to-its-air-china-is-sold-on-sydney-real-estate-20131213-2zct2.html

National Australia Bank (NAB) (2015). *NAB residential property survey: Q1 2015*. Retrieved from http://business.nab.com.au/wp-content/uploads/2015/04/Quarterly-Aus tralian-Residential-Property-Survey-Q1-2015-PDF202KB.pdf

NAB (2016). *NAB residential property survey: Q4 2015*. Retrieved from http://business.nab.com.au/wp-content/uploads/2016/02/Residential-Prop-Survey-Q4-2015.pdf

Newszulu (2015, May 30). *Sydney party for freedom protest 'Chinese real estate invasion'*. Retrieved from http://www.newzulu.com.au/en/photos/australia/2015-05-30/10376/syd ney-party-for-freedom-protest-chinese-real.html#f=0/109313

Ong, A. (1999). *Flexible citizenship: The cultural logics of transnationality*. Durham, NC: Duke University Press.

Ouchi, W.G. (1980). Markets, bureaucracies and clans. *Administrative Science Quarterly, 25*(1), 129–142.

Ray, B.K., Halseth, G., & Johnson, B. (1997). The changing 'face' of the suburbs: Issues of ethnicity and residential change in suburban Vancouver. *International Journal of Urban and Regional Research, 21*(1), 75–99.

Robertson, S. (2013). *Transnational student-migrants and the state: The education–migration nexus*. Basingstoke: Palgrave Macmillan.

Rogers, D., Lee, C.L., & Yan, D. (2015). The politics of foreign investment in Australian housing: Chinese investors, translocal sales agents and local resistance. *Housing Studies, 30*(5), 730–748.

Ross, S. (2011). A model for examining foreign direct investment in real estate. *Journal of New Business Ideas & Trends, 9*(2), 23–33.

Sassen, S. (2001). *The global city, New York, London, Tokyo*. (2nd ed.). Princeton, NJ: Princeton University Press.

Scott, A.J. (1998). *Regions and the World economy: The coming shape of global production, competition and political order*. Oxford: Oxford University Press.

Sheelhan, P. (2014, March 10). Cashed-up Chinese are pricing the young out of the property market. *Sydney Morning Herald*. [Comments]. Retrieved from http://www.smh.com.au/comment/cashedup-chinese-are-pricing-the-young-out-of-the-property-market-20140309-34f9k.html

Sheller, M., & Urry, J. (2006). The new mobilities paradigm. *Environment and Planning A, 38*, 207–226.

Smith, M.P. (2001). *Transnational urbanism: Locating globalisation.* Malden, MA: Blackwell.

Smith, M.P. (2005). Transnational urbanism revisited. *Journal of Ethnic and Migration Studies, 31*(2), 235–244.

Stalder, F. (2002, November). *The status of objects in the space of flows.* Paper presented at the Door of Perception conference, Amsterdam. Retrieved from http://felix.openflows.com/html/objects_flows.pdf

Standing Committee on Economics (2014). *Report on foreign investment in residential real estate.* Canberra: Parliament of the Commonwealth of Australia.

Storper, M. (1995). The resurgence of regional economies, ten years later: The region as a nexus of untraded interdependencies. *European Urban and Regional Studies, 2*(3), 191–221.

Sydney Property Conveyancing (2009). *Understanding the latest changes in Australia's foreign ownership laws.* Retrieved from http://www.sydneypropertyconveyancing.com.au/sites/default/files/media-article/FIRB.pdf

Urban Taskforce Australia (2014). *Urban taskforce submission on foreign investment.* Retrieved from file://ad.uws.edu.au/dfshare/HomesPTA$/30029304/Desktop/final%20urban%20taskforce%20submission%20on%20foreign%20investment%208%20may%202014.pdf

Waldinger, R., Aldrich, H., Ward, R., Blaschke, J., Boissevain, J., Bradford, W., ...Wilson, P. (1990). *Ethnic entrepreneurs: Immigrant business in industrial societies.* Newbury Park, CA: Sage.

Warren, R. (2010, November 12). China towns. *Financial Times.* Retrieved from http://www.ft.com/intl/cms/s/2/4cf60cf2-ed17-11df-8cc9-00144feab49a.html#axzz2yb1O7JFY

Whirlpool (2013, June 28). *Chinese pushing up property prices—part 1* [Discussion forum]. Retrieved from http://forums.whirlpool.net.au/archive/2120699

Wilmot, B., & Thistleton, R. (2012, April 30). Chinese demand stays strong. *Australian Financial Review.* Retrieved from http://wmkarchitecture.com/assets/Uploads/The-Quay-in-Financial-Reveiw-April-2012.pdf

Window to China (2012). *Chinese Sydney property expo magazine.* Sydney: Chinese Media Group.

Young, I. (2014, February 12). Canada's immigrant investor scheme: How the rug has been pulled from under the rich. *South China Morning Post.* Retrieved from http://www.scmp.com/news/world/article/1426636/rug-pulled-under-rich

Chinese investment in Australian housing: push and pull factors and implications for understanding international housing demand

Sha Liu and Nicole Gurran

The increasing integration of the globalised financial market and real estate has resulted in growing levels of international investment in property markets. Yet research on the factors driving international housing demand remains limited. This paper examines the underlying drivers encouraging the involvement of Chinese developers and individuals in the global property market, focusing on the interface between both 'push' factors and 'pull' factors driving them 'overseas'. Ostensibly, domestic policy settings, such as China's anti-speculation measures (introduced between 2004 and 2014) might be expected to displace housing investment to other markets. This paper examines the relative influence of such measures along with other domestic 'push' and international 'pull' factors through in-depth interviews with real estate agents, developers, and a Chinese local government official. In exploring the intersection between 'push' and 'pull' factors, the focus is specifically on international investment in Sydney, Australia.

Introduction

Increasing levels of international investment in real estate have raised a number of concerns about the implications for receiving nations (Duca, Muellbauer, & Murphy, 2010; Rogers, Lee, & Yan, 2015). Rising Chinese foreign investment in particular has sparked affordability concerns in recipient nations, including the United States (US), the United Kingdom (UK), Australia, Canada and some European countries (Rogers, Lee, & Yan, 2015; Rolnik, 2013). Broad explanations for the global phenomenon have been posited (i.e. the search for financial 'safe havens', the need to accommodate multi-national firms or international students, second home ownership for vacations or retirement) (Cheng & Kwan, 2000; Javorcik, Özden, Spatareanu, & Neagu, 2011; Paris, 2013a, 2013b). However, the impact of domestic housing (or other) policy settings on demand to purchase 'overseas' remains under-researched. Similarly, the pull factors attracting particular investors to specific Australian or other housing markets warrant further scrutiny. This paper contributes to such work by examining reasons why Chinese developers and individual investors have decided to develop and/or purchase properties overseas, focusing in particular on the impacts of China's changing domestic housing policies over the period 2004 and 2014. In particular, the 'Purchase Restriction' policy, widely ratified in 46 large Chinese cities in 2011 to reduce real estate speculation in China, provides a specific point of focus as a potential explanation for increased outbound investment. The paper draws on the results of a qualitative study involving 16 in-depth interviews conducted with four groups of participants (Chinese developers who have developed/purchased projects in overseas markets, senior staff working in real estate consultancy/investment firms in China and abroad, a Chinese local government official, and sales agents targeting Chinese buyers in Sydney, Australia). The interviews, conducted between July 2014 and January 2015, enable a nuanced understanding of how domestic policy changes within a country of origin may create additional impetus for outbound housing investment, and the intersection between such 'push' factors and the specific 'pull' factors attracting investors to a particular housing market – Sydney, Australia.

Examining a particular segment of the international housing market (Chinese investment in Sydney, Australia) allows more detailed exploration of the balance between the 'push factors' motivating Chinese investors to seek foreign housing markets and the 'pull factors' attracting them to specific nations or cities. In the case of Australia, there is limited official data on the extent of foreign investment in the housing market (Foreign Investment Review Board, 2014), although in the context of growing domestic affordability pressures there has been increasing government and public concern that Chinese investment is contributing to price inflation (Parliament of Australia, 2015; Sydney Morning Herald, 2014). Of course, the very buoyancy of the Australian housing market, which escaped the Global Financial Crisis (GFC) relatively unscathed (Yates & Berry, 2011), will attract international investors to Australian cities alongside other global real estate destinations such as London, New York, or Vancouver (Ley, 2010; Moos & Skaburskis, 2010; Paris, 2013a, 2013b).

The first part of the paper situates the study in relation to wider literature on the international financialisation of housing. It then focuses on the Chinese case, outlining the range of policies for addressing housing affordability introduced by the Chinese government over the past decade. This policy context provides a basis for understanding the range of 'push' and 'pull' factors which may influence Chinese interest in global housing markets (Australia as a specific example), as explored through the interviews for this study. Wider research and policy implications in relation to Chinese foreign housing investment in particular, and the intersections between domestic 'push' factors and international 'pull' factors are highlighted in conclusion.

International financialisation of housing markets and domestic affordability pressures

A number of processes have provoked fundamental changes to housing markets over the past four decades. These include the rapid development of information technology and increasing information flows, which reduce locational barriers (Adair et al., 1999), financial innovation, which supports new lending products (Coakley, 1994) and diversification of investment which encourages interest in new markets (Adair et al., 1999). In the 1980s, under neoliberalism, housing was greatly marketised and commodified through mortgaged homeownership (Aalbers, 2015). Consequently, the notion of housing 'financialisation' emerged, as 'the transformation of hitherto physical and illiquid assets into types of financial assets', which are 'saleable and liquid entities' (Coakley, 1994, p. 708). The internal complexity of real estate and housing, which as a commodity combines a use value to end users with an exchange value to financial investors, makes residential property a 'quasi-financial' asset (Coakley, 1994). All of these factors have meant that demand for housing increasingly reflects the value of housing as a source of and repository for wealth, rather than on demographic drivers. Aalbers (2015) supported this argument in a recent publication:

> Homeownership is valued less for its use value and more for its exchange value. Not only do lenders and investors prioritise exchange value, but even homeowners increasingly come to think of their home in terms of investment rather than consumption... (Aalbers, 2015, p. 52)

Similarly, Wu (2015) explains how contemporary housing markets are driven by capital accumulation, reflecting wider economic processes:

> The theory of capital switching goes beyond the supply and demand relation in the housing market and relates the development of housing to the more general development dynamics of capitalism... [it] relates the sector to the wider economy, capital accumulation, and regulation. (Wu, 2015, pp. 8–9)

Along with globalisation, housing market actors, including sales agents, buyers, developers and financiers, operate more internationally (Aalbers, 2015). Therefore, a significant consequence of the integration of housing and the globalised financial market is that cross-border investments in housing have increased considerably in receiving nations (Duca et al., 2010). International investment demand contributes to local demand pressures, potentially exacerbating price inflation and undermining affordability for aspiring first home buyers who struggle to compete with upgraders and investors (Rolnik, 2013). In these contexts, credit constrained households seeking secure and affordable accommodation, and an increasingly open ended pool of speculative investors anticipating financial gain, are often in contest for the same housing stock. Even when investor demand fuels new housing production – as occurred in the case of Spain and Ireland in the lead up to the GFC – new supply typically fails to dampen price inflation during a speculative boom (Coq-Huelva, 2013; Romero, Jimennez, & Villoria, 2012; Waldron & Redmond, 2014).

The design of housing assistance policies has become more complex in this era of globally porous property markets. The suite of policy instruments used by governments – income subsidies to assist with rental payments or home purchase; funding or incentives for low cost rental housing provision or ownership – tend to support (rather than restrain) the market through demand-side or supply-side interventions. Relatively few nations have sought to address affordability by directly restraining demand and deliberately attempting to reverse price inflation, with the few exceptions mostly associated with anti-speculation provisions for east Asian contexts (Ha, 2013). In this sense, China's suite of housing policies – which span both demand-side and supply-side measures including strong anti-speculation regulation – are distinct.

China, as a transitional economy which is shifting toward marketisation, has faced rising speculative housing investment over the past three decades (by its rapidly expanding middle and higher income groups), along with growing housing affordability problems (for moderate and lower paid workers). In recent years the government has attempted to reduce house price speculation by constraining demand-side pressures, through heavy taxation on investment housing. It has also imposed less favourable mortgage terms on second-home purchases and new 'Purchase Restrictions' on the number of investment properties able to be acquired, in 46 large cities. Although a number of studies analysing China's housing reform and housing policies can be found (Cao & Keivani, 2014; Chen, Guo, & Wu, 2011; Deng, Shen, & Wang, 2011; Li & Driant, 2014; Liang, 2013; Wu, 2015; Wu, 2001; Yang & Chen, 2014; Ye & Wu, 2008; Zhang, Yuan, & Skibniewski, 2011), most focus on examining the impacts of these policies on the domestic housing market and China's macro economy. Little attention has been paid to the potential effects these policies may have had in driving Chinese investors towards global real estate opportunities. Within the wider financialisation of housing literature, a contribution of this study is to explore the potential impacts of China's housing demand constraint policies on the behaviour of Chinese real estate investors and their propensity to seek opportunities in foreign markets.

China's anti-speculation housing policies

In 1979, the Chinese government embarked on a series of wide ranging housing reforms. These have gradually transformed the state-sponsored welfare housing system to a market-oriented model (Liang, 2013). In 1998, to boost the national economy after the 1997 Asian Financial Crisis, the provision of state housing was abolished. Better-off households were able to access mortgage finance for home ownership, and housing gradually became an important asset for households and investors (Wu, 2015). Overall the housing reform process significantly improved urban housing conditions in China, contributing to the country's economic growth, and accelerating urbanisation. However, housing marketisation and commodification has also exacerbated economic and social disparities in contemporary China (Chen et al., 2011; Wu, 2001; Zhang et al., 2011).

In response, the Chinese central government launched a series of intervention policies since 2004 (Figure 1), to curb rapid housing inflation and improve housing affordability for middle- and low- income families (Ye & Wu, 2008). Specifically, on the demand-side, Chinese central government has utilised heavy taxation, less favourable mortgage terms and 'Purchase Restriction' measures to combat housing speculation and control excessive investment demand (Cao & Keivani, 2014). On the supply-side, to address the housing needs of disadvantaged urban groups, a comprehensive urban housing framework was constructed and several affordable housing programmes were put forward, including the Economical and Comfortable Housing (ECH) programme, the Housing Provident Fund (HPF) programme, the Cheap Rental Housing (CRH) programme, and the Public Rental Housing (PRH) programme (Deng et al., 2011; Li & Driant, 2014; Yang & Chen, 2014). In addition, during the 12th Five-year Plan (2011–2015), the Chinese central government announced that 36 million non-market housing units under those schemes would be constructed to produce a security net for the nation's urban poor (Cao & Keivani, 2014).

Among these interventions, the 'Purchase Restriction' policy, first imposed in 2010 in the first-tier cities[1] and then widely ratified in 2011 across 46 large Chinese

Figure 1.   Key anti-speculation policies to improve housing affordability issued by Chinese central government 2004–2014.
Source: State Council of China; People's Bank of China; Ministry of Finance of China; Ministry of Housing and Urban-Rural Development of China (2004–2014)

cities, has been regarded as the most powerful measure. Specifically, it restricts registered local residents (permanent residents with local 'hukou') who already own one unit of housing, to purchase only one additional unit. Non-registered local residents (that is, temporary residents in cities without local 'hukou') must have a record of paying one year's local personal income tax or social insurance (five consecutive years' in Beijing) to be eligible to purchase only one unit (Cao & Keivani, 2014). This policy was designed to curb speculative price inflation and to reduce barriers to first home ownership. The policy was partially wound back in mid-2014 but remained fully operational in the four largest cities, including Beijing, Shanghai, Guangzhou and Shenzhen, at the time of writing.

According to the National Bureau of Statistics of China (2011–2014), since the enactment of the 'Purchase Restriction' policy in 2011, both Chinese developers and individual investors greatly reduced their investments in the Chinese housing sector (Figures 2 and 3). Although the growth rate of total Chinese housing sales surged between 2012 and 2013 (Figure 3), when more first-home buyers and upgraders entered the market (Zoharo, 2013), this declined dramatically after 2013.

Furthermore, from around 2011, individual Chinese investors as well as development firms appeared to dramatically expand investment in the global real estate market. The implementation of the China's 'Purchase Restriction' policy in that year, may have acted as a 'push' factor, driving Chinese investors and developers to source new investment opportunities overseas.

Figure 2. Total investment in housing in China, accumulated growth rate, Feb 2011–Dec 2014.
Source: The authors, drawing on information from National Bureau of Statistics of China, 2011–2014.
*Data refer to corporate investment in China.

Figure 3.   Total sale of housing in China, accumulated growth rate, Feb 2011–Dec 2014.
Source: The authors, drawing on information from National Bureau of Statistics of China, 2011–2014
*Data refer to individual investment in China.

Chinese outbound investment in global real estate markets

The National Bureau of Statistics of China (2009–2016) reports that China's net outbound investment in real estate began to rise in 2009 and surged dramatically in 2013. By 2015, over 9 billion US dollars were invested in global real estate markets, over 25 times the amount in 2008 (Figure 4).

This growing market has been documented in numerous reports conducted by global consultancy and investment firms (CBRE Global Research & Consulting

Figure 4.   China's net outward investment in real estate 2008–2015.
Source: The authors, drawing on information from National Bureau of Statistics of China, 2009–2016

2013; Juwai 2013; Cushman & Wakefield 2014; Knight Frank 2014; Visas Consulting Group 2014). According to Cushman & Wakefield (2014), Chinese outbound real estate investment amounted to around US$33.7 billion from January 2008 to June 2014, growing more than 200-fold during that time (Cushman & Wakefield 2014, p. 3). In the USA, Chinese investors spent over USD $7.5 billion in 2012 alone, as the second largest group of investors after Canadians (National Association of Realtors 2013, pp. 2 and 16). According to the same source, between March 2013 and 2014, buyers from China purchased U.S. properties estimated at $22 billion in total value, 'approximately a quarter of total international sales' (National Association of Realtors, 2014, p. 23). In Europe, the UK has been the focus for Chinese investors seeking high yields, with central London alone attracting USD$2.1 billion from Chinese investors in 2013 (JLL, 2014). In Australia, Credit Suisse reported that Chinese buyers spent AUD $8.7 billion on Australian residential properties between 2013-2014, an increase of 60% over the previous twelve months (SMH, 2015). However, it is difficult to confirm these figures via official sources, and it appears that few countries maintain clear or consistent data on the extent of foreign investment in their housing market.

It appears that individual Chinese investors have preferred the mature markets in North America, Europe and Asia, which include the USA, the UK, Australia, Canada and Singapore (CBRE Global Research & Consulting 2013; Juwai 2013; Cushman & Wakefield 2014). Further, the introduction of 'Golden Visa' schemes in Portugal, Spain, Cyprus and Malta (Knight Frank 2014) and The Business Immigration programme (BIP) in Canada (Ley, 2017) made these destinations attractive to wealthy Chinese buyers seeking European and Canadian residency. Chinese developers and institutional investors have targeted the world's leading cities of London, Paris, New York, Los Angeles, San Francisco, Vancouver, Toronto, and Singapore (KnightFrank, 2014; Visas Consulting Group, 2014).

In addition to (or perhaps as a partial consequence of) direct interventions by the Chinese government, perceived oversupply of housing has also slowed price growth and increased perceptions of investment risk within China's domestic housing market. At the same time, the gradual easing of global credit conditions, the appreciation of the Chinese currency, the rising demand from wealthy Chinese and the desire of Chinese firms to internationalise have all been factors associated with outbound real estate investment (CBRE Global Research & Consulting 2013; Knight Frank 2014). More specifically, with regard to individual investors, considerations of immigration, children's education opportunities and increasing interest in asset protection and taxation strategies reportedly influence motivation to purchase overseas (Knight Frank 2014). In contrast to individual investors, Chinese developers are seeking growth opportunities, diversification, and brand positioning, while the relatively low cost of overseas financing is also an attraction. Chinese development firms are also well placed to serve Chinese individuals' overseas purchasing demand (CBRE Global Research & Consulting 2013; Cushman & Wakefield 2014; Knight Frank 2014).

After a brief introduction to the Australian context, the following sections of the paper examine the extent to which these factors appear to have played a part in the phenomenon of increasing Chinese investment in Australia's housing market, focusing particularly on the nation's largest city, Sydney.

Australian housing market and Chinese foreign investment in Australian housing

Unlike other advanced economies, Australia escaped the GFC, and its house prices seemed largely impervious to the effects of the GFC (Yates & Berry, 2011). Sydney, in particular, has experienced double-digital growth between late 2013 and early 2016 (ABS, 2016). By mid-2016, the median price of residential dwellings across Australia's eight capital cities reached AUD$623,000 (ABS, 2016), while the Sydney's median house price was around AUD$1 million (Domain, 2016).

Foreigners wishing to purchase Australian real estate must apply to the Foreign Investment Review Board for approval. Approval is generally restricted to new dwellings only, although temporary residents can purchase established dwellings if the properties are for their own use. Operationally, developers of new housing are able to apply to the Foreign Investment Review Board for approval to sell up to 100% of units in new housing projects to international investors, reducing administrative barriers for purchasers.

The policy of limiting foreign real estate purchases to new dwellings is intended to ensure that international investment contributes to new housing supply. In the wake of the GFC however, the regulations governing foreign real estate investment were changed in 2009, extending the definition of 'new dwellings' to homes constructed within twelve months of purchase (FIRB, 2014). Restrictions on 'off the plan' sales within a development (previously capped at 50%) were also lifted, and foreign purchasers of vacant land were awarded 24 months to undertake housing development (up from one year). Finally, notification requirements for temporary residents acquiring established homes for their own use were abolished. In addition, foreign owned companies were permitted to purchase established dwellings for their own use for Australian staff, provided they are sold or rented if left vacant for more than six months. Finally, price ceilings affecting the price of new properties purchased by those on a student visa were also lifted.

During the same period that Australia was relaxing its regulations on foreign investment in housing, China was implementing the anti-speculation measures to dampen domestic housing demand, as outlined above. Whether or not as a consequence of these policy shifts, Chinese investment in Australian real estate has risen

Figure 5.   Chinese investment in Australian real estate 2009–2015.
Source: Compiled from data in Foreign Investment Review Board Annual Reports 2009–10;
2010–11; 2011–12; 2012–13; 2013–14; 2014–15
*Data refer to the sum of both individual and corporate investment.

steadily since 2009 (FIRB, 2010; FIRB, 2015; Gauder, Houssard, & Orsmond, 2014). By 2015, investment by Mainland Chinese purchasers in the Australian real estate market had grown to AUD$24,349 million almost double the rate recorded in the previous year, and more than ten times in 2010 (FIRB, 2010, 2011, 2012, 2013, 2014, 2015) (Figure 5).

Another indicator of growing Chinese interest in Australia's housing market is the ratio of Chinese investment in real estate over its total investment in all sectors in Australia. According to the Foreign Investment Review Board (2010), in 2009, 99% of Chinese investment went to the mineral exploration and development sector (FIRB, 2010). From 2010 to 2015 however, a significant proportion of Chinese investment has shifted to Australian property. By 2015, over half of Chinese capital flew into the real estate sector in Australia (FIRB, 2010, 2011, 2012, 2013, 2014, 2015) (Figure 6).

Research design

Behavioural economics, which applies psychological insights to explain economic decision making, offers a lens for understanding the motivations of housing invest-ors and developers (Gibb, 2009). Although the approach has not been used exten-sively by housing researchers, behavioural perspectives are particularly helpful in illuminating the psychological and sociological factors which influence investor sentiment and decisions (Shiller, 2003; Shiller, 2007). A range of qualitative and quantitative methods – from in-depth interviews and survey questionnaires to quasi-experimental approaches have been used in behavioural research on the prop-erty market, to expose how information and expectations about the property market are formed and shared (Gallimore & Gray, 2002; Sah, Gallimore, & Sherwood

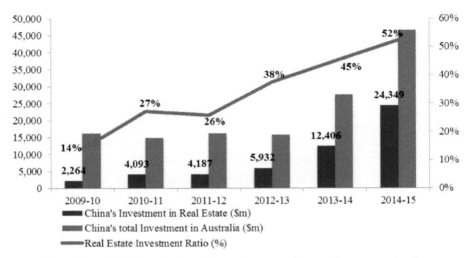

Figure 6.   Chinese investment in Australian real estate and its total investment in all sectors, 2009–2015.
Source: Compiled from data in Foreign Investment Review Board Annual Reports 2009–10; 2010–11; 2011–12; 2012–13; 2013–14; 2014–15
*Data refer to the sum of both individual and corporate investment.

Clements, 2010). For this study, which seeks to understand the dynamics of Chinese interest in foreign housing markets, including the role of domestic 'push factors' encouraging outbound investors, and the influence of external 'pull factors' towards particular overseas destinations, the behavioural approach offers a useful framework.

A series of 11 in-depth interviews with Chinese housing investors and developers were undertaken in two Chinese cities (Shanghai and Chengdu) between July 2014 and January 2015. To focus particularly on factors influencing investment in the Australian housing market, Sydney in particular, five interviews were also conducted with sales agents in Sydney over the same period.

Interviews were conducted in Shanghai and Chengdu, China as well as Sydney, Australia. Shanghai and Chengdu are important national (Shanghai) and regional (Chengdu) economic centres as the first and the fourth largest cities in China (in terms of population), respectively. Both Shanghai and Chengdu reflect the contemporary dichotomies in China's modern society – with rising incomes and assets amongst the wealthy elite driving house price inflation, while a significant proportion of the population remains unable to achieve home ownership, or afford appropriate accommodation on the private rental market. The housing markets of both cities have been rigorously intervened by central government policies designed to curb housing speculation, which makes wealthy households there seek alternative investment opportunities elsewhere actively. Sydney, as the focus Australian city, was selected as it has been a particular destination for Chinese investors and developers in recent years.

Recognising the risks that particular individuals could provide biased or misleading information, given the high stakes nature of real estate investment and commercial interests in development, it was important to recruit a range of participants for the study. Four groups of participants were selected for interview: five Chinese developers who have developed/purchased projects in overseas markets; five senior staff working in real estate consultancy or investment firms; one Chinese local government official; and five sales agents in Sydney who target Chinese buyers. The inclusion of a Chinese government insider was also regarded important for better understanding the domestic policy setting influencing investment decisions in Shanghai and Chengdu, noting particular constraints associated with the provision of certain types of information. All interviewees participated in an anonymous capacity as individuals rather than as representatives of a particular firm or organisation, and care was taken to preserve their anonymity in recording and presenting results.

Of the Chinese developers (two in Shanghai and three in Chengdu), all have developments in overseas countries, including Australia, the USA, the UK, Portugal, Japan and Hong Kong. Four are small or medium-sized developers, specialising in residential development; while one, as a Hong Kong listed company with 10 business lines in 26 cities in China, covers a wider range of sectors in the global markets, including residential, retail, office and hotel sectors.

Of the four participants from real estate consultancy firms, two are full-service consultancy firms serving Chinese developers, while another two serve individual Chinese investors seeking overseas real estate. One investment firm evaluates projects and offers finance to developers. Three are multinational companies while the other two are based only in China. In addition, one local government official accepted the interview invitation. As a senior member of a local government with expertise on local housing matters, he was able to offer high-level insights on China's housing policies and their impacts.

In Sydney, five sales agents targeting Chinese buyers in Sydney were interviewed. In order to better serve Chinese communities and offshore buyers, all the sales agents have employed a number of Chinese background sales staff who can speak either Mandarin or Cantonese. One of the largest agents interviewed has three sales offices across Sydney so as to increase exposure for projects. Among the three offices, one is located in Chinatown. Through capitalising on 'walk in' enquiries, this agent attempts to attract more Chinese buyers who reside in or are visiting Sydney.

The interviews were semi-structured around a series of themes relating to the underlying drivers of Chinese outbound investment in real estate, the main types of investors and developers likely to seek international investment opportunities, preferred international markets and housing products, financing mechanisms, the intended purpose and duration of foreign investment (i.e. permanent rental, personal use, or short-term capital gain), and the potential interaction between China's anti-speculation housing policies and the increasing Chinese investment in the Australian housing market. In other words, a key question for this study is whether domestic purchase restrictions on investment within large Chinese cities have increased interest in foreign housing markets such as Australia. A parallel question is the ways in which domestic policy settings and changes in other nations – such as Australia – might also contribute to the factors attracting inbound investors from Chinese cities.

Potential interviewees were sent information about the study, and invited to contact the research team to arrange an interview. Almost all invitees accepted the invitation to participate. Interviews were conducted by a member of the research team who is fluent in Mandarin. They were tape recorded, transcribed, and then translated to English for analysis. Overall, the in-depth interview approach used in this study provides valuable behavioural insights into the reactions of Chinese investors and developers to changing domestic and international policy settings alongside wider drivers of real estate investment. The qualitative, behavioural lens offers insights as to investor sentiment and behaviour, which are not discernible from available sources of quantitative data. Nevertheless, as with any qualitative study, the findings are not strictly generalisable. Rather the findings outlined below provide perspectives on particular aspects of foreign real estate investment drivers, particularly Chinese real estate investment in Australia, which may then be further explored through subsequent qualitative and quantitative research.

Push factors: Changing domestic housing market and policy environment

As outlined above, China's changing domestic housing policies, in particular the 'Purchase Restriction' regulations were designed specifically to limit housing investment within China itself. The impact of this policy, and wider changes to the domestic housing policy framework, was a key focus for the interviews.

From the perspective of the government interviewee, strong housing policies designed to curb housing inflation (such as the 'Purchase Restrictions' law) were effective in dampening demand. A local housing official observed:

> In general, we have found that the market performed stably when the 'Purchase Restriction' was first enacted. But, a bit later, housing transaction volumes kept declining, and, in 2014, housing prices in many big cities started falling… So, we think the policies are very effective: they have combated housing speculation and made housing more affordable for first-home buyers and upgraders. (Chinese local government official interviewed in Chengdu, July 2014)

However, interviewees advised that uncertainty about the impact of these and potentially other policy changes contributed to wider concerns about the state of the Chinese housing market and a slowing-down of the economy:

> Housing market in China has reached its limit, and it needs time to do self-adjustment. Due to a number of factors, including the slowing-down economy, housing policy changes, serious housing bubbles and so on, housing price in China is not expected to increase further quickly while rental returns remain very low, so investors have to seek alternative investment opportunities elsewhere to secure their wealth. (Investment firm interviewed in Shanghai, July 2014)

These economic effects played on the minds of Chinese real estate investors:

> All my clients are worried about the housing oversupply, which is very risky, especially when the government enacted the 'Purchase Restriction' policy. Besides, to be honest, China's future economy is not optimistic. (Real estate consultancy company interviewed in Chengdu, July 2014)

Chinese developers expressed the view that the 'Purchase Restriction' policy would exacerbate perceived oversupply in the Chinese housing market (excess numbers of vacant housing units), which they regard as very dangerous when the domestic economy is slowing down.

In addition to the purchase restriction policy encouraging Chinese buyers to invest in overseas housing markets, a developer interviewee advised that the policy was also turning his interest to overseas destinations as well:

> The problem of oversupply in the Chinese housing market is serious. When the government implements the 'Purchase Restriction' policy, this problem will become even worse, and it will definitely take a longer time to take up the current stock. So, I won't develop properties in China until the government changes the policies completely. (Chinese developer interviewed in Chengdu, July 2014)

However, perspectives varied on the ways in which the changing policy environment had impacted on levels of domestic and foreign outbound investment. Another developer with projects in New York, London, Tokyo and Hong Kong, offered an alternative perspective:

> The majority of our company's assets are still allocated in China because the company believes, even during the most restrictive policy-control period, there are still a lot of good investment opportunities in China... We think the housing policy is only one important factor the company will consider. Generally, we make development or investment decisions case by case... (Chinese developer interviewed in Shanghai, August 2014)

Thus it may be too simplistic to assert that 'push factors' such as uncertain domestic housing policies and market trends alone, explain increased levels of outbound Chinese real estate investment to nations like Australia.

In addition to the changing housing policies discussed above, informants also advised that the volatile Chinese policy environment, including changes to property taxes and fees, is also influential. Property taxes remain small and experimental in selected Chinese cities, but interviewees expressed concern over uncertainty as to future taxes that may be imposed. Consequently, due to this uncertainty, interviewees advised that Chinese investors with multiple housing units have sought to divest these assets in favour of overseas opportunities, even if they may face heavier taxes in the destination countries. Certainty as to tax regimes was seen to be more important than the actual amount that needed to be paid.

Pull factors

In exploring the key 'pull factors' attracting investors to Australia's housing market, future immigration or education opportunities featured heavily. Real estate consultants advised that environmental and lifestyle considerations, combined with the prospects of immigration opportunities, were very influential:

> My clients bought overseas properties for future immigration considerations. As we all know, environmental pollution in China is very bad now. So many of them want to send their family or kids overseas for a better living environment or lifestyle... (Real estate consultancy company interviewed in Chengdu, August 2014)

Asset diversification was an oft-cited reason for Chinese investors to seek international real estate opportunities, reflecting the role of housing as a vehicle for mobile capital:

> When China's property market is cooling down, many of my clients have gradually realized the importance of global asset allocation and become very interested in overseas investment options. Now, they are more clear about that asset diversification is a good way to help minimise investment risks... (Real estate consultancy company interviewed in Chengdu, July 2014)

In addition, growing international travel by the Chinese middle class, and increased awareness of other markets increased both dissatisfaction with the Chinese housing market, and perceptions of better value abroad:

> Chinese people now travel a lot all over the world. Lots of my clients told me housing price in many western countries is much cheaper than China. It is very attractive for them. We believe housing price in China is overpriced while properties in those developed countries are significantly undervalued after the GFC, so it is the best time to purchase properties overseas. (Real estate consultancy company interviewed in Chengdu, July 2014)

Developer informants were keenly aware of this growing Chinese interest in international housing opportunities. They responded to this trend by increasing their development activities in countries seen to be most popular among Chinese buyers.

These are clearly the nations perceived to have liberal immigration policies including the USA, Australia and Canada, and Southern European countries like Portugal, Spain, Greece and Cyprus:

> We have projects in Portugal. According to its immigration policy, investors, who would like to spend 500 thousand Euros to purchase housing in Portugal, can be granted a temporary residence visa. After five years, they can get a permanent residence visa and become citizens after six years. During the first five years, they are only required to stay in Portugal or European Schengen countries for seven days per year. It's so simple, right? (Chinese developer interviewed in Shanghai, August 2014)

> Properties in Portugal are very attractive for Chinese investors who intend to change their passports through investing housing...Based on our knowledge, 90% of foreign investors in Portuguese property market are Chinese. (Chinese developer interviewed in Shanghai, August 2014)

In this way, the value of foreign residency and citizenship is becoming capitalised in the global housing market.

Chinese foreign investment in Australian housing

In relation to pull factors attracting Chinese investors to Australia overall, and Sydney in particular, real estate agents in China and Australia were a key source of advice for this study. They referred to two types of Chinese investors who are attracted to the Australian housing market. These are Chinese high-net-worth individuals seeking to secure their wealth or immigrate to Australia, and the rising middle class who also have education or immigration aspirations:

> As we all know, the property market in China is not promising right now. My Chinese clients try to transfer their assets from China to Australia. They try to exchange Chinese housing for Australian housing through selling their investment properties in China... (Sales Agent Sydney, January 2015)

In contrast to the Canadian situation (Ley, 2017), where the majority of Chinese investors are wealthy entrepreneurs immigrating through the BIP, the profile of investors in Australian market seems more diverse. In addition to super wealthy Chinese individuals, an increasing number of middle-class Chinese are also active investors in Australia's housing market:

> As I observed, before 2013, most of my Chinese clients were super-rich individuals. But in recent years, I have found more and more middle-class Chinese start investing in the Australian housing market as well. (Sales Agent Sydney, January 2015).

In many cases the selection of Australia as an investment destination, especially by the middle-class group, is influenced by prior experience as a student or through employment:

> Many investors know the Australian housing market quite well because lots of them had working or studying experience in Australia before. (Sales Agent Sydney, January 2015)

As for Chinese developers, interviews revealed a significant increase in activity from the year 2013, when one of the largest Chinese developers, Greenland Group, entered the Sydney market. Since this time both large and numerous smaller Chinese developers have emerged in Sydney, such as the Wanda Group, Country Garden, China Poly Group and so on.

The agents described a specific set of housing preferences. A number of informants advised that their clients prefer projects in Chinese ethnic communities. According to a sales agent in Sydney,

> The percentage of Chinese-background buyers of developments in particular communities can reach up to 90%. For example, 95% of purchasers in recent Chinatown developments were ethnic Chinese. 99% of buyers in Chatswood new developments were ethnic Chinese. (Sales Agent Sydney, November 2014)

Of course, in this instance the agent is not able to distinguish between ethnic Chinese with Australian residency or citizenship, who also account for a significant proportion of demand, and foreign purchasers. As for individual projects, informants perceived that the percentage of Chinese buyers is much higher in projects developed by Chinese developers than those by Australian developers:

> If a project is developed by a Chinese developer, Chinese background buyers can account for 70-80%. Among the 70-80%, 10-20% are pure investors from China. But, if a project is developed by a local developer, the percentage of Chinese buyers is much lower, normally no more than 30%. (Sales Agent Sydney, January 2015)

The agent also explained that some Australian banks have lending restrictions on the percentage of foreign buyers in a development. Thus developers seeking Australia finance are often required to show that foreigners do not account for more than 30% of pre sales. Some banks even request that non-residents and non-citizens are not allowed to purchase properties in Australia. These finance constraints likely explain why the percentage of Chinese buyers is much lower in developments by Australian based firms. However, those requirements are implemented by the banks (and contrast to the looser government regulations on foreign investment), and do not apply for all projects.

In relation to preferences for particular housing types, apartments appear to be the most popular housing products among Chinese investors for Sydney. As well as a higher proportion of new housing development in Sydney being in the apartment sector, sales agents reported that it is easier to finance apartments (due to lower deposit requirements) and that apartments may offer prospects of higher rental yields:

Compared with houses, apartments generally require lower down payments while enjoy higher investment yields in short term. So, investors can make more efficient use of money if they purchase apartments. (Sales Agent Sydney, November 2014)

In Australia, apartments are also more likely to be located in proximity to public transport than detached dwellings, which makes them more popular with Chinese buyers.

Compared with houses, the location of apartments is generally better, and they are normally more accessible with convenient public transport. (Sales Agent Sydney, November 2014)

In terms of the mechanisms for financing purchases, informants advised that financing arrangements for Chinese investors have shifted from predominantly cash transactions, to loans from Australian banks (before early 2016 when mortgage restriction on foreign income buyers was implemented by major banks in Australia). The availability of finance has fuelled demand for multiple dwellings:

With our help, most of our clients have learnt they can borrow money from local banks, normally 70-80% of the total housing prices. So now, they generally choose mortgage payment. In this way, they can buy more than one unit per time with the same amount of money. (Sales Agent Sydney, December 2014)

However, one informant advised that some local banks have become more cautious in relation to approving loans to foreign purchasers, for apartments in major development areas:

… Recently, some banks have been refusing to lend if future supply is too large in some areas, like Zetland and Rhodes in Sydney. (Sales Agent Sydney, January 2015)

Furthermore, in April 2015, a home loan broker for Westpac, one of Australia's four largest banks, announced:

All temporary visas must be living in Australia and have income from Australia for Westpac to approve the loan. (MyHomeLoan, 2015)

This suggests that the availability of Australian or other sources of finance in future may limit demand from a certain sector of the Chinese investment market. (In early 2016, after the writing of this paper, major banks in Australia restricted loans for foreign income buyers, which made many foreign investors without local incomes unable to settle their presale housing and forced to resell the uncompleted properties under market prices. These measures in Australia may have wider impacts on Chinese foreign investment as well as local housing market, which need to be studied further).

Given that Australia's foreign real estate investment policy is intended to boost the supply of new housing, an important question for this study is whether Chinese purchasers intend to make their properties available to rent on the open market. In China, investment consultants advised that it is not uncommon for new housing units in Chinese cities to remain empty or be reserved for occasional self use, on the expectation of eventual capital gain. However, the interviews for this study suggest that by and large, the majority of homes purchased in Australia are for investment purposes rather than for self use, and most of this investment housing is subsequently made available for rent. Consultants advised that Australia's capital gain tax laws, which require owners to pay a large amount of tax if the housing has not been self-used for one year before sale (and if sold within a short period of time), mean that most Chinese buyers purchase Australian housing for long-term investment rather than short-term capital gains.

Finally, all informants interviewed for this study advised that the relaxation of some of the Chinese government's anti-speculation measures in 2014 would do little to reverse the trend for Chinese investors to 'go overseas'. In part, this reflects the going accumulation of wealth and interest in global investment amongst aspirational Chinese individuals and firms, as well as concerns about the instability of the domestic policy environment and economy.

Conclusion

This paper uses the lens of behavioural economics to examine the push and pull factors influencing Chinese foreign investment in Australian housing. It has a particular emphasis on the potential impact of China's domestic housing policies as a catalyst for displacing Chinese housing investment to international markets. Sixteen in-depth interviews with real estate consultants in Shanghai, Chengdu, and Sydney, as well as Chinese development firms and a Chinese housing official highlighted the importance of China's anti-speculation measures – in particular, the 'Purchase Restriction' policy, within the domestic housing market. However, the interviews suggested that the domestic policy and economic settings were only one of a series of considerations, with 'pull factors' associated with lifestyle and immigration factors a major drawcard to nations like Australia. By no means the only influence on Chinese international investment – with immigration aspirations, education, and environmental amenities major drawcards for China's globally mobile elite, the domestic housing policy setting has certainly impelled investors and developers to 'go overseas'. While the policy appeared to control speculative housing demand, moderating prices to enable more first-home buyers and upgraders to achieve ownership, it also exacerbated existing problems within the domestic market, in particular the perception of oversupply, thus encouraging Chinese investors and developers to seek international opportunities.

At the same time, in this paper the focus on a particular destination for Chinese housing investment, Australia, highlights the dualistic nature of domestic policies as a factor in the increasing globalisation of the housing market. In the case of Australia, pull factors also include Australia's own housing policy and investment settings applying to both local and foreign buyers. It is particularly pertinent that restrictions on foreign ownership in Australia were being eased around the same period that the environment for domestic housing investment was tightening in China. Just as there are concerns about the impacts of Australia's tax settings on domestic housing demand and price inflation (Yates, 2010), it is significant to note the importance of these settings in driving foreign investment, along with the availability of international and local sources of finance, all factors that have arisen in the course of this study. What is less clear is whether the policies surrounding property investment in either country have helped meet domestic housing goals. If the exodus of domestic funds may have pulled down property prices in China, long-term implications for affordable home ownership are less clear. Similarly, the extent to which increasing inbound foreign housing investment, will contribute to the supply of affordable dwellings in Australia overall and Sydney in particular remains unknown. The informants to this study are clearly acting on expectations of on-going price inflation in Australia, which may support new housing production even if affordability for aspiring local purchasers continues to decline. In these ways, this study highlights how two very distant domestic housing policy environments (China, Australia) and settings (Shanghai, Sydney, Chengdu) intersect across the increasingly porous global housing market.

This study also demonstrates that when housing is financialised and housing market becomes global, houses are no longer simply fixed assets only, with demand solely determined by local demographic changes, economic development or other domestic drivers. Instead, houses have become a vehicle for mobile capital, the demand and supply of which are influenced by a set of more complicated phenomena. Housing policy makers and urban planners need to be cognisant of these drivers, ensuring that new housing developments and programmes address local needs and pressures, while seeking to optimise potential opportunities presented by global investors and developers.

Disclosure statement

No potential conflict of interest was reported by the authors.

Note

1. First-tier cities in China refer to Beijing, Shanghai, Guangzhou and Shenzhen, which are the largest four Chinese cities. Second-tier cites in China include capital cities of each province, like Chengdu, Nanjing, Wuhan, Fuzhou, etc., as well as some developed coastal cities, such as Xiamen, Dongguan, Wenzhou, Tianjin and so on.

References

Aalbers, M.B. (2015). The great moderation, the great excess and the global housing crisis. *International Journal of Housing Policy, 15*(1), 43–60.

ABS. (2016). *Australian bureau of statistics*. Canberra.

Adair, A., Berry, J., McGreal, S., Sýkora, L., Parsa, A.G., & Redding, B. (1999). Globalization of real estate markets in Central Europe. *European Planning Studies, 7*(3), 295–305. doi: 10.1080/09654319908720519

Cao, J.A., & Keivani, R. (2014). The limits and potentials of the housing market enabling paradigm: An evaluation of China's housing policies from 1998 to 2011. *Housing Studies, 29*(1), 44–68. doi: 10.1080/02673037.2013.818619

CBRE Global Research & Consulting. (2013). An expanding horizon: Chinese capital tapping into overseas real estate markets [Press release]. Retrieved from http://www.cbre.com.cn/EN/aboutus/mediacentre/mediaarchives/Pages/07102013.aspx

Chen, J.H., Guo, F., & Wu, Y. (2011). One decade of urban housing reform in China: Urban housing price dynamics and the role of migration and urbanization, 1995-2005. *Habitat International, 35*(1), 1–8. doi: 10.1016/j.habitatint.2010.02.003

Cheng, L.K., & Kwan, Y.K. (2000). What are the determinants of the location of foreign direct investment? The Chinese experience. *Journal of International Economics, 51*(2), 379–400. doi: 10.1016/s0022-1996(99)00032-x

Coakley, J. (1994). The integration of property and financial markets. *Environment and Planning A, 26*(5), 697–713.

Coq-Huelva, D. (2013). Urbanisation and financialisation in the context of a rescaling state: The case of Spain. *Antipode, 45*(5), 1213–1231. doi: 10.1111/anti.12011

Cushman & Wakefield. (2014). China's outbound boom: the rise of Chinese investment in global real estate [A Cushman & Wakefield research publication]. Retrieved from http://www.cushmanwakefield.com/en/news/2014/10/chinese-outbound-investment-booming/

Deng, L., Shen, Q.Y., & Wang, L. (2011). The emerging housing policy framework in China. *Journal of Planning Literature, 26*(2), 168–183. doi: 10.1177/0885412210390220

Domain. (2016). Sydney's median house price falls below $1 million: Domain Group. *Domian*. Retrieved from http://www.domain.com.au/news/sydneys-median-house-price-falls-below-1-million-domain-group-20160420-go9kie/

Duca, J.V., Muellbauer, J., & Murphy, A. (2010). Housing markets and the financial crisis of 2007–2009: Lessons for the future. *Journal of Financial Stability, 6*(4), 203–217.

FIRB. (2010). *Foreign investment review board annual report 2008-2009*. Canberra: Commonwealth of Australia.

FIRB. (2011). *Foreign investment review board annual report 2009-2010*. Canberra: Commonwealth of Australia:.

FIRB. (2012). *Foreign investment review board annual report 2010-2011*. Canberra: Commonwealth of Australia.

FIRB. (2013). *Foreign investment review board annual report 2011-2012*. Canberra: Commonwealth of Australia.

FIRB. (2014). *Foreign investment review board annual report 2012-2013*. Canberra: Commonwealth of Australia.

FIRB. (2015). *Foreign investment review board annual report 2014-15*. Canberra: Commonwealth of Australia.

Foreign Investment Review Board. (2014). *Annual report 2012-13*. Canberra: Commonwealth of Australia.

Gallimore, P., & Gray, A. (2002). The role of investor sentiment in property investment decisions. *Journal of Property Research, 19*(2), 111–120. doi: 10.1080/09599910110110671

Gauder, M., Houssard, C., & Orsmond, D. (2014). *Foreign investment in residential real estate*. Reserve Bank of Australia. Retrieved from https://www.rba.gov.au/publications/bulletin/2014/jun/pdf/bu-0614-2.pdf

Gibb, K. (2009). Housing studies and the role of economic theory: An (Applied) disciplinary perspective. *Housing, Theory and Society, 26*(1), 26–40. doi: 10.1080/14036090802704262

Ha, S.K. (2013). Housing markets and government intervention in East Asian countries. *International Journal of Urban Sciences, 17*(1), 32–45.

Javorcik, B.S., Özden, Ç., Spatareanu, M., & Neagu, C. (2011). Migrant networks and foreign direct investment. *Journal of Development Economics, 94*(2), 231–241. doi: 10.1016/j.jdeveco.2010.01.012

JLL. (2014). Chinese commercial real estate buyers pump record $7.6B into foreign investments in 2013 [press release]. Retrieved from http://www.us.jll.com/united-states/en-us/news/2680/chinese-commercial-real-estate-buyers-pump-record-7b-into-foreign-investments-in-2013

Juwai. (2013). Top destinations for Chinese property buyers [Juwai research publication]. Retrieved from https://list.juwai.com/bundles/juwailist/pdf/Juwai-map-FINAL.pdf

Knight Frank. (2014). The wealth report 2014: The global perspective on prime property and wealth. In Shirley A., (Ed.), *The wealth report*. London. (Vol. Accessed at http://www.knightfrank.ae/resources/kf-wealthreport.pdf (20 July 2015))

Ley, D. (2010). *Millionaire migrants: Trans-pacific life lines*. Oxford: Blackwell-Wiley:.

Ley, D. (2017). Global China and the making of Vancouver's residential property market. *International Journal of Housing Policy, 17*(1), 15–34.

Li, M., & Driant, J.-C. (2014). Affordable housing policies in urban China. In *Affordable Housing in the Urban Global South: Seeking Sustainable Solutions* (pp. 204–218). Taylor and Francis.

Liang, S.Y. (2013). Planning and its discontents: Contradictions and continuities in remaking China's great cities, 1950-2010. *Urban History, 40*, 530–553. doi: 10.1017/s0963926812000752

Moos, M., & Skaburskis, A. (2010). The globalization of urban housing markets: Immigration and changing housing demand in Vancouver. *Urban Geography, 31*(6), 724–749.

MyHomeLoan. (2015). [Explanation for Westpac latest home loan policy for foreign investors] [Press release]. Retrieved from http://myhomeloan.net.au/overseas-investor-loan/2015-april-westpac-overseas-income-loan-policy-changes/

National Association of Realtors. (2013). *2013 profile of international home buying activity*. Chicago, IL: National Association of Realtors.

National Association of Realtors. (2014). *2014 profile of international home buying activity*. Chicago, IL: National Association of Realtors.

Paris, C. (2013a). The homes of the super-rich: Multiple residences, hyper-mobility and decoupling of prime residential housing in global cities. In *Geographies of the Super-Rich* (pp. 94–109). Edward Elgar Publishing.

Paris, C. (2013b). The super-rich and the globalisation of prime housing markets. *Housing Finance International, XXVII*(4), 18–27.

Parliament of Australia. (2015). *Out of reach? The Australian housing affordability challenge, senate economics references committee inquiry report*. Canberra: Parliament of Australia.

Rogers, D., Lee, C.L., & Yan, D. (2015). The politics of foreign investment in Australian housing: Chinese investors, translocal sales agents and local resistance. *Housing Studies 30*(5), 730–748.

Rolnik, R. (2013). Late neoliberalism: The financialization of homeownership and housing rights. *International Journal of Urban and Regional Research, 37*(3), 1058–1066. doi: 10.1111/1468-2427.12062

Romero, J., Jimennez, F., & Villoria, M. (2012). (Un)sustainable territories: Causes of the speculative bubble in Spain (1996-2010) and its territorial, environmental, and sociopolitical consequences. *Environment and Planning C: Government and Policy, 30*, 467–486.

Sah, V., Gallimore, P., & Sherwood Clements, J. (2010). Experience and real estate investment decision—making: A process—tracing investigation. *Journal of Property Research, 27*(3), 207–219. doi: 10.1080/09599916.2010.518402

Shiller, R.J. (2003). From efficient markets theory to behavioral finance. *Journal of Economic Perspectives, 17*(1), 83–104. doi: 10.1257/089533003321164967

Shiller, R.J. (2007). *Understanding recent trends in house prices and home ownership* (National Bureau of Economic Research Working Paper No. 13553). Cambridge, MA: National Bureau of Economic Research.

SMH. (2015). China's $60 billion Australian property splurge. *Sydney Morning Herald.*

Sydney Morning Herald. (2014). Locals priced out by $24b Chinese property splurge. *Sydney Morning Herald 5/3/14.*

Visas Consulting Group. (2014). Immigration and the Chinese HNWI 2014. Accessed 21 July 2015. http://up.hurun.net/Hufiles/201504/20150427162743845.pdf Shanghai: Hurun Research Institute.

Waldron, R., & Redmond, D. (2014). The extent of the mortgage crisis in Ireland and policy responses. *Housing Studies, 29*(1), 149–165. doi: 10.1080/02673037.2013.825694

Wu, F. (2015). Commodification and housing market cycles in Chinese cities. *International Journal of Housing Policy, 15*(1), 6–26.

Wu, F.L. (2001). China's recent urban development in the process of land and housing marketisation and economic globalisation. *Habitat International, 25*(3), 273–289. doi: 10.1016/s0197-3975(00)00034-5

Yang, Z., & Chen, J. (2014). *Housing affordability and housing policy in urban China.* Dordrecht: Springer.

Yates, J. (2010). Protecting housing and mortgage markets in times of crisis: What can be learned from the Australian experience. *Paper na konferenci Housing: The next, 29*(2), 361–382. doi: 10.1007/s10901-013-9385-y

Yates, J., & Berry, M. (2011). Housing and mortgage markets in Turbulent times: Is Australia Different? *Housing Studies, 26*(7-8), 1133–1156. doi: 10.1080/02673037.2011.609328

Ye, J.P., & Wu, Z.H. (2008). Urban housing policy in China in the macro-regulation period 2004-2007. *Urban Policy and Research, 26*(3), 283–295. doi: 10.1080/08111140802301740

Zhang, J.K., Yuan, J.F., & Skibniewski, M.J. (2011). The analysis on the policy of access to economically affordable housing in China: An area calculation model based on the incentive mechanism design. *International Journal of Strategic Property Management, 15*(3), 231–256. doi: 10.3846/1648715x.2011.613236

Zoharo. (2013). [Zoharo Annual Review] Accessed 22 July 2015. http://www.zoharo.cn/B_market.aspx Chengdu: Zoharo Research.

Ethnic connections, foreign housing investment and locality: a case study of Seoul

Hyung Min Kim

A new trend in global cities has been the increasing volume of foreign capital flowing into property markets with cross-border housing investment becoming a focus for international migrants. However, how ethnicity plays out in the housing market, particularly for home ownership, along with global migration, has not been well explored in emerging economies despite the increase in human and capital mobility. The aim of this paper is to identify the main housing investors with respect to ethnic connections and to explore intra-urban spatial expressions of foreign housing investment using Seoul as a case study. The result reveals that knowledge of local circumstances, usually via previous residency or shared ethnicity, can be significantly strengthened via ethnic and/ or family ties. Koreans living in high-income Western Anglophone countries such as the USA, Canada, Australia and New Zealand have been the key source of inbound funds in Korea. Foreign housing investment has appeared in three key areas where different groups of foreign nationals and translational class have been concentrated.

Introduction

A new trend in global cities is the increasing volume of foreign capital in their property markets (Lizieri, 2009). Advancements in transport and communication technologies (Friedmann, 1986), and changing cross-border real estate investment, education and migration practices (Rogers, Lee, & Yan, 2015) are being underwritten by the increasing mobility of real estate investors. The literature has recognised that foreign investment is a reflection of increasing integration of the global economy, and that ownership of foreign properties is also a strategy in corporate asset management (Kim, O'Connor, & Han, 2015; Newell & Worzala, 1995; Tiwari & White, 2010; Zhu, Sim, & Zhang, 2006).

Institutions and individuals have enacted foreign property investment since regulations on foreign investment were relaxed in many countries (Adair et al., 1999; Hsing, 2006; Keivani, Parsa, & Mcgreal, 2001; LaPier, 1998). The literature has acknowledged the significance of ethnicity in global capital flows and spatial outcomes of inflows of ethnic groups in host cities (Gao, 2003; Javorcik, Ozden, Spatareanu, & Neagu, 2011; Lee, 2014). However, how ethnicity plays out in the housing market, particularly for home purchase, along with global migration, has not been fully explored amongst emerging economies despite the increasing mobility of people and capital. In addition, the spatial dimension of foreign housing investment has been under-researched. The aim of this paper is thus to identify key housing investors, investigate the role of ethnic connections in the housing market and explore spatial expressions of foreign housing investment. Using Seoul as a case study, this research pays attention to the following research questions: who are foreign housing investors; how significant are ethnic connections in foreign housing investment; and how has foreign housing investment been expressed spatially? This paper uses housing transaction data in the period January 2006 to June 2010 to answer the research questions. In addition, this research carried out interviews with buyers (home owners), brokers, government officials and foreign nationals staying in Korea to provide in-depth understanding of foreign housing investment behaviours.

In modern Korean history, international immigration has been rare (Hill & Kim, 2000) and foreign nationals have played only a minor role in Seoul's housing market. However, the number of immigrants staying long term is increasing significantly,[1] while the Korean population is relatively stable. Since the Korean government removed regulations on foreign housing investment in 1998 – subsequent to the Asian financial crisis – the share of foreign housing investment has been gradually on the increase in Seoul's housing market.

The following three sub-sections provide, by means of literature review, an outline of global trends in foreign housing investment, its facilitating factors and its spatial characteristics. This is followed by a discussion of data collection and methods applied in our study. The paper goes on to consider our findings on the regulatory frameworks of foreign housing investment, the significance of ethnicity and spatial expressions of investment practices in Seoul. We draw on case studies of key foreign housing investment locations in Seoul, before moving on to the conclusions.

A global trend in foreign housing investment

Foreign property investment is an outcome of global economic integration (Hines, 2001; Kim et al., 2015). Cross-border property investment has advanced in commercial property markets strengthened by global real estate advisory firms and various investment vehicles (LaPier, 1998; Lizieri, 2009; Lizieri & Kutsch, 2006; Tiwari & White, 2010). Also, as high-income nations have accommodated a large number of cross-border immigrants, many countries have experienced investment in housing by non-citizens, for example, immigrants from Hong Kong to Canadian cities in the 1990s (Edgington, 1996), and Japanese real estate investors in Canadian and Australian cities in the 1980s and 1990s (Berry, 1994; Edgington, 1996;

Hajdu, 2005). The 2000s witnessed even greater volumes of inward foreign direct investment (FDI) in real estate in Australia, facilitated by accumulated capital in the Australian housing market, electronic communication technologies, and China's internal policy on housing and outward investment (Rogers & Dufty-Jones, 2015). Rogers and Dufty-Jones (2015) have further claimed that Chinese housing investment has been encouraged by the Chinese cultural trope that 'to buy property is in the Chinese investors' bones' and Australian government policy favouring integration with Asia as seen in 'Australia in the Asian Century'.

While foreign investment in real estate has been observed primarily in Western Anglophone countries, there is emerging evidence that shows a trend in foreign housing investment in non-Western countries such as China (Hui & Chan, 2014), Vietnam (Jung et al., 2013), Singapore (Lim, Adair, & Mcgreal, 2002) and South Korea (Kim et al., 2015). Most of these countries have only permitted property ownership by non-citizens recently. However, the dynamics and evolution of foreign property investment have manifested differently in these countries depending on economic structure and regulatory frameworks. The literature on these countries has focused upon commercial and industrial property. For China, land-use rights were first sold to foreign investors in the Shenzhen Special Economic Zone in 1987 (Lin & Ho, 2005). Under the state landownership regime, FDI in China's real estate has increased. Specifically, FDI in real estate by enterprises from Hong Kong, Macau and Taiwan accounted for 6%−7% of the total real estate investment in the 2000s, while real estate FDI by other foreign enterprises accounted for 4%−6% (Hui & Chan, 2014).

The Vietnamese government adopted an open door policy towards foreign investment in 1986 and foreign property ownership was de-regulated in 2009 (Jung et al., 2013). As foreign nationals preferred apartments, while the locals preferred traditional style villas, foreign developers, mostly from East Asian countries such as Taiwan, Korea, Japan and Singapore, led apartment development projects (Jung et al., 2013). The Singapore government, meanwhile, has strategically adopted state landownership. The city-state owned approximately 80% of all Singapore land in 1992 (Han, 2005a). Despite massive use of leasehold-based land sales (Han, 2005b), Singapore has evolved into a global city, as a financial centre and a centre for regional headquarters (Yeung, Poon, & Perry, 2001), with high numbers of MNEs, inward FDI and expatriates, resulting in expensive private housing markets for both foreigners and upper class and upper−middle class Singaporeans (Tu, 2004).

In South Korea, foreign property ownership was regulated until 1998 as the Korean government opened up the property market in response to the Asian Financial Crisis. There was large-scale foreign investment in commercial property immediately after the opening up as global investors sought out high rates of return in Seoul's office market (Kim et al., 2015). The post-Asian financial crisis saw more integrated and inter-linked Asian property markets (Gerlach, Wilson, & Zurbruegg,

2006). The volume of foreign housing investment has increased although limited groups of investors have been involved (Kim, Han, & O'Connor, 2015). Foreign housing investment was primarily dependent upon government regulation, but the relaxation of rules has been widespread in most countries. In addition to liberalising property markets for the global investors, government policies have played an important role in facilitating or discouraging foreign housing investment. The Korean government de-regulated the property market, and implemented foreigner-friendly policies such as Free Economic Zones in selected areas. However, public animosity against foreign land ownership has also been an issue (Park, Jung, & Jung, 1998).

Facilitators of foreign housing investment

Decisions on housing investment involve multiple considerations. Foreign housing investment adds complexity for individual investors as it involves cross-border capital transfer and international migration into unfamiliar places. Nevertheless, a number of cities have witnessed growing volumes of foreign housing investment associated with 'use values' and 'exchange values' (Haila, 1991; Harvey, 1982). While the use value emphasises the role of housing as a space to live, the exchange value views housing as a financial asset providing economic gains. In line with the increasing number of international migrants, demand for housing is expected to increase in host cities. The decision on international immigration and housing purchase is often tied in with family considerations such as educating children (Rogers & Dufty-Jones, 2015). In the sense that immigrants need a space to stay, their purchases generate 'derived demand' associated with the use value of housing. However, due to the monetisation of property that has transformed property into a financial asset or as a commodity beyond derived demand (Harvey, 1982; Lizieri, 2009), housing investors have also sought out the exchange values through rigorous market analysis. Developers and landowners have been keen to profit, particularly when there is rapid urban transformation, which has also manifested over country boundaries (Edel, 1972; Ha, 2007). From an investment point of view, affluent individuals are likely part of foreign housing investment by virtue of their accumulated wealth (Hay, 2013).

Geographical and cultural distances between home and host countries play an important role in foreign housing investment as seen in FDI flows (Javorcik et al., 2011). In particular, ethnicity via diasporic networks has facilitated international migration and investment in housing (Gao, 2003; Kim et al., 2015; Sassen, 2005; Luo, 1998). The ethnic connectivity is frequently combined with multiple processes through bilingual agencies with global connections including visa application, relocation, education arrangements and housing investment (Rogers & Dufty-Jones, 2015). Property investment has been stimulated by inflows of international immigrants facilitated via ethnic networks as manifested in Canadian cities

(Edgington, 1996). Diasporic networks, often in the form of small-size agencies or individuals, provide investment information without language barriers. While commercial property investment draws upon professional advisory firms (LaPier, 1998), cross-border housing investment tends to rely upon ethnic/family ties as the investment decision is made at the individual household level. The investors, who are in search of exchange values, need housing market information and support for property management that can be provided through ethnic/family ties. As a result, due to the ethnic connections, housing investment is likely geographically concentrated in the city. There are thus potentially long-term self-reinforcing effects in the ethnic enclaves once housing investment has taken place.

These facilitators (i.e., immigration size, gross domestic product (GDP) per capita in the home country, ethnic closeness and geographical distance) will later be used in a regression analysis to explain the origin of foreign housing investment in Seoul in this research.

Spatial characteristics of foreign housing investment within the city

Despite growing evidence of foreign housing investment worldwide, little attention has been paid to intra-urban spatial patterns in most cities, possibly due to unavailable data on foreign housing investment. Jung et al. (2013) provided a comparison of development projects completed by domestic and foreign investors in Ho Chi Minh City. Foreign investors tended to take a more politically risk-averse strategy by choosing areas distant from the central business district (CBD) to avoid potential uncertainties on land tenure in and around the CBD. The apartments, developed by foreign investors, were more expensive than ones by domestic developers. Kim et al. (2015) conducted comprehensive spatial analysis on foreign housing investment in conjunction with the presence of foreign nationals and locations of foreign housing investment in Seoul. Their findings demonstrated that locations of foreign housing investment were reshaping Seoul's spatial structure, but foreign housing investment took place in small geographical areas of Seoul (Kim et al., 2015).

This research broadens the understanding of investors' profiles and location choice in Seoul by categorising ethnic connections and describing the most active areas. Korea has a relatively short modern history of foreign real estate investment. Seoul, as the city at the burgeoning stage of foreign housing investment, has witnessed a growing volume of housing investment associated with ethnic ties that have evolved from immigration, emigration and re-migration (or returning).

The case study of Seoul provides unique characteristics in three aspects. First, most investors had a Korean ethnic background or they were long-term sojourners in Korea. In the sense that the direction of international migration and foreign housing investment was primarily to developed countries, in particular Western Anglophone countries, the Korean case showed a counter-direction associated with the Korean diaspora. Therefore, this research draws upon historic, geographic and economic considerations when categorising countries of origin in Korean contexts. Second, most foreign housing investment in Korea was completed by individuals, not by the corporate investors/developers who played a more pivotal role in developing countries such as Vietnam and China. Third, owing to the spatial data used, this research provides intra-urban location patterns of foreign housing investment.

Data collection

A key data source in this study is a housing transaction database covering the period January 2006 to June 2010, collected from all local governments in Seoul. In 2006, the Korean government started a Real Estate Trade Management System (RTMS) to collect data on real estate transactions for transparent real estate market management. Every single transaction should be reported to the local government (gu).[2] A formal request was made to the local governments in Seoul via the Korea Public Information Disclosure System.[3] The data-set includes 4782 housing transactions by foreign nationals. The collected transaction data include an address, an acquisition date, home country information, foreigners' ethnic background information and a housing type. Due to limited data about the profiles of foreign housing investors, this paper can only provide implications in limited scope such as ethnicity and location choice.

Interviews were also conducted to explore investors' behaviour in greater detail. The Global Village Centre, a government-initiated service centre for foreign nationals in Seoul, was therefore contacted. The Global Village Centre holds information sessions for foreign nationals who immigrate to Korea (mostly without a Korean ethnic background). In addition to attending the information session to identify potential interviewees, a so-called 'snowball' approach was used to secure more participants. Interviewees are composed of Korean emigrants (to Australia), foreign nationals staying in Korea (working in English education, administrative and military services) through the Global Village Centre and representatives of the *Hwagyo*,[4] as well as institutional informants: a real estate broker for overseas Koreans, a government official, an officer of an expat community, and foreign executives of the Global Village Centres. Fifteen interviews were conducted in 2010 (in English or Korean depending on the interviewer's first language). Selected samples are by no means representative of all foreign investors, but they provide details of their decision-making on home purchase. The interviews were recorded or annotated as appropriate. Anonymity has been preserved. Each interview lasted for about 30 minutes on average. Interview questions were semi-structured and flexibly treated during the interviews. Interview responses are directly quoted in this paper to support arguments and provide evidence.

A statistical regression model was used to analyse the origin of foreign housing investment. This regression model analyses the origin of investors and critical factors in housing investment at a global scale. The most active areas in foreign housing investment are identified by hotspot analysis in ArcGIS.

The role of foreign investors in the Seoul housing market

Changes in a regulatory framework in Korea

Enacting foreign land ownership dates back to the Japanese colonial rule in the early twentieth century. The Japanese prioritised the transformation of the Korean land system in order to control the Korean economy as well as for resource extraction (Chang, 1971). Colonial rule conducted a land survey, established the '*Chosun* Civil Area Planning Enactment' in 1934, and introduced the modern property rights system with new land tax under the Governor General of Korea (Jung, 1995). The 'Foreigners' Land Act' was also established in 1925 to enable the Japanese to acquire land (Cumings, 1997, p. 151). These land policies undermined conditions of farmers and stimulated a severe polarisation in land ownership (Jung, 1995).

After independence, the Korean government abolished the Foreigners' Land Act in 1961. Subsequently, foreigners' land acquisition was prohibited for over three decades. Then, in 1994, policy began to embrace foreign land ownership. In this transition period, deregulation of law allowed limited foreign land acquisition. Foreign corporations in manufacturing were allowed to own land for factories, offices, storage and dormitories. For non-manufacturing industries, foreigners were allowed to acquire land only for business and the affiliated dormitories. After a strict approval process, individual foreigners, who had a visa to stay long term (more than five years), were allowed to acquire small plots of land.

The Korean government opened up the property market in 1998. After Korea joined the OECD in 1996, which sped up global trade without limitation (Kim & Choi, 2004), the Korean government had to consider the Multilateral Agreement on Investment (MAI) negotiated between members of the OECD in 1995. Although the OECD eventually stopped implementing the MAI in 1998, the property market was one of the areas covered by the MAI (Jung & Cheong, 1999). In addition, facing the Asian financial crisis, the IMF requested the liberation of the property market in order for Korea to receive aid. As a result of this opening up of the property market, any institutions and individuals have been able to own property in Korea without constraint since 1998.

The trend in housing transactions

Foreign investment in housing has been part of the globalisation process. Greater volumes of inward FDI are associated with foreign employment (Kim & Han, 2014). In more general terms, the greater engagement of Korea in international trade and political affairs is likely to stimulate an increase in foreign residents.

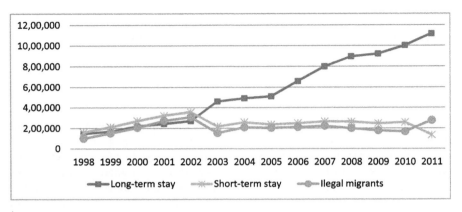

Figure 1.   Number of immigrants in Korea, 1998—2011.
Source: e-National indicators. http://www.index.go.kr

Despite weak immigration tradition in Korean history (Hill & Kim, 2000), the aspects reviewed above have been felt in an increase in the foreign population in Seoul from less than 14,000 in 1995 to 163,000 in 2010 (Figure 1). Moreover, the number of immigrants staying long term has increased remarkably while short-term migrants have remained relatively stable (Figure 1). Long-term immigrant numbers increased from 148,000 in 1998 to 1,117,000 in 2011, exhibiting a 7.6-fold increase over 13 years.

The rise of long-term immigrants ostensibly boosted the possibility of foreign housing investment. In Korea, investment in apartment buildings for rental income by either global or domestic property investors has not been common practice (Ronald & Jin, 2010). Instead, housing investment typically involved the purchasing of apartments or houses by individual investors. Only 30 transactions, or 0.6% of foreign housing investment in the data-set, were made by institutions and companies, suggesting they played a minimal role in foreign housing investment. As a dominant, standardised housing type, apartments accounted for 2925 transactions or 61.2% of the total foreign housing investment. There were 527,201 apartment transactions in the same period identified via the RTMS; foreign nationals accounted for 0.55% of apartment transactions over the analysis period, on average. Despite the increasing presence of foreign activities in Seoul, such as cross-border immigration (Jun, Ha, & Jeong, 2013), inward FDI (Kim & Han, 2014) and global office investment (Kim et al., 2015), the scale of foreign housing investment was small. However, this small role has been increasing as seen in the gradual rise in the share of sales completed by foreign nationals, from 0.37% in 2006 to 0.96% in 2010 (Table 1).

Table 1.   Trend in foreign housing investment in Seoul, January 2006 to June 2010.

Year	Number of apartment transaction* (A)	Number of foreign housing investment	Number of foreign apartment investment (B)	Foreign share (B/A)
2006	191,575	1165	704	0.37%
2007	98,790	844	446	0.45%
2008	95,128	826	487	0.51%
2009	108,488	1443	969	0.89%
2010[+]	33,225	503	318	0.96%
Total	527,206	4781[++]	2924	0.55%

*Source: Onnara Portal, MLTM (www.onnara.go.kr).
[+]2010 includes transactions from January to June.
[++]One transaction is excluded in this table due to lack of the transacted date.

A high spatial concentration of foreign land ownership as in Seoul has also been observed nationwide. In terms of assessed values of foreign owned land, Seoul accounted for 31.4% of the total of Korean foreign-owned land, followed by Seoul's surrounding region, Gyeonggi (18.0%) and the second largest city, Busan (8.1%) (Ministry of Land, Transport and Marine Affairs, 2012). Although there is rapidly growing interest in real estate investment in Jeju Island by the Chinese due to a free economic zone policy (Kwon et al., 2015), Seoul has functioned as the top-tier city in global property investment activities.

Investor behaviour

Identification of major investors

Table 2 reports the top 21 origins most active in housing investment by overseas Koreans. They are the USA, Canada, Australia, Taiwan, mainland China, New Zealand and Japan in order. The USA is an obviously proactive home country, accounting for approximately 60% of total transactions.

In terms of ethnicity, the vast majority of foreign housing investment has been completed by overseas Koreans, citizens of other countries who migrated from Korea. They accounted for 84.7%. Seoul is not seen as a major focus for housing investment in a global sense but rather it is a focus for housing purchase by those with some previous connections to Korea. These different ethnic connections will be analysed below.

Overseas Koreans

Overseas Koreans have major advantages in negotiating housing purchase due to their language skills and local connections. For housing investment,

Table 2. Foreign housing investment in Seoul, January 2006 to June 2010.

	Country	Number of housing Investment by overseas Koreans	Foreigners	Number of overseas Koreans in 2009*
Geographically	Mainland China	141 (3.5%)	136 (19.5%)	2,336,771
close countries	Taiwan	164 (4.0%)	302 (43.3%)	3158
	Japan	57 (1.4%)	69 (9.9%)	912,655
	Russia	13 (0.3%)	6 (0.9%)	222,027
Developed	USA	2758 (68.1%)	76 (10.9%)	2,102,283
countries	Canada	500 (12.3%)	18 (2.6%)	223,322
	Australia	176 (4.3%)	16 (2.3%)	125,669
	UK	18 (0.4%)	6 (0.9%)	45,295
	Germany	43 (1.1%)	6 (0.9%)	31,248
	New Zealand	92 (2.3%)	1 (0.1%)	30,792
	France	16 (0.4%)	10 (1.4%)	14,738
	Italy	7 (0.2%)	2 (0.3%)	4203
	Spain	3 (0.1%)	2 (0.3%)	3647
Developing	The Philippines	1 (0.0%)	0 (0.0%)	115,400
countries	Brazil	6 (0.1%)	0 (0.0%)	48,419
	Indonesia	6 (0.1%)	3 (0.4%)	31,760
	Singapore	4 (0.1%)	2 (0.3%)	13,509
	Argentina	3 (0.1%)	0 (0.0%)	22,024
	Paraguay	2 (0.0%)	0 (0.0%)	5,229
	Vietnam	1 (0.0%)	4 (0.6%)	84,566
	Thailand	1 (0.0%)	2 (0.3%)	20,200
Others		38 (0.9%)	37 (5.3%)	425,691
Total		4050 (100%)	698 (100%)	6,822,602

*Source: Present state of overseas Korean, 2010; Ministry of Foreign Affairs and Trade.
**4782 transactions were identified in total. 30 transactions by institutions were excluded in this table.

local language abilities are essential as the contract for housing transaction is written in the Korean language and all government documents relating to the sale are also in Korean. In addition, many foreigners find it difficult to understand local leasing arrangements, called *Cheonsei*. The *Cheonsei* leasing arrangement is a popular leasing type whereby the tenant deposits a lump sum (about 30%−80% of the property price) for a rental property with no monthly rent payable. Deposits are totally refunded to the tenants at the end of the leasing contract (Kim, 1990; Park, 2014; Ronald & Jin, 2010).

For centuries, Korea has interacted with China, Japan and Russia due to their geographical proximity and these countries were the main destinations of early migration. For political reasons, there were large Korean communities in these adjacent countries in the late nineteenth century. The second phase of migration started in the 1960s. In this period people emigrated to developed countries to seek economic prosperity, often in association with the spread of Korean conglomerates' activities as the Korean industry globalised. These two migration histories are felt in current foreign housing investment.

To see this effect, Table 2 analyses overseas Koreans by geographic closeness, as well as level of development of those with more distant origins. To provide a size context, data on the number of overseas Koreans in each country have also been tabulated. It is clear that only two groups play significant roles in the market: those from geographically close countries and those from developed countries, especially the USA. These will be reviewed in turn.

Ethnic Koreans in geographically close countries. It might be expected that geographically close countries are a source of investors, as the immigrant would be familiar with the local market, better able to participate in negotiations and easily inspect and manage properties. For Korea, these are residents of China, Japan and Russia. However, statistics reveal that geographical closeness has little relevance to foreign property investment although there are numerous overseas Koreans in these countries.

China is the country where the largest overseas Korean population lives. The majority of overseas Koreans in China, the ethnic Korean-Chinese, are called *Chosunjok* or the *Chosun*. Many Koreans escaped from the Korean peninsula to avoid Japanese persecution and remained in China after independence from Japanese colonial rule in 1945. Consequently, *Chosunjok* have been concentrated in areas close to the Korean Peninsula such as *Jilin* Province. *Chosunjok* have come back to Korea steadily since 1988 when Chinese visits to Korea were allowed. The number of *Chosunjok* in Korea in the 2000s reached 170,000, which accounted for approximately two-thirds of the total foreign population in Korea (Hong, Kim, & Lee, 2010). However, this group did not bring high-level skills as they immigrated. Rather *Chosunjok* largely worked in catering services and/or in manufacturing as low-income workers (Piao, 2006) and their wages even in the same industry were typically lower than domestic workers (LeeYu, Lee, Sul, & Park, 2007). This socio-economic context limited the chance of buying a house in Seoul, and they were likely to be renting so the number (141) shown in Table 2 is thus low, despite China having the highest number of overseas Koreans. In many cases members of this group have tended to purchase properties in Chinese cities once they accumulated sufficient capital from work in Korea (Piao, 2006).

The Korean-Japanese are another group whose numbers reflect experience associated with (in some cases) forced removal during Japanese colonial rule, and represent the largest group as foreigners in Japan. Their population reaches over 600,000 and the majority of them are former colonial subjects and their offspring (Tai, 2004). During colonial rule, Japanese industries actively recruited Koreans to meet the increasing demand for labour. In 1939, the Japanese government forced many Koreans to move to Japan to manage their labour shortage. By 1945, many Koreans were working under harsh conditions in mines and factories. The population reached two million, the majority of whom were unskilled labourers and their dependent families (Tai, 2004). After the World War II, 1.3 million Koreans returned back to Korea from Japan, but roughly 600,000 Koreans remained in Japan because of the uncertain political and economic situation in Korea. The Korean-Japanese have a very small involvement in the Seoul housing market.

Although there has long been a Korean community within Russia, its links to modern Korea are very weak, as seen in its small role in the housing market. Geographic proximity (and long-term historical links) alone seem to have had little effect upon housing purchases on Seoul's market. Rather, the demand has come from a later generation of migrants.

Ethnic Koreans from developed countries (EKD). It is apparent that many emigrants to developed countries have accumulated wealth adequate to participate in the Seoul housing market in proportion to the scale of the Korean communities within those countries (Figure 2).

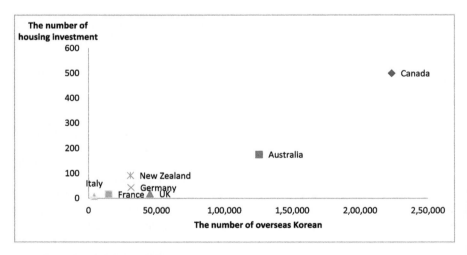

Figure 2. Foreign housing investment and the number of overseas Koreans.
Source: Ministry of Foreign Affairs and Trade.
Note: The USA is not included because the size is exceptionally large.

These emigrants tended to have become middle-class professionals who emerged in the period of rapid industrialisation in Korea since the 1960s (Park, 1997), and who were attracted by migration regulations favouring their skills in Western Anglophone countries, in particular, the USA, Canada, Australia and New Zealand. Housing investment by Korean-Americans alone accounted for 57.7% of purchases, while investors from these four developed countries together accounted for 75.6%. This shows that the financial connections associated with globalisation are focused upon selected countries. Indeed Interviews with house purchasers in this group reveal investment behaviours related to asset management strategies similar to those in commercial property investment (Kim et al., 2015; LaPier, 1998).

The interviews identified that ethnic Koreans from developed countries (EKD) can be categorised into three groups. The first is emigrants who were homeowners in Korea before moving and have not sold their original house. One interviewee explained her migration story. She worked as a secretary and one of her relatives recommended her to invest in a house in Ilsan, a new satellite residential area adjacent to Seoul. With partial support from her parents and financing from the *cheonsei* leasing deposit, she was able to invest in a villa. After she married, her family emigrated to Australia, but she decided to retain the house because she expected capital gains from home value increases. Also, she was unsure about her future due to the uncertainty surrounding migration, and she might want to come back to Korea if Australian life was uncomfortable for her family. She mentioned:

When I came here (Australia), I was unsure about what was going to happen. I decided to just bring the money that could support us for two to three years rather than selling everything... I thought my family could come back... I bought the house in 2002 using cheonsei leverage without any mortgage loans. The housing price was 110 million WON, and the cheonsei deposit was 70 million WON, so I just spent 40 million WON that I had saved to buy the house. Now, the housing price is about 200 million WON. The reason that I purchased the house was that my aunt, who was a real estate agent, said the housing price was going to increase because the house was surrounded by good schools and the previous landlord rushed to sell the house at a cheaper price than market values... Indeed, I bought the house even without inspection because I trusted my aunt. I did not know about housing investment... Because I nominated my father-in-law as a proxy, he works for me to manage the house... The location is good and there is ongoing development in surrounding areas... In about fifteen years, there might be redevelopment.[5]... I do not need that money right now, so I have just held the house. Even though the housing price rose drastically, having ownership is financially better than selling the house.

At the initial stage of migration, she leased the Korean house for monthly rent. Later, she changed the lease contract to *cheonsei* when she needed lump sum money to purchase a house in Australia. Another interview provided another perspective on Korean migrant home purchasing in Seoul. One of the informants, a medical doctor from Korea who migrated to America in the 1960s, settled there but did not apply for American citizenship because he anticipated a return to Korea. As an eldest son, he retained rights to an inherited family property. Over this period the brother of this emigrated doctor lived in this house, illustrating the role of family ties in the global management of the property.

The second group of migrant owners have established themselves overseas, but seek out housing investment opportunities in Korea. This is important in the case of the USA as there are brokers there that facilitate housing investment for the US-based Koreans.[6] These brokers have developed trustworthy relationships via the Korean communities in the US cities. Some of their clients invest in Korean housing even without any inspection, based upon successful prior investment operated by the broker. To some extent family ties and personal trust perform the functions of a broker or a management company in facilitating the investment process. In that sense, it is obvious that cultural closeness, more specifically ethnicity, plays an important role in the investment process and managing properties.

The attraction is often greater expected income and capital gains than in the US housing market and exchange rate variations can favour Korean-based returns. The interview with the broker indicates that purchasers target both expensive areas and redevelopment zones in pursuit of capital gains. There are also some advantages in different taxation levels associated with home ownership in Korea versus the USA. There is capital gains tax, as well as property tax and stamp duties in Korea (see Kim, Hur, & Jang, 2013, for details of Korean property tax systems), but property owned outside the USA might be hidden to avoid the US tax and take advantage of government benefits.

The third group consists of returners or re-migrants who have migrated to developed countries and returned back to Korea for retirement after they completed their migration purpose, such as educating their children or establishing a business. Returners stay in Korea with foreign citizenship. One interviewee in this category ran a successful business trading in textiles in the period of rapid industrialisation in Korea. When the business lost ground due to changing trading environments, he migrated to Australia (in 1989) to provide his two children with good educational opportunities:

> I have travelled overseas since 1976 because I worked in trading. Major trading partners were in America, Japan, and Hong Kong... Many friends were in America for study. Out of 480 colleagues in my secondary school (Gyeonggi secondary school), about 150 went to America to study. When I visited America, I used to stay in my friend's house and I saw children commuting by bicycle and carrying just one small bag, unlike Korean children who carried two to three large bags. So I decided to educate my children in these environments... I found Australia was good for education... I took my family to Australia when my second daughter graduated from her primary school.

His family stayed in Australia while his children attended a secondary school and university. After his children graduated from university and married, he could not find any reason to stay in Australia. Then, his family came back to Korea and he purchased an apartment in a satellite town of Seoul in search of a higher quality living environment. He was from an affluent family and had accumulated sufficient capital.

The above-mentioned interviewees have accumulated sufficient assets to afford housing. In particular, for the first two groups, housing investment has been an instrument to manage their assets and achieve capital gains. Investment has usually been achieved at an individual level using ethnic connections and/or family ties. For those who reside outside Korea, finding someone who can help them manage the property is particularly important.

Non-Korean Asian investors: the Hwagyo

One prominent group was house purchasers/investors with Taiwanese passports. There were 466 housing transactions by the Taiwanese over the analysis period. This group accounted for 43% out of the total non-Korean housing transactions. Their settlements in Korea reflect modern connections between Taiwan, China and Korea in the development of Asian trade, investment and industrial growth. They are labelled the *Hwagyo* and recognised through their Taiwanese passports. The *Hwagyo* are the Chinese diaspora living in Korea. They settled in Korea in the 1880s from mainland China. The current *Hwagyo* are the fourth to fifth generation since their ancestors came to Korea. They obtained Taiwanese nationality following the post-war political changes in China (interview with a manager of the Korean *Hwagyo* association). Nevertheless, they are regarded as foreigners in Korea even though they have been in Korea for more than a century.

Their population has fluctuated due to economic and political reasons. The population reached record highs in the 1970s at 33,000 and gradually decreased; the population of the *Hwagyo* was 22,000 in the 2000s (Yang & Lee, 2004).

Their foreigner status has been reflected in regulations over land ownership. For example, when the Foreign Land Act was enacted in 1961, the *Hwagyo* had to sell their land to Koreans (Yang & Lee, 2004). A CBD redevelopment plan also demolished *Hwagyo* retail clusters in the early 1970s. A retail concentration had been operated by the *Hwagyo* in the middle of the CBD in Seoul since the 1880s. The CBD redevelopment scattered their activities to other areas (Son, 2003). Further, due to their status as foreigners, the *Hwagyo* could not access to mortgage loans from banks despite the fact they were permanently resident in Korea.

For these reasons, the *Hwagyo* are a distinctive group within foreign housing activities in Korea. In this case, housing purchase is a natural result of their long-term settlement, which has produced different outcomes from the other overseas Koreans discussed above.

Investment in housing by the groups outlined above illustrates some of the important features of the way that global property investment operates. It requires an unrestricted movement of funds between two countries, depends upon comparative economic performance of different markets, and requires local knowledge and understanding, which is often supplied through brokers with international connections.

Modelling the country of origin of investors

Different investment groups have been explored in the previous section. This section analyses factors that explain the country of origin of foreign investment in housing. This analysis tests the idea that the volume of foreign investment in housing is a function of demographic characteristics in a host city, geographical closeness, cultural closeness and economic conditions of investors. Four variables were specified. The data-set for an analysis was built with 40 countries in which data were available:

$$\text{Foreign Housing Investment} = f(\text{demographic feature, geographic distance,}$$
$$\text{cultural closeness, economic conditions})$$

The dependent variable is the number of foreign investment transactions in housing pooled by home countries between January 2006 and June 2010. In this analysis, the volume of investment is measured by the pooled number of transactions for a consistent data arrangement.

The number of foreign nationals from each country was used to represent demographic features in Seoul. It was assumed that a high foreign population stimulates housing investment in the housing market. The Chinese population in Seoul was the largest at 190,000. The second largest was migrants from the USA at 13,000.

For geographical proximity, direct distance was measured from Seoul to the capital city of each sample country on Google Earth, assuming travelling time is roughly proportional to this absolute distance.

Evidence presented in the previous part exhibits that cultural closeness, i.e., ethnicity, plays an important role in housing investment in Seoul. Ethnicity was measured by the number of overseas Koreans in these countries. The Ministry of Foreign Affairs and Trade provided statistics on the number of overseas Koreans on a yearly basis. In 2009, largest numbers of overseas Koreans were, in order, in China, the USA, Japan, Canada and Russia.

Finally, economic conditions were measured by the GDP per capita in countries of origin. The economic conditions were assumed to provide an indication of individuals' affluence and hence potential to purchase housing in Korea. The GDP per capita, published in the World Economic Outlook Database by the IMF, was employed to measure investors' economic condition. A summary of statistics is included in Appendix and all the details for regression analysis are presented in Table 3.

Table 3. Multiple regression on foreign investment in housing, Seoul.

Independent variables	Coefficients	Std. error	Standardised coefficients	t-Value	p-Value
Constant	−93.903	74.520		−1.260	.216
Demographic Foreigners in Seoul[1]	−.013	.002	−.836	−7.253	.000
Geographic Distance (km)[2]	.013	.010	.103	1.277	.210
Ethnicity Overseas Korean[3]	.001	.000	1.324	11.739	.000
Economic GDP per capita[4]	<0.001	.002	.003	.041	.968

Notes:
[1]2010, The Seoul Metropolitan Government (http://stat.seoul.go.kr/).
[2]Direct distance is measured on Google Earth from Seoul to the capital city of each home country.
[3]Overseas Koreans 2009, Ministry of Foreign Affairs and Trade.
[4]World Economic Outlook Database October 2010, IMF (unit: US dollars).
R^2 is 0.82 and adjust R^2 is 0.80.

Using four variables, a multiple-regression analysis was conducted to discover the factors relevant to origins of foreign housing investment (Table 3). An ordinary least square method was used in the regression analysis. The model had a high explanatory power; the R^2 is 0.82.

As seen in the multiple-regression analysis, ethnicity was the most important variable in housing investment. The standardised coefficient of overseas Koreans was the highest and statistically significant. This signifies the importance of ethnicity in foreign housing investment, and also that the Korean housing market has not yet been seen as a major opportunity to a broader international market.

By contrast, geographic closeness was not statistically significant. The sign of the coefficient was even positive, which was different from expectations. Although geographical distance has been considered critical in global interactions (Yeung et al., 2001), advanced technologies have facilitated 'time−space compression' to shrink geographical barriers (Harvey, 1990). In foreign housing investment in Seoul, ethnic ties, which shaped access to local information and personal networks, were of importance. This regression result supports the argument that, in Seoul, ethnic connections play a more significant role in foreign capital movement than geographical distance.

Demographic characteristics also proved interesting. The variable, the number of foreign nationals in Seoul, had a negative sign and is statistically significant. The standardised coefficient was −0.836 which is the second highest after the ethnicity variable. It seemed that there was a negative relationship between the number of foreigners and foreign investment in housing. Many foreigners in Seoul were low-waged labourers (as in many global cities) who were unlikely to be able to participate in the housing investment market. Less-skilled workers, such as *Chosunjok*, have typically replaced Korean workers in low-waged catering service sectors and dirty, difficult and dangerous jobs (the so-called '3D' occupations). Not only the *Chosunjok*, but people from developing countries, such as Vietnam, Mongolia and the Philippines, were a fast growing group in these industries.

Most high-income foreigners (i.e., those in professional jobs) were more likely to rent than purchase. However, according to the regression result, the economic variable was unclear. The GDP per capita was positive, but the coefficient was not statistically significant. This could be understood by the limited data source that fails to include individual information. Housing investment has been completed at the individual level, thus, rather than general income levels in home countries, an individual economic status is more appropriate. The flow of funds under these arrangements can have a particular effect on parts of the housing market as they may be targeted at carefully selected locations.

Active areas for foreign housing investment

A concentrated spatial pattern was observed in foreign housing investment activities in Seoul possibly due to the significance of ethnicity. This section, therefore, provides case studies of key places for foreign housing investment. Highly concentrated spatial patterns were observed in the hot-spot analysis (Figure 3). Three major areas were identified with respect to foreign housing investment. They were *Yeonghee dong*, *Yongsan* and *Gangnam*. As discussed, foreign housing investment in Seoul had close relations with ethnic connections and/or Korean ethnic backgrounds. The following three places represent different aspects of foreign housing investment.

Yeonhee dong, *communities of the* Hwagyo

The *Hwagyo* are a typical example of long-term resident foreign nationals in Seoul. In 2006, more than one-quarter of the *Hwagyo* lived in *Seodaemun gu* where *Yeonhee dong* was situated; the population of the *Hwagyo* in *Seodaemun gu* was approximately 2300 and *Yeonhee dong* was a major centre for them. The population of the *Hwagyo* was relatively stable, unlike numbers in other foreign national categories, which tended to rise over time.

Housing investment by the *Hwagyo* revolved around their community and their concentration created an exotic atmosphere in this area. For example, *Yeonhee dong* in *Seodaemun gu* was well known as a cluster of Chinese settlements, and it was the location of a large number of restaurants operated by the *Hwagyo*. The concentration of Chinese restaurants was not a direct result of foreign home ownership,

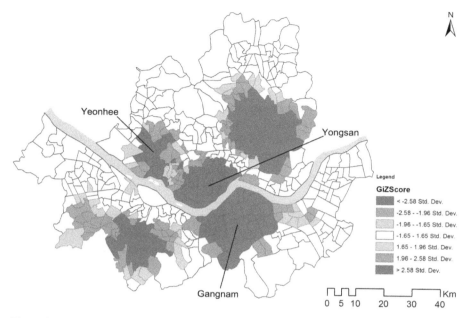

Figure 3.   The result of hot-spot analysis, Seoul.

but rather was related to their long-term settlement which has strengthened their role in economic activities in *Yeonhee dong*. These activities have expanded and diversified recently due to increased inflows of Chinese residents and visitors. For instance, large Chinese restaurants, Chinese medical centres and a wedding hall were established, consolidating a Chinese commercial area along the street where the *Hwagyo* clustered (Kim & Kim, 2006). In addition, there were cultural events during the 2002 FIFA World Cup to entertain Chinese visitors. For these reasons, the SMG considered the designation of a Chinatown in *Yeonhee dong* in 2008 although the plan has not been implemented to date.

Yongsan, *a hybrid town*

Yongsan is an area where there are diversified global influences. Here the popula- tion analysis identifies many origins of residents so that *Yongsan* is a multicultural area providing unique streetscapes. There are diverse shops targeting foreign nationals such as foreign brand shops, currency exchange vendors, foreign book stores and restaurants with multilingual signs (Kim & Kim, 2006, p. 72). A typical area for foreign activities is *Itaewon* in *Yongsan*. Originally, *Itaewon* was developed in response to the establishment of the US military camp. Subsequently, there has been an influx of ethnically diverse people. For example, an Islamic Mosque was built in 1976 and Islamic communities have gathered in *Itaewon* (Kim & Kim, 2006). The foreign Muslims were mostly from Asian countries such as Pakistan, Bangladesh and Indonesia. This cultural context has played a contributory role in attracting more foreign migrants from Muslim countries.

Property ownership by foreigners embeds their culture and fosters the diversity of this place. In 1997, the government designated *Itaewon* as a special district for tourism in recognition of its hybrid culture. Since then, there has been a tourism festival every year. *Yongsan* illustrates the way a global village emerges following foreign migration and foreign housing investment.

Gangnam, *a global elite town*

Gangham is an area in the south of the Han River, shaded dark red in the map on the left-hand side of Figure 4. It is one of the main business centres (Kim & Han, 2012). Considerable housing investment in *Gangnam* is attributable to Korean emigrants. *Gangnam* has become a residence for the bourgeois, owing to high-quality public infrastructure and prestigious education facilities. Housing prices, especially apartment prices, are well above the Seoul average. In terms of economic structure, *Gangnam* has attracted internationally networked advanced services—firms that are a core driver in the post-modern economies.

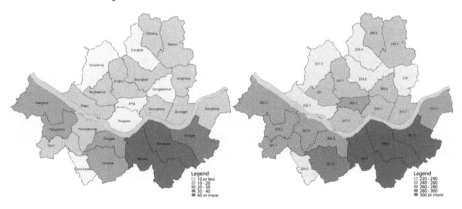

Figure 4. High-income household (left) and average household income (right) in Seoul, 2006.
Source: SMG (2006, p. 403).
Note: Left is the number of high-income households, more than five million WON per month (unit: 1000 households). It is calculated by multiplying the number of households and the share of high-income household in each area. Right is the average household income (unit: 10,000 WON).

High-income households are concentrated in *Gangnam*. Households in *Seocho gu* and *Gangnam gu* were the highest income earners on average in the entire city. In 2006, one-quarter of high-income households lived in these two areas (Figure 4).

The predominant group in *Gangnam* is characterised by the 'transnational class' originally from South Korea. Their global connections have been developed through studying abroad and travelling internationally for business. In some cases, these connections have led them to emigrate, and when they return, they seek out home ownership in *Gangnam*. This global mobility has stimulated the transformation of *Gangnam* into a global elite town.[7] Rather than foreign-driven changes due to a massive influx of foreigners, changes in *Gangnam* could be motivated by links with Koreans in offshore countries.

Conclusion

Deregulation of property markets has encouraged free flows of capital into the housing market by individuals, although foreign housing investment accounted for a small portion in Korea. Ethnicity is a key factor that explains foreign investment in Korean housing at this moment. Geographical distance is more easily overcome than information barriers in a technologically advanced society. An influx of low-wage foreign labourers has little relevance to housing investment. Instead, economically qualified foreigners seem to be implicated in housing investment although processes of capital accumulation have not been fully explored due to the lack of relevant data in this research.

Spatial expressions of foreign housing investment have demonstrated concentrations around the ethnic community for the long-term resident Chinese, a globalising multicultural area and a newly emerging global elite town. All these three active areas have a close relation with ethnic connections to either foreign nationals or the Korean diaspora.

The findings illustrate some of the key dimensions in foreign investment in housing. Knowledge of local circumstances, usually via previous residency or shared ethnicity, can be important. These dimensions have shaped foreign residential real estate investment outcomes in Seoul. It is apparent that a free flow of funds across the globe is a first step, which depends on the removal of regulation in destination countries. Second, there needs to be a source of investment funds, generated by relatively high-income employment in developed countries. Then, there needs to be institutional arrangements, usually in the form of brokers and professional services providing trustworthy market information in countries of origin. The change of regulation on foreign ownership has opened up the market. However, Koreans living in Western Anglophone high-income countries have been the key source of inbound funds often seeking exchange values of the property. Although some markets, such as the USA, the UK, Singapore and Australia, seem to be open to a wide array of investors and purchasers (Arth, 2011, Rogers et al., 2015, Tu, 2004), the

Korean market is less well known, possibly due to recent operation, a short history of immigration, language barriers and localised housing investment institutions. A very recent rise of Chinese real estate investment, especially in the Jeju Island, may indicate the next stages of global property market integration, which requires further research.

Acknowledgements

This paper is partially from the PhD thesis 'Global Property Investment in a Global City, Seoul: Dynamics of office and housing markets (2012)' completed in the University of Melbourne. The early idea was presented at the conference 'Spaces and Flows', Prato, Italy, in 2011. I appreciate my supervisors, Prof. Sun Sheng Han and Emeritus Prof. Kevin O'Connor, for their insights and support. I would like to thank to Guest Editors Dr. Sin Yee Koh and Dr. Dallas Rogers and anonymous reviewers for their constructive feedbacks.

Disclosure statement

No potential conflict of interest was reported by the author.

Notes

1. The origins of foreign nationals staying in Korea are diverse. Top origins were China (50.3%), the USA (7.3%), Thailand (4.9%) and the Philippines (2.9%) in 2015 (Korea Immigration Service). However, not all immigrants have been active in housing investment activities in the destination city, which will be discussed in the findings section.
2. *Gu* is an administrative (mostly autonomous) district. Seoul comprised of 25 autonomous *gu*s (or local governments).
3. https://www.open.go.kr
4. The *Hwagyo* means Chinese-Korean.
5. In Korea, redevelopment is commonly recognised as the process that generates huge amount of capital gains that are pocketed by landlords.
6. The interviewed broker was an accredited real estate agent working individually.
7. A Korean popular song named '*Gangnam Style*' by Psy from 2012 reflected the emergence of *Gangnam* as a global elite town.

References

Adair, A., Berry, J., Mcgreal, S., Sýkora, L., Parsa, A.G., & Redding, B. (1999). Globalization of real estate markets in central Europe. *European Planning Studies, 7*, 295–305.
Arth, L. (2011). *Top 5 real estate investment markets – commercial and residential* [Online]. Retrieved from http://howtobuyusarealestate.com/top-5-real-estate-investment-markets-commercial-and-residential
Berry, M. (1994). Japanese property development in Australia. *Progress in Planning, 41*, 113–201.
Chang, Y. (1971). Colonization as planned changed: The Korean case. *Modern Asian Studies, 5*, 161–186.

Cumings, B. (1997). *Korea's place in the sun: A modern history*. New York, NY: W.W. Norton & Company.

Edel, M. (Ed.) 1972. *Planning, market or warfare? Recent land use conflict in American cities*. New York, NY: The Macmillan Company.

Edgington, D.W. (1996). Japanese real estate investment in Canadian cities and regions, 1985–1993. *The Canadian Geographer, 40*, 292–305.

Friedmann, J. (1986). The world city hypothesis. *Development and Change, 17*, 69–83.

Gao, T. (2003). Ethnic Chinese networks and international investment: Evidence from inward FDI in China. *Journal of Asian Economics, 14*, 611–629.

Gerlach, R., Wilson, P., & Zurbruegg, R. (2006). Structural breaks and diversification: The impact of the 1997 Asian financial crisis on the integration of Asia–Pacific real estate markets. *Journal of International Money and Finance, 25*, 974–991.

Ha, S.-K. (2007). Housing regeneration and building sustainable low-income communities in Korea. *Habitat International, 31*, 116–129.

Haila, A. (1991). Four types of investment in land and property. *International Journal of Urban and Regional Research, 15*, 343–365.

Hajdu, J. (2005). *Samurai in the surf: The arrival of the Japanese on the gold coast in the 1980s*. Canberra: Pandanus.

Han, S.S. (2005a). Global city making in Singapore: A real estate perspective. *Progress in Planning, 64*, 69–175.

Han, S.S. (2005b). Polycentric urban development and spatial clustering of condominium property values: Singapore in the 1990s. *Environment and Planning A, 37*, 463–481.

Harvey, D. (1982). *The limits to capital*. Oxford: Basil Blackwell.

Harvey, D. (1990). *The condition of postmodernity*. Oxford: Blackwell.

Hay, I. (2013). *Geographies of the super-rich*. Cheltenham: Edward Elgar.

Hill, R.C., & Kim, J.W. (2000). Global cities and developmental state: New York, Tokyo and Seoul. *Urban Studies, 37*, 2167–2195.

Hines, M.A. (2001). *Investing in international real estate*. Westport, CT: Quorum Books.

Hong, S.-K., Kim, S.-J., & Lee, H.-S. (2010). *Social cohesion policy for foreigner in Seoul*. Seoul: Seoul Development Institute.

Hsing, Y.-T. (Ed.). (2006). *Global capital and local land in China's urban real estate development*. New York, NY: Routledge.

Hui, E.C.M., & Chan, K.K.K. (2014). Foreign direct investment in China's real estate market. *Habitat International, 43*, 231–239.

Javorcik, B.S., Ozden, C., Spatareanu, M., & Neagu, C. (2011). Migrant networks and foreign direct investment. *Journal of Development Economics, 94*, 231–241.

Jun, M.-J., Ha, S.-K., & Jeong, J.-E. (2013). Spatial concentrations of Korean-Chinese and determinants of their residential location choice in Seoul. *Habitat International, 40*, 42–50.

Jung, H.N. (1995). The evolution of Korean land policies since liberalization, 1945–1995. *The Korea Spatial Planning Review, 23*, 127–145. (Korean).

Jung, H.N., & Cheong, W.-H. (1999). Reform and impact of foreign land policy. *Land Studies, 9*, 90–109. (Korean).

Jung, S., Huynh, D., & Rowe, P.G. (2013). The pattern of foreign property investment in Vietnam: The apartment market in Ho Chi Minh City. *Habitat International, 39*, 105–113.

Keivani, R., Parsa, A., & Mcgreal, S. (2001). Globalisation, institutional structures and real estate markets in central European cities. *Urban Studies, 38*, 2457–2476.

Kim, E.M., & Kim, J.-H. (2006). *Global city Seoul project*. Seoul: Seoul Development Institute. (Korean).

Kim, H.M., & Han, S.S. (2012). City profile: Seoul. *Cities, 29*, 142−154.

Kim, H.M., & Han, S.S. (2014). Inward foreign direct investment in Korea: Location patterns and local impacts. *Habitat International, 44*, 146−157.

Kim, H.M., Han, S.S., & O'Connor, K.B. (2015). Foreign housing investment in Seoul: Origin of investors and location of investment. *Cities, 42*, 212−223.

Kim, H.M., Hur, Y.-K. & Jang, K.-S. (2013). The estimation of property tax capitalisation in the Korean taxation context. *Current Urban Studies, 1*, 110−116.

Kim, H.M., O'Connor, K.B. & Han, S.S. (2015). The spatial characteristics of Global Property Investment in Seoul: A case study of the office market. *Progress in Planning, 97*, 1−42.

Kim, K.-H. (1990). An analysis of inefficiency due to inadequate mortgage financing: The case of Seoul, Korea. *Journal of Urban Economics, 28*, 371−390.

Kim, Y.-C., & Choi, Y. (Eds.). (2004). *The theory of Korean foreign direct investment*. Burlington,VT: Ashgate.

Kwon, N.-K., Hong, S.-W., Sung, Y.-J., Bae, J.-S., Yoon, H.-J., Min, S.-S., ... Sang, Y.-J. (2015). Chinese superrich looking to Korean market. *The Korea Herald*.

Lapier, T. (1998). *Competition, growth strategies, and the globalization of services: Real estate advisory services in Japan, Europe, and the United States*. London: Routledge.

Lee, K.-Y., Yu, G.-S., Lee, H.-C., Sul, D.-H., & Park, S.-J. (2007). *Foreign labour market analysis and mid- and long-term management*. Seoul: Korea Labour Institute. (Korean).

Lee, W. (2014). Development of Chinese enclaves in the Seoul−Incheon metropolitan area, South Korea. *International Development Planning Review, 36*, 293−311.

Lim, L.C., Adair, A., & Mcgreal, S. (2002). Capital flows into the Singapore real estate market: An analysis of the land sales program. *Journal of Real Estate Literature, 10*, 265−277.

Lin, G.C.S., & HO, S.P.S. (2005). The state, land system, and land development processes in contemporary China. *Annals of the Association of American Geographers, 95*, 411−436.

Lizieri, C. (2009). *Towers of capital: Office markets & international financial services*. Chichester: Wiley-Blackwell.

Lizieri, C., & Kutsch, N. (2006). *Who owns the city 2006: Office ownership in the city of London*. London: The University of Reading Business School.

Luo, Y. (1998). Strategic traits of foreign direct investment in China: A country of origin perspective. *Management International Review, 38*, 109−132.

Ministry of Land, Transport and Marine Affairs. 2012. *Current status of landholdings*. Gyeonggi: Author.

Newell, G., & Worzala, E. (1995). The role of international property in investment portfolios. *Journal of Property Finance, 6*, 55−63.

Park, H.-J., Jung, H.N., & Jung, W.-H. (1998). *Foreigners' land acquisition and management policies*. Gyeonggi: Korean Research Institute of Human Settlements. (Korean).

Park, J. (2014). The division of spatial housing submarkets: A theory and the case of Seoul. *Environment and Planning A, 45*, 668−690.

Park, K. (1997). *The Korean American dream*. Ithaca, NY: Cornell University Press.

Piao, G.X. (2006). Labor flux of Korean Chinese and social changes in a global era (PhD thesis). Seoul National University, Seoul.

Rogers, D., & Dufty-Jones, R. (2015). 21st-century Ausralian housing: New frontiers in the Asia-pacific. In *Housing in 21st-century Australia: People, practices and policies*. Burlington, VT: Ashgate.

Rogers, D., Lee, C.L. & Yan, D. (2015). The politics of foreign investment in Australian housing: Chinese investors, translocal sales agents and local resistance. *Housing Studies, 30*, 730−748.

Ronald, R. & Jin, M.-Y. (2010). Homeownership in South Korea: Examining sector underdevelopment. *Urban Studies, 41*, 2367–2388.

Sassen, S. (Ed.). (2005). *Global cities and diasporic networks*. New York, NY: Springer.

Seoul Metropolitan Government (SMG). (2006). *Seoul survey*. Seoul: Seoul Metropolitan Government. (Korean).

Son, J.M. (2003). *Seoul urban planning story 2*. Seoul: Hanul. (Korean).

Tai, E. (2004). Korean Japanese: A new identity option for resident Koreans in Japan. *Critical Asian Studies, 36*, 355–382.

Tiwari, P., & White, M. (2010). *International real estate economics*. Basingstoke: Palgrave Macmillan.

Tu, Y. (2004). The dynamics of the Singapore private housing Market. *Urban Studies, 41*, 605–619.

Yang, P., & Lee, J. (2004). *The country without a China town: Yesterday and today of Korean Hwagyo economy*. Seoul: Samsung Economic Research Institute. (Korean).

Yeung, H.W.-C., Poon, J., & Perry, M. (2001). Towards a regional strategy: The role of regional headquarters of foreign firms in Singapore. *Urban Studies, 38*, 157–183.

Zhu, J., Sim, L.-L., & Zhang, X.-Q. (2006). Global real estate investments and local cultural capital in the making of Shanghai's new office locations. *Habitat International, 30*, 462–481.

Appendix. **Summary of statistics for multiple regression on foreign investment in housing**

	N	Minimum	Maximum	Mean	Std. deviation
Foreigners in Seoul	40	113.0	191,237	6324.8	30,106.6
Distance (km)	40	940.0	17,543	6590.4	3497.0
Overseas Korean	40	374.0	2,336,771	167,541.5	500,635.7
GDP per capita (US$)	40	453.8	65,699.4	19,041.3	21,028.4

Further Reading

This book offers a brief snapshot of the globalisation of real estate via case studies from Canada, Hong Kong, Singapore, Russia, Australia and Korea. It is not intended to be a comprehensive overview. We offer below a further reading list as a starting point for a more in-depth engagement with this book's theme.

Atkinson, R. (2016). Limited exposure: Social concealment, mobility and engagement with public space by the super-rich in London. *Environment and Planning: A, 48(7)*: 1302–1317.

Atkinson, R., Parker, S., & Burrows, R. (2017). Elite Formation, Power and Space in Contemporary London. *Theory, Culture & Society, 34*(5–6): 179–200.

Burrows, R., Webber, R., & Atkinson, R. (2017). Welcome to 'Pikettyville'? Mapping London's alpha territories. *Sociological Review, 65*(2): 184–201.

Christophers, B. (2016). For real: Land as capital and commodity. *Transactions of the Institute of British Geographers, 41*(2), 134–148.

DeVerteuil, G., & Manley, D. (2017). Overseas investment into London: Imprint, impact and pied-à-terre urbanism. *Environment and Planning A, 49*(6), 1308–1323.

Fernandez, F., Hofman, A., & Aalbers, M. (2016). London and New York as a safe deposit box for the transnational wealth elite. *Environment and Planning A, 48*(12): 2443–2461.

Forrest, R. (2015). The ongoing financialisation of home ownership: New times, new contexts. *International Journal of Housing Policy, 15*(1), 1–5.

Forrest, R., Koh, SY., & Wissink, B. (2017). *Cities and the Super-Rich: Real Estate, Elite Practices and Urban Political Economies* (eds) Basingstoke: Palgrave Macmillan.

Goldstein, J. E., & Yates, J. S. (2017). Introduction: Rendering land investable. *Geoforum, 82*, 209–211.

Hay, I. (2013). *Geographies of the Super-Rich* (eds) Cheltenham: Edward Elgar Publishing.

Ho, HK., & Atkinson, R. (2017). *Looking for big 'fry': The motives and methods of middle-class international property investors. Urban Studies* (iFirst).

Koh, SY. (2017). Property Tourism and the Facilitation of Investment-Migration Mobility in Asia. *Asian Review, 30*(1): 25–43.

Lees, L., Shin, HB., & López-Morales, E. (2016). *Planetary gentrification*. Cambridge: Polity Press.

Ley, D. (2011). *Millionaire Migrants: Trans-Pacific Life Lines*. West Sussex: Wiley-Blackwell.

Roberston S., & Rogers, D. (2017). Education, real estate, immigration: brokerage assemblages and Asian mobilities. *Journal of Ethnic and Migration Studies, 43*(14): 2393–2407.

Rogers, D. (2017). *The Geopolitics of Real Estate: Reconfiguring Property, Capital and Rights*. London: Rowman & Littlefield International.

Rogers, D., Nelson, J., & Wong, A. (2017). Public perceptions of foreign and Chinese real estate investment: intercultural relations in Global Sydney. *Australian Geographer*, *48*(4): 437–455.

Rogers, D., Lee, C., & Yan, D. (2015). The Politics of Foreign Investment in Australian Housing: Chinese Investors, Translocal Sales Agents and Local Resistance. *Housing Studies*, *30*(5): 730–748.

Rogers, D. (2017). "Uploading real estate: Home as a digital, global commodity" in Cook, N., Davison, A., & Crabtree. L., (eds) *Housing and Home Unbound*. London: Routledge.

Rogers, D. (2015). Becoming a super-rich foreign real estate investor: Globalising real estate data, publications and events in Forrest, R., Wissink, D., & Koh, SY., (eds) *Cities and the Super-Rich: Real Estate, Elite Practices and Urban Political Economies*. Basingstoke: Palgrave Macmillan.

Rogers, D., & Dufty-Jones, R. (2015). "21st Century Australian housing: New frontiers in the Asia-Pacific" in Dufty-Jones, R., & Rogers, D., (eds) *Housing in Twenty-First Century Australia: People, Practices and Policies*. Aldershot: Ashgate.

Rogers, D., Nelson, J., & Wong, A. (2018). Geographies of Hyper-Commodified Housing: Foreign Capital, Market Activity and Housing Stress. *Geographical Research* (iFirst).

Seabrooke, W., Kent, PS., & How, HHH. (2004). *International real estate: An institutional approach* (eds) Oxford; Malden: Blackwell Publishing Ltd.

van Loon, J., & Aalbers, MB. (2017). How real estate became 'just another asset class': The financialization of the investment strategies of Dutch institutional investors. *European Planning Studies*, *25*(2), 221–240.

Webber, R., & Burrows, R. (2016). Life in an alpha territory: Discontinuity and conflict in an elite London 'village'. *Urban Studies*, *53*(15): 3139–3154.

Index

Note: Page numbers in *italics* refer to figures
Page numbers in **bold** refer to tables
Page numbers with "n" refer to notes

absentee investors 6
Additional Buyer's Stamp Duty (ABSD), Singapore 67
affordability *see* housing affordability
Agency for Housing Mortgage Lending (Russia) 81
anti-speculation housing policies, China 123–125, *124*, 138
apartments: in Australia 136–137; in South Korea 150
Asia: lifestyle capital for super-rich, Singapore as 61–63; real estate investors in 4; *see also* China; Seoul (South Korea), foreign housing investment in
Asia Pacific Economic Co-operation (APEC) 18
assemblage theory 11; and geopolitics 79–80
asset diversification 134
Australia 97–98; Asian Century strategy 113; Chinatown as node for diasporic transnational real estate networks 103–104; Chinese capital and Chinatown's transnational real estate 104, 106; Chinese foreign real estate investment in 2, 5, 22, 101–103, 127; Foreign Ownership Law 115n4; geography of Chinatown and Chinese transnational real estate practices 106, *107*, 108; Korean population in 155, 156; new mobility paradigm, global

cities and transnational urbanism 98–100; racialised media representation of Sydney's transnational real estate 109, **110**, 111–112; racialised public discourse in 114; residential buildings funded/developed by Chinese capital in Chinatown and CBD South **105**; Sydney as global city and middle-class Chinese immigrants 100–101
Australian Bureau of Statistics (ABS) 98
Australian housing, Chinese investment in 120–121, 128–129, *129, 130*, 145; apartments 136–137; Chinese ethnic communities 136; domestic housing market and policy environment in China 132–134; finance constraints 136; foreign *vs.* local developers 136; mechanisms for financing 137; profile of investors 135; pull factors 134–135; push factors 132–134; relaxation of regulations 128; research design 129–138

Bausparkassen 81, 90n2
BE100 103
behavioural economics 129, 138
Beijing Bureau of Land and Resources 47
Beijing Olympics (2008) 87
brokers, in South Korea 156
Büdenbender, M. 75
Bulgaria, presence of Russians in 85

INDEX

passport insurance 20
planetary gentrification 11
political capital 9
political cooptation, in China 41–42
political economy, Pacific Rim 17–19
politics of discontent, in Singapore 65–70
popular politics, in China 44–49
Pow, C.P. 56
prime property, definition of 71n1
private housing, in Singapore 64, 66–67;
    accessibility *67*; affordability 66; vacancy
    rates 67, *68*, 69
privatisation, in Russia 80
property expos 103, 104
Property Investors Alliance 103
property rights, in China 47–49
property state, Singapore as 10, 58, 60, 64,
    65, 69–70
property tax: in China 134; in Singapore 69
property types, in foreign real estate
    investment 3–7
public housing, in Singapore 66–67, 69,
    71n2
Public Rental Housing (PRH) programme,
    China 124
Purchase Restriction policy (China) 121,
    123, 124–125, 132, 133, 138
Putin, Vladimir 82, 86

Quay, The (Chinatown, Sydney) 106

Real Estate Board of Greater Vancouver
    (REBGV) region 24, 27
Real Estate Trade Management System
    (RTMS), South Korea 148
recession, in Canada 17
redevelopment, in China 47–49
regulation, of foreign real estate investment
    7–9; in Australia 128; in South Korea 149
RE/MAX 25
Rogers, D. 1
Royal Pacific Realty 24–25
Russia: foreign real estate investment of 9,
    82; geopolitics of state-led projects
    85–88; housing finance system in 81;
    internationalisation of real estate in 76,
    80–83; Korean population in 154;
    outward real estate investment of 83–85;
    sanctions against 82, 84, 85
Russian Orthodox Church (ROC) 86

Russian Orthodox Spiritual and Cultural
    Centre (Paris) 86
Russian world 86

safe tax havens 77
sales, transnational 23–25
Saverin, Eduardo 62
Sberbank 84
secondary migration 20
securitisation 59, 90n3; mortgage-backed
    81, 90n4
Sentosa Cove, Singapore 64, 65, 71n5
Sentosa Development Corporation 64
Seoul (South Korea), foreign housing
    investment in 144; active areas for
    160–163; brokers 156; changes in Korean
    regulatory framework 149; country of
    origin of investors, modelling 158–160;
    data collection 148–149; demographic
    characteristics 158, 159–160; ethnic
    Koreans from developed countries
    154–157; ethnic Koreans in
    geographically close countries 153–154;
    Gangham 162–163; high-income and
    average income households *162*; hot-spot
    analysis *161*; identification of major
    investors 151; investor behaviour
    151–158; multiple regression **161, 167**;
    non-Korean Asian investors 157–158;
    overseas Koreans 151–157, *154*; role of
    foreign investors 149–160; spatial
    characteristics 147–148; trend in housing
    transactions 149–151, **151**; 2006–2010
    152; *Yeonghee dong* 160–161; *Yongsan*
    161–162
Shenzhen Special Economic Zone (China)
    145
Shui On 48
Singapore 56–58; as Asia's lifestyle capital
    for super-rich 61–63; cooling measures
    67; decoupling of prime residential
    districts 66; foreign real estate investment
    in 2, 145; luxury property market 63–65;
    as property state 10, 58, 60, 64, 65, 69–70;
    revenue from land/property-related
    transactions 69; social-spatial polarisation
    66; spatial fix strategy of 10, 57–58, 62,
    63, 64, 65, 69, 70; super-rich and politics
    of discontent 65–70; taxation in 62
Sino-British Joint Declaration 19, 41

175

INDEX

For Product Safety Concerns and Information please contact our EU
representative GPSR@taylorandfrancis.com
Taylor & Francis Verlag GmbH, Kaufingerstraße 24, 80331 München, Germany

www.ingramcontent.com/pod-product-compliance
Ingram Content Group UK Ltd.
Pitfield, Milton Keynes, MK11 3LW, UK
UKHW021611240425
457818UK00018B/490